MW00811289

# Film and Sexual Politics

# Film and Sexual Politics

Edited by

## Kylo-Patrick R. Hart

CAMBRIDGE SCHOLARS PRESS

Film and Sexual Politics, edited by Kylo-Patrick R. Hart

This book first published 2006 by

Cambridge Scholars Press

15 Angerton Gardens, Newcastle, NE5 2JA, UK

British Library Cataloguing in Publication Data
A catalogue record for this book is available from the British Library

Copyright © 2006 by Kylo-Patrick R. Hart and contributors


All rights for this book reserved. No part of this book may be reproduced, stored in a retrieval system,
or transmitted, in any form or by any means, electronic, mechanical, photocopying, recording or
otherwise, without the prior permission of the copyright owner.
ISBN 1-84718-037-X

# TABLE OF CONTENTS

**Part III: Controversial Cinematic Representations**

**Part IV: Cinematic Strategies, Identification, and Spectatorship**

## Part V: Gay Men on Film and Video

For Polly, Telly, Dizzy, Skishy, and X

# INTRODUCTION

# KYLO-PATRICK R. HART

From the birth of cinema to the present, a wide range of social actors have been concerned about the various ways that sex, gender, and sexual orientation are represented in films of all kinds. Their concerns have stemmed largely from the concept of dystopian fears associated with cinematic reception—which typically regard film images as potentially evil forces capable of producing social chaos and a range of negative social effects—as well as from complex, related processes pertaining to cinematic spectatorship and identification in its various forms. While some individuals have historically regarded such phenomena as threatening and deleterious, others have viewed them as offering utopian potentialities in the ongoing cultural struggle to achieve equal acceptance, balanced power dynamics, and positive social constructions of individuals of all kinds, no matter what their specific sex, gender, and/or sexual orientation may be.

This collection features eighteen noteworthy critical essays—all addressing power, domination, and representation in their numerous forms—that explore the evolution and social construction of sex, gender, and sexual orientation in films from the early days of cinema to the early twenty-first century. Contrary to popular perceptions of films as relatively simplistic forms of "entertainment," these essays demonstrate clearly how the act of producing meaning through the use of cinematic verbal and visual signs is far from a simple process, but rather one with substantial social, political, and cultural consequences for the lived realities of individuals of all backgrounds and lifestyles.

The essays in Part I explore the impact of restrictive Motion Picture Production Code regulations, enacted in the early 1930s, on the contents of Hollywood films. With regard to screwball comedies, Jane Greene demonstrates that there were two distinct phases of industry self-regulation during the decade of the 1930s that substantially affected the development and contents of films of this kind, including their representations of women in relation to men. Catherine Burke examines how the Production Code restrictions dramatically transformed the lovemaking scenes in the films of Warner Baxter, one of the most popular Hollywood actors during the early years of talking pictures, by restricting the range of sexual acts and actions that could be presented on the screen. David Lugowski reveals the range of "queerness," prohibited from explicit depiction

INTRODUCTION

by the Production Code, that demanded expression and is therefore readily identifiable in Orson Welles' classic film *Citizen Kane*.

The essays in Part II investigate various forms of sexual politics evident in films of the postwar 1950s, the contents of which continued to be restricted by the regulations of the Motion Picture Production Code. In my own essay exploring *From Here to Eternity*, I demonstrate that, even though overtly homosexual characters and homosexual storylines were prohibited from appearing on screen, the film contains a substantial subtext that reveals itself to be a gay love story between Sergeant Milton Warden (played by Burt Lancaster) and Pvt. Robert E. Lee Prewitt (played by Montgomery Clift), its two attractive, masculine leading male characters. Nate Brennan offers an in-depth analysis of *The Incredible Shrinking Man*, focusing on its allegorical representations of male anxiety and restrictive gender-role constructions in the postwar era. Tamar Jeffers McDonald explores how the bodies of actresses in "virginity-dilemma films" visibly indicate their virginal or non-virginal status during an era in which mainstream society, as well as mainstream films, preferred not to reveal such information in plain language. Whitney Strub applies Janet Staiger's concept of perverse spectators to Los Angeles law-enforcement officials in the 1950s and beyond, with regard to their official responses to gay-themed films and gay social spaces and the resulting obscenity prosecutions that served as repeated attacks on the formation of stable, secure gay communities.

The essays in Part III explore controversial cinematic representations from the early twentieth century to the early twenty-first century. Heather MacGibbon focuses on influential cinematic portrayals of abortion and the individuals who sought and performed them during the first half of the last century. Melissa Ooten investigates the phenomena of censorship and rejection of sex-hygiene films by members of Virginia's movie-censorship board during the period from 1922 to 1965, as well as the messages they communicated about socially valued and devalued individuals based on race, class, gender, and other attributes. By focusing on Pier Paolo Pasolini's film *Porcile* from the late 1960s, Mattias Frey investigates complex, controversial representations of bestiality, savagery, and cannibalism in an eye-opening example of how the country of Germany functioned historically in Italian postwar cinema as a site of national transference, with Germans frequently being represented as possessing and demonstrating "deviant" forms of sexuality and social behaviors. Analyzing *Jackass the Movie*, Mary Pagano reveals how, rather than offering a subversive representation of masculinity, the human jackasses in the film maintain mainstream media's traditional boundary between acceptable homosocial bonding and threatening homosexual impulses at the start of the current millennium.

The essays in Part IV offer advanced investigations into cinematic strategies, cinematic identification, and cinematic spectatorship. Focusing on the U.S. film *Female Perversions* and the Dutch film *A Question of Silence*, Cynthia Lucia demonstrates how both of these works strive intentionally to fulfill the desires of feminist female spectators in traditionally patriarchal societies. Jaime Bihlmeyer analyzes *Elizabeth* in ways that expand upon existing poststructuralist approaches to exploring gender imaging in mainstream films. Jack Beckham utilizes an audio-visual approach to more adequately decode the complexities of *The Matrix*—in relation to themes of birth, reproduction, and gender construction—than traditional approaches focusing primarily on the cinematic image allow. Sarah Sinwell explores the phenomenon of cinematic identification in relation to the groundbreaking independent film *Being John Malkovich* and its challenging postmodern privileging of mobility, fluidity, and multiplicities of identity and identification.

The essays in Part V focus on noteworthy representations of gay men on film and video. Offering an in-depth analysis of *My Own Private Idaho*, Christine Pace demonstrates how that film efficiently projects a powerful political unconscious stemming from the paradoxical social construction of gay men in U.S. society. Alina Patriche demonstrates the historically important role that heritage films, such as *Maurice* and *Wilde*, have played in restoring representations of homosexuality to history as well as to mainstream visual culture. Hollis Griffin concludes this collection with his pioneering exploration into the forms and functions of bareback pornography, which has emerged as a contentious albeit increasingly popular subgenre in the field of gay adult film and video over the past decade.

# Part I
# Sexual Politics and the Motion Picture Production Code

CHAPTER ONE

RETHINKING SCREWBALL COMEDY

JANE M. GREENE

Critics and historians have long recognized a unique relationship between industry self-regulation and screwball comedy. While all genres were affected by censorship in the 1930s, screwball comedy supposedly owes its existence to changes in regulatory policy. Andrew Sarris was the first critic to advance this argument in his 1978 essay "The Sex Comedy Without Sex," in which he links screwball comedy's characteristic verbal and physical battling to changes in censorship that made "the act and the fact of sex" forbidden after 1934. Channeling a Hollywood screenwriter from the 1930s, Sarris writes:

> Here we have all these beautiful people with nothing to do. Let us invent some substitutes for sex. The wisecracks multiply beyond measure, and when the audiences tire of verbal sublimation, the performers do cartwheels and pratfalls and make funny expressions. (13)

Hence, 1934 is crucial in the history of the romantic comedy genre. First, it marks the formation of the Production Code Administration (PCA), headed by Joseph Breen. Created by the Motion Picture Producers and Distributors of America (MPPDA), the Hollywood industry's trade organization, in response to growing public protest over film content, the PCA reviewed scripts and films in light of the Motion Picture Production Code, a series of guidelines based upon the presumed response of external censorship groups. PCA censors worked with producers, suggesting changes and deletions to ensure that films would not encounter any difficulties with state and local censorship agencies. Second, according to traditional histories, 1934 also marks the debut of screwball comedy with the releases of Frank Capra's *It Happened One Night* and Howard Hawks' *Twentieth Century*.

Most studies of screwball humor and censorship focus on the slapstick-comedy characteristic of the genre: Carole Lombard sparring with Fredric March in *Nothing Sacred* (1937); Katherine Hepburn and Cary Grant tumbling down hills in pursuit of a dog and dangling from a collapsing brontosaurus skeleton in *Bringing Up Baby* (1938); Henry Fonda tripping on Barbara Stanwyck's outstretched leg and upsetting a multitude of waiters in *The Lady Eve* (1941). As Sarris' remarks suggest, this eccentric behavior is often explained via a lay psychoanalytic reading: the sexual energy suppressed under the watchful eye of the PCA finds its expression in an acceptable physical and verbal loonyness. By this line of reasoning, the wisecracks, pratfalls, and funny expressions of screwball comedy are both a replacement for and symbolic of sexual desire, as when Sarris compares the "subterfuges of screwballism" to the dance duets of Fred Astaire and Ginger Rogers, arguing that they "achieved much of their seductive charm through the need for a new symbolic language of motion and gesture to circumvent repression" (13). Similarly, Ed Sikov contends that screwball violence in particular was the inevitable result of repression:

> Prevented by the Production Code from expressing human sexuality, screwball characters are in an unbearable emotional bind; if they were unable to express the rage they so abundantly feel, they'd go mad.... When we see and hear screwball characters berating, hitting, insulting, and denouncing one another,...we are witnessing personal liberation in its purest and most therapeutic form, the end of repression and the beginning of a healthy life. (217)

It is true that the producers of screwball comedies could not explicitly represent a couple's sexual union or reunion and therefore found alternative ways to demonstrate the couple's suitability and desire. For example, in the 1937 screwball version of *The Awful Truth*, the filmmakers substituted an escalating battle of social embarrassment for the comic seduction of the 1922 play (Greene 356). However, most censorship accounts remain limited in their portrayals of the self-regulatory process, the style of screwball humor, and the impact of the former on the latter.

First, they rest on the faulty assumption that industry self-regulation did not exist or was ineffective prior to 1934. Sikov, for example, contends that if the genre could be traced to one single event, it would be "the establishment in 1934 of the now infamous Production Code" (20). William K. Everson echoes this assertion, noting that "Hollywood's self-censoring Production Code [was] imposed at the end of 1933" (15). However, the Production Code was first implemented in 1930 and was administered by the Studio Relations Committee (SRC), a forerunner to the PCA, until 1934. While the SRC was originally thought to be largely ineffectual, recent work on self-regulation has demonstrated that this was hardly the case. Under the SRC, industry censorship may not have been as rigorous or as systematic as under the PCA, but MPPDA members were still required to submit scripts and completed films for review, and the agency did affect the form and content of films. Hence, to understand how changes in self-regulation influenced the development of screwball comedy, one must first establish how censorship functioned prior to 1934.

Second, many screwball comedies were problematic with industry censors and outside interest groups. The remarriage variations faced special problems with the Catholic Legion of Decency, the industry's most vocal external pressure group, during the late 1930s and early 1940s. According to Frank Walsh, over half of the Legion's B classifications ("morally objectionable in part") in 1940 resulted from the light treatment of marriage or divorce (169), and between 1939 and 1941, the Legion gave a C rating ("immoral") to four films, two of which were screwball remarriage comedies: *This Thing Called Love* (1940) and *Two-Faced Woman* (1941) (163). Walsh explains:

> In an attempt to circumvent the Code, producers were using unusual marriage situations, such as a trial marriage or a husband or wife, long thought dead, who returns to find the spouse remarried, to introduce suggestive scenes and dialogue. They reasoned that such screenplays would enable them to get away with situations that would be rejected if the couple were unmarried. A string of such films were released between 1939 and 1941: *He Married His Wife*, *My Favorite Wife*, and *Too Many Husbands* all squeaked by with a B rating. (165)

This demonstrates that filmmakers were not simply replacing sex with cartwheels, at least by the latter half of the 1930s. If it were this simple, it seems unlikely that the films would have encountered any difficulty with the PCA, and they certainly would not have provoked the condemnation of the Legion.

Revisionist work on industry self-regulation also indicates that the relationship between the screwball genre and censorship is more complicated than previous studies have suggested. Lea Jacobs contends that screwball comedies were a source of frustration for censors "because they were so adept at exploiting the sorts of denial mechanisms typically favored by the Production Code Administration" (113). "Denial mechanism" is a term used by Jacobs to describe methods employed by filmmakers to create ambiguity around transgressive situations, setting up one interpretation of an event, say that a couple engaged in premarital sex, while simultaneously denying it. Jacobs describes a scene from the 1936 film *Camille*, in which the heroine and her lover, Armand, arrive at a cottage in the country. Armand carries Camille over the threshold, an action that suggests they will spend the night together. However, the following scene shows Camille waking up alone in her bedroom the next morning, and in a conversation with her maid, she reveals that Armand spent the evening at a nearby inn. As Jacobs points out, because the PCA pushed for greater ambiguity via the use of denial mechanisms, "in many cases such as that of *Camille*, it is difficult for the spectator to pinpoint with certainty when or how the...sexual transgressions occur" (111-113).

The PCA's methods worked well for dramas like *Camille*. But the gag structures, character behaviors, and comedic situations that characterize screwball comedy were, in fact, strategies developed by filmmakers to represent risqué situations in a Code-approved manner. The negotiations between producers and the PCA reveal that censors struggled to rein in writers and directors who had essentially discovered a loophole in the Code, developing a style of humor and gag structures that simultaneously satisfied the letter of the law but defied its spirit. Moreover, there are two distinct phases of censorship following the formation of the PCA, and the style of humor characteristic of later screwball comedies was simply not possible earlier in the decade. Films such as *My Favorite Wife* (1940), *This Thing Called Love* (1940), and *Love Crazy* (1941) are quite distinct from mid-1930s romantic comedies in their representation of sexual desire (particularly with a marriage) and in the way they use sexuality to create gags and humorous situations. Hence, the earlier films commonly thought of as screwball comedies are better characterized as sentimental comedies, a distinct cycle of romantic comedy.

## Sophisticated Comedy

To understand the unique characteristics of screwball humor, especially as it functions to subvert the Code, it is useful to consider romantic comedy precedents. The dominant form of romantic comedy in the 1920s and early 1930s was sophisticated comedy, sometimes referred to as "comedy of manners" in trade and popular press reviews. Sophisticated comedies have upper-class settings and, in the remarriage variants, the cause of marital discord is typically infidelity. At the very least, one or both members of the main couple are seriously tempted by or attracted to someone other than their spouse. Many sophisticated comedies were adaptations of theatrical properties, and their humor is rather suggestive, based on the open representation of adultery or the expression of modern ideas about marriage, divorce, and infidelity.

An example from the 1931 film *Private Lives* illustrates the style of humor typical of sophisticated romantic comedies. The source material for the film was the Noel Coward play of the same name, which centers on a divorced couple, Amanda and Elyot, who have just remarried and are embarking on honeymoons with their new spouses Victor and Sybil. As luck would have it, the couples wind up in the same hotel, where Amanda and Elyot encounter each other on a terrace that adjoins the two suites. After some initial bickering, they begin reminiscing about their marriage and are soon professing their love for one another. Vowing never to argue again, they abandon their new spouses and run away together. In the play, the next act opens in a flat in Paris. The stage directions indicate that a few days have elapsed since Act One. It is about ten o'clock in the evening, and Amanda and Elyot, wearing pajamas and a dressing gown respectively, are enjoying coffee and liqueurs. The following exchange indicates that they haven't left the flat since arriving in Paris:

ELYOT: I'm glad we didn't go out tonight.
AMANDA: Or last night.
ELYOT: Or the night before. (54)

When MGM submitted the play to the SRC for review, the censors were particularly concerned with the representation of adultery suggested by this scene. In his initial response to the script, censor Lamar Trotti noted:

The fact that Amanda and Elyot are married and that they run off together on the first night of their honeymoon is, in my opinion, contrary to the Code provision governing the institution of marriage, as well as the provision respecting adultery, which is not only justified but made extremely attractive. Yes extremely. (4 Feb. 1931)

After several months of negotiation, the censors and studio agreed that the problematic material could be fixed by eliminating what they referred to as "the time element." As Trotti described it:

If it can be played so Amanda and Elliot [*sic*] run off together and have their fight and are discovered before anything actually could have happened, the implication is much less serious. (4 June 1931)

In response to this suggestion, the producers not only accounted for most of Amanda and Elyot's time together, but found in this requirement a method of creating humor—that is, making a joke out of the couple's inability to be alone and re-consummate their love. Immediately after Victor and Sybil discover that their new spouses have abandoned them, there is a fade, followed by an intertitle that reads, "Came the dawn." The next shot, a close-up, shows Elyot in profile, sleeping. He wakes up and smiles. The camera then pans right, in the direction he is looking, revealing Amanda facing him, still asleep. As Elyot tries to wake her, she moves closer to him and the camera pans left and tracks back slightly, leaving them in a two-shot. The initial framing of the shot and the behavior of the couple encourage the viewer to surmise that they have re-consummated their relationship. But after a few minutes of dialogue, the camera tilts up and tracks back to a long shot, revealing that Amanda and Elyot are not alone. Rather, they are sleeping in the middle of an enormous bed, sharing it with at least five other people.

In his essay "Notes on the Sight Gag," Noël Carroll classifies this type of gag as the switch image. According to Carroll:

> In these cases, the image is given to the audience under one interpretation, which is subverted with the addition of subsequent information. The initial image is subsequently shown to be radically undermined. At first, it seems to mean one thing unequivocally in terms of its visual information, but then it means something entirely, and unexpectedly, other. (151)

Carroll points to an example of a switch-image gag in the 1917 Charlie Chaplin comedy *The Immigrant*. The opening shot shows Chaplin from behind, leaning over the railing of a boat, moving in such a way as to suggest that he is seasick and vomiting. A few moments later, Chaplin turns around to reveal that he has actually been struggling to land a big fish.

As noted previously, the opening moments of the Alpine bed gag in *Private Lives* invite the audience to surmise that Amanda and Elyot have slept together. Yet SRC censors did not object because the track out to a longer shot reveals that this interpretation was incorrect. Responding to the gag at the script stage, Jason Joy, head of the SRC, even referred to it as a model for covering "the time element" throughout the film:

> In the first appearance of the runaway couple, you have taken care of this situation by placing Amanda and Elyot in an Alpine bed with half a dozen other persons, and this encourages us to believe that you can find a way to cover this situation throughout. (27 Aug. 1931)

Yet, in order for the gag to work, the spectator has to make the risqué assumption invited by the beginning of the shot. As Carroll points out, "Once the initial image is subverted, part of our pleasure involves noting the way in which our first identification of the image was misguided" (152). In fact, this visual joke in *Private Lives* is a small-scale illustration of the way the SRC employed its compensating moral values policy. Just as the punishment or redemption of a character at the end of a film could compensate for his or her earlier transgressions, the suggestion that Amanda and Elyot have been unfaithful in the first moments of the gag is recuperated by the assurance, at the gag's conclusion, that they have not transgressed.

An example from the 1934 sophisticated comedy *Easy to Love* illustrates how this gag structure could be extended across an entire sequence. The lead couple, John and Carol Townsend, have been married for twenty years and have a seventeen-year-old daughter, Janet. When Carol discovers that John has been having an affair with her best friend, she asks for a divorce. Meanwhile, Janet grows increasingly frustrated with her parents' behavior. She and her fiancé, Paul, announce that they no longer have faith in marriage so they have decided to forgo matrimony and simply live together. The two run off with Janet's parents in pursuit. Carol and John follow the young couple to a hotel and, after summoning a justice of the peace, force their way into the room to find Paul and Janet lying under the covers of two twin beds. Carol and John soon realize how foolishly they have been acting and agree to reconcile. Janet then reveals that she and Paul were married earlier that day, unbeknownst to her parents and the audience.

Like the Alpine bed gag in *Private Lives*, the hotel room gag in *Easy to Love* is based on the incongruity between a risqué initial interpretation and a later, innocent truth. I call these "switch-assessment gags" to reflect the fact that the humor is not simply rooted in the visual elements of a shot or scene; dialogue, plot, and our knowledge of character psychology contribute to the incongruous sequential interpretations. Reviewing this scene in the script stage, the SRC did ask the studio to eliminate some dialogue and elements of mise-en-scene that would have made the suggestion that Janet and Paul are in bed together in the hotel room more explicit—for example, eliminating "the action of clothes being thrown on the sofa" and "shots of the underclothing scattered around the room," as well as the line, "As soon as we can get some clothes on, Mother" (Wingate 4 Nov. 1933). The producers adopted some of these changes, but the finished film still clearly invites the risqué interpretation; John and Carol and the audience are meant to think that Janet and Paul have gone to the hotel to have premarital sex.

The script for *Easy to Love* was submitted to the SRC just a few months before Joseph Breen and the PCA censors took over the task of regulating film content. The change in personnel and policy after 1934 meant that the producers of screwball comedies did not have recourse to suggestive switch-image and switch-interpretation gags and instead relied on more indirect representations of intimacy.

## Screwball Comedy

In 1934, self-regulation did become more restrictive and systematic. The PCA monitored films more closely than the SRC, elaborating on strategies that had been used earlier in the decade. For example, Jacobs demonstrates that post-PCA, filmmakers could no longer use an ellipsis to suggest an action that could not be explicitly represented. Instead, censors began considering how an ellipsis functioned within a scene to determine what it was meant to suggest (111). In other words, if a dissolve or fade clearly indicated that a couple had engaged in sex, it was not acceptable. The PCA wanted producers to create greater ambiguity around taboo actions. As discussed earlier, they frequently advocated the use of denial mechanisms, which involved setting up one interpretation of an event while simultaneously denying it. This strategy worked fairly well in dramas, but in the later 1930s, filmmakers began exploiting this technique to make their comedies more suggestive.

It is important to make a distinction between switch-image and switch-assessment gags and the type of denial mechanism one finds in a film like *Camille*, since there are structural similarities. In the Alpine bed gag in *Private Lives* and the hotel room gag in *Easy to Love*, there is little or no ambiguity because the first stage of each gag purposely misleads the viewer into making a risqué interpretation. In contrast, the shot of Armand carrying Camille into the country house *may* be interpreted as an indication that they are spending the night together, but there is nothing that directly confirms this interpretation.

Switch-image and switch-assessment gags depend on a complete lack (or minimum) of ambiguity to be truly effective, since they are built on the incongruity between earlier and later interpretations. And purposely misleading the audience to believe that a character has committed a transgression would have been quite difficult under the PCA, especially if this were done for comedic effect. This is not to say that screwball comedies never employ switch-image or switch-assessment gags but, given censorship restrictions, these are typically not suggestive. The sexually oriented switch gags that do appear do not mislead the audience as explicitly as those in sophisticated comedies and, I would argue, are not as funny.

To illustrate this, consider the only switch interpretation gag in the 1937 screwball comedy *The Awful Truth*. Jerry Warriner, who is separated from his wife Lucy, overhears her on the phone with her music teacher, Armand Lavalle. Lucy confirms a meeting with Armand for the following afternoon but then tells Jerry she was speaking with her masseuse. This lie and the mysterious nature of Lucy's appointment create doubt for both the spectator and Jerry, suggesting that she is carrying on an affair. These suspicions prove unfounded in the following scene, when Jerry goes to Armand's apartment expecting to catch Lucy and her voice teacher "in the clinch" and instead finds them in the middle of a recital, surrounded by an admiring audience. The restricted narration in the earlier scene creates some curiosity about Lucy's appointment, but it does not trick the audience into believing that she is having an affair, particularly since the film never definitely establishes that she has been unfaithful. Thus, when Jerry finds her engaged in an innocent activity, there is a moment of comic surprise, but the degree of incongruity is not that great. In contrast, the Alpine bed gag in *Private Lives* does trick the spectator into believing that Amanda and Elyot have committed adultery by using close framing and character behavior;

in other words, the *most* logical interpretation of the beginning of the shot is that they have slept together, *not* that they are in a large bed with a group of people.

Most of the humor in the recital scene in *The Awful Truth* is the result of Jerry's screwy or slapstick behavior, which might be understood as a supplement to the less incongruous switch-assessment gag. When Jerry arrives at the door of Armand's apartment, a butler tries to prevent him from entering. Jerry forces his way in and the butler trips him, exclaiming, "Me ju jitsu!" Rising from the floor, Jerry pretends to shake hands with the butler only to flip him onto the floor, stating, "Me ju jitsu, too." Jerry then bursts into the main room of the apartment to find Lucy and Armand in the middle of a song. Embarrassed, he takes off his hat and moves to a chair in the back of the room. After sitting properly for a moment, he leans back in the chair and then falls over, taking a small end table with him. Trying to recover his dignity and straighten out the situation proves impossible when his arm gets caught in the chair and his leg gets caught in the table. The filmmakers may have added this series of slapstick antics to build up the scene's comedy, recognizing that the switch-assessment gag alone was not funny enough to sustain the scene. Much of the humor in the scene arises from the incongruity between Jerry's ridiculous behavior and the quiet civility of the gathering he has interrupted, but this incongruity is quite different from the suggestive switch-assessment gags typical of sophisticated comedy.

Many screwball gags are best understood in comparison to another sight gag discussed by Noël Carroll: "the mutual interference or interpenetration of two (or more) series of events (or scenarios)" (148). In this type of gag, a scene is "staged in such a way that an event, under one description, can be seen as two or more distinct, and perhaps in some sense mutually exclusive, series of events that interpenetrate each other" (148). Carroll's description of a scene from Alfred Hitchcock's *The 39 Steps* (1935) offers an effective example:

> The character played by Robert Donat has been manacled to a woman who positively hates him. They come to an inn, where the landlady takes them to be intensely affectionate newlyweds. Their closeness is in fact mandated by the handcuffs, and when Donat pulls his prisoner toward him, this in order to get more control over her. The landlady misinterprets these gestures as further signs of the "lovers'" infatuation, although we hear them exchanging hostilities. The scene is shot and blocked in such a way that we not only know how things actually stand between the "lovers," but also simultaneously see how someone in the landlady's position could systematically misinterpret the situation. Our amusement is generated by the fact that the scene is staged to show not only what is actually going on but how that set of events could also visually support an alternative, and in this case, conflicting interpretation. (146-147)

The mutual-interference gag is, in its structure, a mechanism of denial. In fact, it goes even further than the denial mechanism in *Camille* because it ensures that the audience knows the innocent "truth." For example, the 1939 screwball comedy *Bachelor Mother* is based on an extended mutual-interference gag: a shop girl named Polly finds a baby on a doorstep and, due to a series misunderstandings, is forced to keep the baby in order to keep her job. All of the characters in the film believe that the baby is Polly's and, moreover, most of them believe that the child is illegitimate. In one scene, Polly takes the baby out for a walk in the park with David Merlin. David is the son of John "J. B." Merlin, who owns the department store where Polly works. J. B. has come to believe that David is the father of the child. He follows his son to the park to confirm his suspicions and approaches the couple, who are unaware that he believes the baby is his grandchild. Wiping tears from his eyes, he proclaims, "I'd know that chin anywhere." He then asks the baby's name, and when Polly informs him that it is John, J. B. tells his son, "Well, thanks for *that* anyway."

There are three distinct points of view in the *Bachelor Mother* scene: (1) J. B.'s, who believes the child is his grandson; (2) Polly and David's, who are confused by the old man's behavior; and (3) the truth, known only to the audience, which is that J. B. has been misinformed, and the child is not even Polly's, let alone David's. All of the events in the gag interpenetrate, or have overlapping elements that make each interpretation possible. As Carroll explains:

> The relevant conflict of interpretations emerges from the disjunction of the character's point of view—which is a function of the situation being laid out in such a way that the spectator can see why the character fails to see it properly— and the way the situation is. (150)

With a switch-image gag, humor is created by the incongruity between the spectator's initial interpretation and a later (more accurate) understanding of the event made possible by the revelation of additional information. In contrast, with mutual-interference gags, two (or more) interpretations are simultaneously available and the incongruity between the points of view creates humor.

Lea Jacobs points to *Bachelor Mother* as an example of the way screwball comedies employed mechanisms of denial "to introduce notions of sexual deviance which would otherwise have been taboo" (113). She explains:

> Many of the jokes are predicated upon the disparity between the heroine's (and spectator's) knowledge and that of the other characters.... The story thus develops "as if" the heroine had had an illegitimate baby, although the film assures us that she "really" did not. (113-114)

The very structure of the mutual-interference gag, with its complicated hierarchy of knowledge, allowed the filmmakers to deny Polly's transgressions (the audience knows that she is not the child's mother) while at the same time playing upon illegitimacy for comedic effect, as when Mr. Merlin insists the child has his chin or grudgingly thanks his son for naming the boy after him.

It is important to note that, in order to get the joke (or to even understand the film), the audience must understand that the characters believe Polly has had an illegitimate child. The PCA censors were not unaware of this, and they monitored dialogue, actions, and performance to ensure that the characters' misinterpretations about the baby's illegitimacy or paternity were not made too explicit. The ending of the film was particularly problematic in this regard. In the original script, David Merlin proposes to Polly, and she asks him if he still thinks she is the baby's mother. When he says he does, she responds, "And have I got a surprise for you!" (Breen 3 Mar. 1939). The PCA objected to this line in several memos to the studio, and when it remained in the completed film, Joseph Breen wrote to producer J. R. McDonough:

> I regret to be compelled to advise you that the "tag line" of the picture appears, in our judgment, to be unacceptable and, unless you delete this, it will be necessary for us to withhold approval of the film. (Breen 13 May 1939)

Ultimately, RKO replaced the line, and in the film as released, the closing exchange appears as follows:

> DAVID: I've got a surprise for you. We're going to be married tonight.
> POLLY: And you still think I'm the mother of that baby?
> DAVID: Of course.
> POLLY: Ha, ha!

Polly's original closing line ("And have I got a surprise for you!") too explicitly acknowledged David's belief that Polly has had sex, suggesting that he will be surprised to discover that she is a virgin. In the revised scene, Polly's "Ha, ha!" could be taken as a reference to the more innocent but still incorrect assumption that she is the baby's mother. The change does not completely rule out or deny the sexual interpretation but simply makes it more indirect. And significantly, the PCA censors left the structure of the mutual-interference gags intact, demonstrating that they functioned successfully as denial mechanisms.

Screwball behavior itself could function as a mechanism of denial when used in a double-meaning gag. Like mutual-interference gags, double-meaning gags make multiple interpretations simultaneously available to the viewer. However, they are not built upon the incongruity between the audience's knowledge and the misinterpretations of characters. Rather, they are similar to a double-entendre in that they offer two interpretations of characters' actions, one innocent and one risqué. Hence, aside from just substituting for sex, screwball behavior could act as kind of camouflage; a scene could offer a sexually suggestive way to understand characters' behavior while simultaneously providing a second, innocent interpretation—namely, the characters are behaving this way because they are screwy.

Take, for example, the double-meaning gag in the opening scene of the 1941 screwball comedy *Love Crazy*. Steve Ireland arrives home on the evening of his fourth anniversary, clearly happy and excited. In the back of the cab, he sings along to a new portable phonograph record he has purchased as a gift for his wife, Susan: "It's delightful to be married. There's nothing quite so jolly as a happy married life." On the way up to his apartment, the elevator gets stuck and Steve tells the operator, "We can't be stuck. I've got the most important date of the year tonight." He then encourages the elevator: "Oh, come on elevator, nice old elevator. Get me upstairs and I'll put you out to pasture in a beautiful green meadow." Entering his apartment, Steve greets the maid, reminding her, "Tonight's the night." The maid informs him that Susan has been primping since breakfast. Steve sets up the phonograph and hides behind a curtain as Susan enters the room. She finds him and they dance into the bedroom so Susan can finish preparing for their evening together. Susan then tells Steve to ask their maid for her walking shoes and heavy gloves, noting that she will need them for the four-mile walk and the rowing. The ensuing exchange reveals their plans for the evening, as well as the fact that Steve has a different idea.

> STEVE: Do you think we want to go through with all that rigmarole tonight?
> SUSAN: Rigmarole?! … Oh darling, we swore that every year we'd do exactly what we did when we were married.… I love that walk to the justice of the peace.
> STEVE: Four miles.
> SUSAN: But he always gives us sherry when we get there.
> STEVE: One finger.
> SUSAN: Then I row you up the river.
> STEVE: That takes an hour.
> SUSAN: And you read our future in the stars. That's the part I like best.…
> STEVE: Say, look, I've got an idea. Why don't we do everything we did last year, and the year before, and the year before that, only, uh, in reverse.
> SUSAN: In reverse? … But that would mean we would have to take our four-mile walk at midnight and backwards at that.
> STEVE: Yes.…
> SUSAN: Oh yes.… Well, then I don't see why we shouldn't do just as you say.

Steve then instructs the maid to serve them dinner at the regular time, but backwards. He returns to the bedroom, yawning and noting that it is one o'clock. "What was the first thing I did?" he muses, trying to recall the exact order of events on their wedding night. Just as Steve turns out the light, however, the doorbell rings. "Whoever it is," he vows to Susan, "they shall not pass." However, when he answers the door he finds his mother-in-law, who invites herself for dinner.

A viewer could find humor in this scene simply for its representation of a happily married, slightly eccentric couple about to celebrate their anniversary. There is also a comic incongruity between this apparently elegant couple on this supposedly romantic evening and Susan's sudden request for walking shoes and heavy rowing gloves. Steve in particular is the source of much of the comedy: singing in the cab, pleading to the elevator, and hiding behind the curtain to surprise Susan. Moreover, his idea to perform the ritual backwards has an innocent explanation, indicated by his responses to Susan's recitation of the ritual ("Four miles," "One finger," "That takes an hour"). It makes sense that, after four years, he would like to avoid the four-mile walk, long boat ride, and delayed supper.

On another level, the scene is about a husband rushing home and trying to get into bed with his wife as quickly as possible. This level of interpretation really comes into play after Steve suggests reversing the order of the evening, when Susan's response (an emphasis and drawing out of the line, "Oh yes") indicates that she understands Steve's underlying motives. I would not deny that the risqué meaning is fairly obvious. Moreover, once a viewer takes that leap, Steve's earlier actions (singing in the cab, pleading with the elevator) can be reinterpreted and enjoyed for a very different reason than may have initially been the case. However, if the viewer has no inkling of the risqué meaning, the scene still makes sense and is still funny.

This was crucial; the PCA did recognize the suggestiveness of the opening scene of *Love Crazy* and asked the filmmakers to eliminate or change details of performance and dialogue that encouraged a risqué interpretation. For example, censors pointed to dialogue that referred to the wedding night and Steve's desire to perform "the marital act." In some cases, they requested subtle changes, as when they asked producers to change Susan's line, "We swore that every year we'd do exactly what we did on our wedding night" to "we'd do exactly what we did when we got married" (Breen 24 Jan. 1941). Censors also examined script directions, identifying problematic facial expressions described after Susan's mother arrives: "The business of [Steve and Susan] exchanging a hopeless look is questionable as an indication of their desire to cohabit and, as such, must be omitted" (Breen 21 Jan. 1941).

The best evidence that both filmmakers and censors were aware of the way the double-meaning gag functioned can be found in Steve's request to perform the ritual backwards. As discussed above, there is an innocent and not-so-innocent interpretation of this suggestion, but originally the filmmakers attempted to slip a third, even more risqué meaning into the exchange. In the original script, Susan agrees to Steve's request to perform the ritual backwards with the following line, "Well, then, I don't see why we shouldn't do *everything* backwards...just the way you say" (Breen 21 Jan. 1941). The PCA memo places emphasis on the word "everything" by underlining it, although it's not clear if it was emphasized in the script. In this instance, censors did not object to the suggestion of sex, as they did with other dialogue in the scene, but to the "intimation of sex perversion" (Breen 21 Jan. 1941). Similarly, in a memo to Will Hays, president of the MPPDA, Breen noted that the original script for *Love Crazy* contained "offensive sex suggestiveness and perversion" (24 Jan. 1941). The phrase "sex perversion," which is not used in reference to any other scenes in the film, suggests that censors interpreted Susan's agreement to do "everything" backwards as a reference to *coitus a tergo*. While that interpretation could still be made with the reply in the finished film ("Well, then, I don't see why we shouldn't do just as you say"), the elimination of select words in Susan's reply makes it a more difficult leap to make.

The fact that Susan and Steve are married is significant. The degree of sexual innuendo that remains in the film would not have been acceptable in a scene involving an unmarried couple, no matter how well disguised by screwball antics. Producers appear to have recognized the benefits of the remarriage plot, as the number of screwball comedies featuring a married, separated, or divorced couple rose significantly, from a few films per year between 1935 and 1937, to six films in 1938, to nine films in both 1940 and 1941. A shift in censorship policy also contributed to the rise of remarriage comedies and the PCA's acceptance of the double-meaning gag as a mechanism of denial. An examination of the few remarriage comedies produced in the years immediately following the formation of the PCA indicates that producers did not have recourse to the same gag structures that characterize later screwball comedies and, for that reason, these films may be more effectively thought of as a distinct subgenre.

## Sentimental Comedies

Only two remarriage comedies regularly appear on screwball filmographies prior to 1937: *She Married Her Boss* (1935) and *The Bride Walks Out* (1936). Yet these films, along with many other so-called screwball comedies released between 1934 and 1937, are actually better understood as sentimental comedies, a subgenre of romantic comedy distinct from screwball in its frequently dramatic and moralizing tone and indirect representation of sexuality.

I have borrowed the term "sentimental comedy" from theater, where it refers to a movement that began at the turn of the eighteenth century, a reaction against the lewd wit and amoral tone of such comedies of manners as William Wycherley's *The Country Wife* (1674-1675) and William Congreve's *The Way of the World* (1700). The comparison brings to light many salient features of mid-1930s romantic comedies, particularly with regard to changes in self-regulation. Just as theatrical sentimental comedies such as Colley Cibber's *Love's Last Shift* (1696) and William Whitehead's *The School for Lovers* (1762) sprang in part from a desire to reform the stage, Hollywood sentimental comedies of the mid-1930s reflect an attempt to reform the movies, a rejection of the risqué humor and situations characteristic of pre-PCA sophisticated comedy. As Kenneth Muir notes in *The Comedy of Manners*, "The sentimentalists believed their plays would have a beneficial effect on the morals of audiences, who duly approved—even if they were not improved" (154). Similarly, Hollywood censors hoped, if not to improve the moral standards of spectators, at the very least to avoid corrupting impressionable viewers, as was made clear in the Production Code, which states, "No picture shall be produced which will lower the moral standards of those who see it" (Maltby 53).

To that end, sentimental comedy characters are virtuous and moral, and although plots may deal with domestic tribulations, they typically avoid any real threat of adultery or demonstrate the sincere repentance of the guilty party. In fact, as James E. Cox notes in *The Rise of Sentimental Comedy*, a defining feature of the theatrical genre is its "zealous defense of marriage" (5-6). Cox also provides a succinct description of the sentimental approach to comedy in contrast to other forms, noting:

> Sentimental comedy is that species of comedy in which man is made to act as the author thinks he should act, to the end that virtue may be commended; as opposed to the orthodox notion of comedy in which man acts foolishly, even viciously (as in real life) to the end that folly and vice may be discredited through ridicule. (2-3)

Hollywood sentimental comedies were produced throughout the 1930s and 1940s, but following the formation of the PCA, a large proportion of them focused on the tribulations of a newly married couple such that, by 1938, *Variety* identified *Thanks for the Memory* as "another in the newlywed cycle" (9 Nov. 1938). The review does not name other films in the cycle, but I would include *Maybe It's Love* (1935), *The Moon's Our Home* (1936), *Small Town Girl* (1936), *Three Married Men* (1936), *A Bride for Henry* (1937), *As Good as Married* (1937), *Live, Love and Learn* (1937), *Wife, Doctor and Nurse* (1937), *The First Hundred Years* (1938) and *Men Are Such Fools* (1938). This group of films actually represents a nascent attempt to circumvent the Code with recourse to the remarriage plot, exploiting the couple's marital status to present sexually suggestive material.

*The Bride Walks Out* (1936) illustrates the basic conventions of the sentimental comedy plot. Michael Martin, a struggling young engineer, wants to marry his girlfriend, Carolyn, a beautiful and somewhat spoiled model. Although she loves Michael, Carolyn resists his proposals, saying she does not want to get by on Michael's $35 a week when her job as a model would contribute $50 a week to the household income. But Michael refuses to let his wife work. Eventually, Carolyn gives in and the couple is married in a rushed civil ceremony. During the first few months of marriage, Carolyn gives Michael the impression that she is handling the household finances, but their bills are actually past due because she cannot resist buying expensive clothes. Eventually, she returns to modeling and, when Michael finds out, he tries to leave her. But Carolyn beats him to the punch, storming out of their apartment with the words, "Goodbye Mr. Martin, and give my love to your budget!" After their separation, Carolyn begins dating a wealthy playboy, and Michael takes a dangerous but lucrative assignment in South America. When Carolyn finds out, she rushes to stop him. The two are reunited and the film ends with Carolyn promising to quit her job to manage the "home office."

The defining characteristic of sentimental comedies that separates them from screwball comedies is the emphasis on serious, everyday concerns of married life and, arising from this, the dramatic tone of the breakup. Finances and careers are almost constantly referred to in *The Bride Walks Out*, even during the film's comedic moments. The couple's financial difficulties are not treated lightly during the breakup scene, when Carolyn rushes out of the apartment in tears. Sentimental comedies also present a conservative moral or lesson. The most radical notion in *The Bride Walks Out*—Carolyn's insistence that women should be allowed to work outside the home—is ultimately discarded, as she simply renounces her ideals and resolves to be a traditional, supportive, stay-at-home wife. A similarly conservative agenda can be found in *She Married Her Boss* (1935). The heroine, Julia Barclay, is a respected, successful working woman who desires nothing more than to marry and have a family. Granted, she is in love with her boss, Richard, and wants to marry him in particular. However, Julia's desire to be a traditional wife and mother is also marked as a rejection of the modern career woman's lifestyle. This is most apparent when Julia's female assistant reveals that she has been her "ideal," noting, "There's nothing in the world I'd rather be than someone like you. You see, my career means everything to me." Julia asks if she has a boyfriend, and the assistant admits she does but hastens to add, "My career comes first and he understands that." Carolyn then insists that the woman leave the office immediately, explaining:

You're not going to work tonight or any other night if I can help it. You go call up your beau. Take a ride out to Willow Grove, sit in the moonlight and hold hands, read poetry, ride on roller coasters. Do something important, really important.... Don't let a career fool you. It's something that sponges up your whole life and leaves you empty.

Aside from their frequently dramatic tone and conservative plots, sentimental comedies are also separated from later screwball comedies in their handling of potentially suggestive material. *The Bride Walks Out* includes a scene very similar to the anniversary evening in *Love Crazy* that illustrates a very different reaction from the PCA censors. In the finished film, the newly married couple arrives at the apartment Michael has leased and furnished. He shows Carolyn around the apartment, pointing out the new furniture as she makes approving comments. They try out the new couch, sitting on opposite ends, and Michael suggests that Carolyn remove her hat and gloves. He then suddenly blurts out, "What's the matter with us? We're acting as though we just met. We're married. Husband and wife." Carolyn goes out the door and, standing in the hallway, asks Michael to carry her over the threshold. The scene fades to black as he obliges his bride.

As this scene appears in the film, Michael and Carolyn are suddenly shy with one another; at one point, it appears that Michael is trying to express his feelings or make a romantic statement, but he can only stutter and finally turns Carolyn's attention to the new sofa. But the PCA case file indicates that the script played up this awkwardness for comic effect. For example, censors objected to a line of dialogue that followed Michael's suggestion that Carolyn remove her hat and gloves: "Well, I guess there's nothing else you can take off. Say, I didn't mean that—not exactly" (Breen 14 Apr. 1936). The degree of Breen's concern with the script version of this scene is also apparent in the redundancy of his warning to the producers:

Care should be taken throughout with the handling of this scene where Carolyn and Michael first arrive at their apartment after being married.... Use of the material on this page is extremely delicate and questionable. It will be acceptable only if handled with the greatest care and tact. If this material is used, much will depend upon the manner in which it is handled. We suggest that you keep in mind the necessity for great caution, with the understanding that we reserve final opinion as to the acceptability of these scenes until the picture is reviewed. (Breen 14 Apr. 1936)

A month later, when the studio submitted revised pages, Breen again objected to the wedding night scene:

We note that in the dialogue and action here there is an attempt to play up the embarrassment of the two newlyweds on their wedding night. This material is open to objection and should be deleted or changed. Any suggestiveness of this nature is unacceptable. (23 May 1936)

There is no record of the PCA's reaction to the finished film, so it seems likely that the studio made the suggested changes before shooting or during editing. As the scene appears in the film, Michael and Carolyn are suddenly shy and awkward with each other, but there is no dialogue or action that even indirectly links their nervousness to sex. Most importantly, the scene does not, indeed the filmmakers *could not*, play up the impending consummation for comedy (as the line "I guess there's nothing else you can take off" would have). Rather, Michael and Carolyn display a general awkwardness that could easily be attributed to their uncertainty about how to behave now that they are husband and wife, and the scene has a tender, serious tone that is quite unlike the indirect suggestion of *Love Crazy* and other screwball comedies from the later 1930s and early 1940s.

Based upon the PCA's response, the original script for *She Married Her Boss* also used the honeymoon night for suggestive comedy, although much of the material was deleted before filming. The case is slightly different from *The Bride Walks Out* because the groom is not nervously anticipating consummating his marriage but trying to avoid it. In the film, Richard Barclay marries his secretary, Julia, to prevent her from going to Paris. Julia has been in love with Richard for years and, although she is aware that he thinks of their relationship as a business arrangement, she is also hoping that it will develop into something more. In the script, an associate of Richard's (a man called Goodrich) arrives at the Barclay manor to discuss business matters on the eve of the wedding. When he realizes this, he mistakenly assumes that the new groom must be eager to be alone with his bride.

In a memo responding to the first incomplete draft of the script, Breen reported that only one element, "easily corrected," was problematic: "That material which plays upon the idea of the intimacies of the marriage night is open to grave objection, and should be deleted or changed." Breen went on to cite several lines and actions that would have indicated Goodrich believes Richard wants to join his wife in the marital bed. For example, Breen suggested that the studio cut the dialogue and action when Goodrich jabs Richard in the ribs following the line, "My wife's waiting up for me. So is yours, my boy." He also noted, "Richard's reaction to Goodrich's line, and his frightened look to the ceiling, and Goodrich's chuckle, and Richard's smile should be changed. There should be nothing suggestive in his eagerness to keep Goodrich with him." Later in the scene, when Richard finally goes upstairs to Julia's room, Breen asked the studio also to make sure that there was nothing suggestive in his reaction to the sight of his bride, noting in particular, "He should not be nervous." And later, when Julia locks her husband out of the room, Breen suggested, "Richard's relieved reaction should not be shown" (Breen 1 June 1935).

In response, the studio eliminated the portion of the scene dealing with Goodrich's visit, leaving only a suggestion of the "intimacies of the marriage night." Julia is shown in her bedroom, wearing a dressing gown. After arranging her hair and applying perfume, she sits on a divan. When she hears Richard climbing the stairs, whistling to himself, she lies back on the divan, raising one arm over her head. Richard stops outside Julia's door and checks his watch. He apparently decides it is too late to disturb his new wife and, instead of knocking on her door, he retires to his bedroom. Julia is then shown listening as his whistle grows fainter and, when she hears his bedroom door open and close, she sits up with a puzzled expression on her face. As in the case of the honeymoon night scene from *The Bride Walks Out*, this scene avoids almost any suggestion of sexual desire or nervousness and, perhaps more importantly, the filmmakers eliminated all attempts to create comedy out of either the desire for, or the delay of, sexual intimacy.

## Conclusion

The representation of sexuality in romantic comedies from the mid-1930s and the PCA's response to attempts to play upon honeymoon night scenes for suggestive comedy in *The Bride Walks Out* and *She Married Her Boss* indicate that censorship policy shifted across the decade. Reflecting these two stages of censorship are two distinct types of romantic comedy. Sentimental comedies from the mid-1930s are important precursors to later screwball comedies; in their efforts to exploit the couple's marriage license in order to introduce sexually suggestive material, the producers of sentimental comedies pointed to a new direction in romantic comedy. By moving the sexually suggestive action away from the honeymoon night and by drawing on gag structures that mimic denial mechanisms, filmmakers gradually built up a method of presenting adult-themed romantic comedies. However, even these strategies would not have been acceptable were it not for the aforementioned shift in industry self-regulation. Hence, in contrast to what Sarris and others would have us believe, screwball comedy is not characterized by a complete repression of sexuality but rather by indirect methods of representing sexual desire, particularly within the context of a remarriage plot.

In general, romantic comedy has not been subject to the more rigorous or systematic distinctions or analysis that characterize the study of other genres such as film noir, the musical, and the western. This lack of rigor has led, at best, to overgeneralizations and oversimplifications of the genre's conventions, characters, and style of humor. At worst, it has given rise to erroneous claims about the genre's history and its significance vis-à-vis American society and the Hollywood industry. This chapter has suggested how these types of distinctions can help us to better understand variations in the romantic comedy genre and, in turn, paint a more accurate picture of the representation of sexuality in classical Hollywood cinema.

## Works Cited

Breen, Joseph. Letter to B. B. Kahane. 14 Apr. 1936. *The Bride Walks Out* Production Code Administration File. Margaret Herrick Library. Academy of Motion Picture Arts and Sciences, Los Angeles.

—. Letter to B. B. Kahane. 23 May 1936. *The Bride Walks Out* Production Code Administration File. Margaret Herrick Library. Academy of Motion Picture Arts and Sciences, Los Angeles.

—. Letter to Harry Cohn. 1 June 1935. *She Married Her Boss* Production Code Administration File. Margaret Herrick Library. Academy of Motion Picture Arts and Sciences, Los Angeles.

—. Letter to J. R. McDonough. 3 Mar. 1939. *Bachelor Mother* Production Code Administration File. Margaret Herrick Library. Academy of Motion Picture Arts and Sciences, Los Angeles.

—. Letter to J. R. McDonough. 13 May 1939. *Bachelor Mother* Production Code Administration File. Margaret Herrick Library. Academy of Motion Picture Arts and Sciences, Los Angeles.

—. Letter to Louis B. Mayer. 21 Jan. 1941. *Love Crazy* Production Code Administration File. Margaret Herrick Library. Academy of Motion Picture Arts and Sciences, Los Angeles.

—. Letter to Louis B. Mayer. 24 Jan. 1941. *Love Crazy* Production Code Administration File. Margaret Herrick Library. Academy of Motion Picture Arts and Sciences, Los Angeles.

—. Letter to Will Hays. 24 Jan. 1941, *Love Crazy* Production Code Administration File. Margaret Herrick Library. Academy of Motion Picture Arts and Sciences, Los Angeles.

Carroll, Noël. *Theorizing the Moving Image*. Cambridge: Cambridge University Press, 1996.

Coward, Noel. *Private Lives: An Intimate Comedy in Three Acts*. Garden City, NY: Doubleday, Doran & Company, 1930.

Cox, James E. *The Rise of Sentimental Comedy*. New York: The Folcroft Press, 1969.

Everson, William K. *Hollywood Bedlam: Classic Screwball Comedies*. New York: Carol Publishing Group, 1994.

Greene, Jane M. "The Road to Reno: *The Awful Truth* and the Hollywood Comedy of Remarriage." *Film History* 13 (2001): 337-358.

Jacobs, Lea. *Wages of Sin: Censorship and the Fallen Woman Film, 1928-1942*. Berkeley: University of California Press, 1997.

Joy, Jason. Letter to Irving Thalberg. 27 Aug. 1931. *Private Lives* Production Code Administration File. Margaret Herrick Library. Academy of Motion Picture Arts and Sciences, Los Angeles.

Maltby, Richard. "Documents on the Genesis of the Production Code." *Quarterly Review of Film and Video* 15.4 (1995): 33-63.

Muir, Kenneth. *The Comedy of Manners*. London: Hutchinson University Library, 1970.

Sarris, Andrew. "The Sex Comedy Without Sex." *American Film* Mar. 1978: 8-15.

Sikov, Ed. *Screwball: Hollywood's Madcap Romantic Comedies*. New York: Crown Publishers, 1989.

Rev. of *Thanks for the Memory*. *Variety* 9 Nov. 1938: 16.

Trotti, Lamar. Letter to Jason Joy. 4 Feb. 1931. *Private Lives* Production Code Administration File. Margaret Herrick Library. Academy of Motion Picture Arts and Sciences, Los Angeles.

—. Letter to John V. Wilson. 4 June 1931. *Private Lives* Production Code Administration File. Margaret Herrick Library. Academy of Motion Picture Arts and Sciences, Los Angeles.

Walsh, Frank. *Sin and Censorship: The Catholic Church and the Motion Picture Industry*. London: Yale University Press, 1996.

Wingate, James. Letter to Warner Bros. 4 Nov. 1933. *Easy to Love* Production Code Administration File. Margaret Herrick Library. Academy of Motion Picture Arts and Sciences, Los Angeles.

# CHAPTER TWO

# COMMODITY KISSES: LOVE SCENES IN THE FILMS OF WARNER BAXTER (A PRE-CODE/POST-CODE ANALYSIS)

## CATHERINE R. BURKE

Warner Baxter (1889-1951) was one of the most popular and highest paid Hollywood movie actors of the pre-World War II period. Beginning as a leading man in the silent era, he made a startling transition to sound by winning the Academy Award for his very first talkie, *In Old Arizona* (1929), and continued on as a major star and box-office draw throughout his career. Due to his charm and good looks, Baxter built a reputation as a "great lover" and, having been paired with a variety of leading ladies of the day, his films abound with kissing scenes and other types of heterosexual lovemaking.

Baxter was an intelligent actor, and he devised a system around which he based all of his romantic characters. At the same time, he developed a long-term career plan in which he alternated romantic and character roles to prepare him for the day when the public would no longer accept him as a "great lover." Baxter's long and prolific career spans the period during which the Motion Picture Production Code came into effect and transformed the way lovemaking was allowed to be presented in the movies. The purpose of this chapter, therefore, is to analyze the lovemaking scenes in the films of Warner Baxter from three distinct perspectives: (1) his lovemaking system; (2) his alternating career plan; and (3) the Production Code influence.

## Career Overview

Baxter began his movie career in 1921 as a featured player at the tiny Realart Studio and advanced quickly to become Ethel Clayton's leading man at Paramount. In 1922, Baxter and Clayton performed together in *Her Own Money* and *If I Were Queen*. These two films revealed the "polished manners and full projection of his personality" that soon made him famous as one of the great screen lovers of the day (Stuart 43). For the next several years, he played in every type of story from comedy to drama, and from tragedy to farce. As a male lead, he supported many prominent actresses, including Madge Bellamy, Clara Bow, Bebe Daniels, Dolores Del Rio, Billie Dove, Gilda Gray, Margaret Livingston, Patsy Ruth Miller, Colleen Moore, Blanche Sweet, and Florence Vidor.

After making nearly forty films, Baxter received top billing for the first time in *A Woman's Way* (1928), a melodrama of the Parisian underworld in which he portrays an American in love with a café dancer. However, it was *Ramona* (1928), based on the tragic novel by Helen Hunt Jackson, that was his first breakthrough film. Baxter's dignified and sincere performance in the role of Alessandro, the Indian lover of Ramona, brought him great acclaim. The following year, a freak accident motivated further changes in Baxter's career. Raoul Walsh, directing and playing the part of the Cisco Kid in the first outdoor all-talking picture, *In Old Arizona*, was injured during a drive back from location shooting and Baxter was chosen as a last-minute replacement.

Based on O. Henry's short story *The Caballero's Way*, *In Old Arizona* was a daring experiment and its success proved to be a complete vindication of talking films (Everson 109). The casting and blending of a variety of foreign and regional accents was superb. Baxter, who up until that time had been known as a solid leading man, gave a performance that was nothing short of a triumph. According to Elinor Hughes:

> As the irresistible bandit who could love, steal, and avenge himself without hate, Warner Baxter was the living embodiment of hitherto impalpable illusions: gay, charming, lovable, and marvelously convincing. (82-83)

The role increased Baxter's reputation as a romantic player and earned him the Academy Award of 1929 for best actor. The characterization was so popular, in fact, that it was followed by *The Cisco Kid* (1931), *The Return of the Cisco Kid* (1939), and a series of other Latin-themed westerns.

Fox Films, to whom he was under contract, made an effort to maintain Baxter as a romantic actor and, at the same time, vary his roles. Between 1929 and 1932, Baxter made nineteen films and performed in a wide variety of genres, including sophisticated comedies, courtroom dramas, melodramas, musicals, mysteries, war films, and westerns. However, it was a loan-out to another studio that brought Baxter renewed popularity at the box office and placed him at the top of the industry in earnings for the remainder of the decade. In 1933, he was borrowed by Warner Bros. to play the role of Julian Marsh, the hard-driving stage director of *42nd Street*. His frenetic, over-the-top performance of a desperate man approaching a nervous breakdown struck a chord with Depression-era audiences. Due to the success of this and other loan-outs, Fox Films rushed Baxter from picture to picture, and he continued to make as many as eight films a year over the next several years.

By the late 1930s, ill health and severe arthritis caused Baxter to limit his output. He suffered a nervous breakdown in 1941 from what he described as "the result of twenty-two years of competitive picture making" (qtd. in Greene n. pag.) and retired for two years to undergo psychoanalysis. In 1943, he went freelance and made a spectacular double comeback that returned him to his former status as high-wage earner and fan favorite. First, Paramount Studios cast him in an important featured role in the lavish Technicolor musical *Lady in the Dark* (1944). As Kendall Nesbitt, married love interest of Ginger Rogers, Baxter proved he still could portray a romantic leading man with humor and charm. At the same time, he began a series of *Crime Doctor* movies, turning out conscientious and engrossing performances in ten films.

## Lovemaking System

By the time he came to talking pictures, Baxter had been a silent star with the reputation of being a dashing leading man. He was handsome and sturdily built, with black hair and hazel eyes. Being only of average height, he dispelled the myth that one had to be tall in order to excel as a romantic actor. As Elinor Hughes remarked:

> Warner Baxter is under six feet in height, though he looks tall on the screen, yet he can put more active charm, more convincing romance, and more glamour into his playing than any two or three stars whom you might choose to name. (89-90)

Clean-shaven in his early career, he grew a small moustache in the mid-1920s and often wore a fedora hat, both of which became his trademarks in real life and on the screen.

Baxter was an intelligent artist who had a philosophy of acting and developed dramatic formulas that he used for all of his film characterizations. For example, in 1924, he offered the following rules for on-screen lovemaking:

> (1) The screen lover must maintain a woman's mystery, heighten her elusiveness, and be puzzled by her remoteness; (2) He must assume a protective attitude and register his desire to fight for and shield her; (3) He must be self-centered yet willing to sacrifice for his love and make the impossible possible for her; and (4) Since a woman's nature is to live for others, the lover should portray a greater contrast by acting to the contrary. (Baxter n. pag.)

Although written in 1924, these rules evidence themselves in lovemaking scenes throughout his entire body of work. Through the use of eye contact, body language, and gesture, Baxter's love scenes consistently register mystery, protection, sacrifice, and self-absorption. This system is as readily present in *Behind That Curtain* (1929) as it is in *Earthbound* (1940).

Consider the following example from *Penthouse* (1933). Gertie (played by Myrna Loy) has just saved Jack's (played by Warner Baxter) life. He has been too self-absorbed with other matters but, upon recognizing her sacrifice, is emotionally moved. As he prepares to kiss her, she backs away, saying, "No, don't kiss me." He reacts in puzzlement. "Don't ever kiss me unless you really mean it," she says. He stops, noticeably changes his manner, slowly picks up her hand and places it to his lips. Then, cradling her head protectively, he bends her back into a prolonged kiss. In short, his "self-absorption" with other matters is broken by her act of "sacrifice"; the "mystery" of her hesitation is answered by his kiss of "protection."

The themes of sacrifice and protection, in particular, often are taken to an extreme in Baxter's films. They manifest themselves most notably by his picking up the female character and carrying her around. For example, in *West of Zanzibar* (1928), after declaring his love, he picks up a woman and carries her around throughout the remaining twenty minutes of the film. In *Linda* (1929), he gently lifts a woman down from a tree and picks her back up again. In *Penthouse*, after she consents to marry him, he picks up a woman and throws her into the air ecstatically. In *Grand Canary* (1934), he carries a woman, who is shivering with fever, up a long series of steps and around the estate. In *Barricade* (1939), he knocks a woman down, picks her back up, and throws her over his shoulder to prevent her from leaving.

Baxter's press interviews also revealed a personal acting philosophy based on naturalness and verisimilitude. "Naturalness in acting," he said, "is the result of careful study and experience and is not simply the use of types from real life" (Baxter n. pag.). He strived to add verisimilitude to the characters he was portraying. For example, he mastered the boleodoro, a leather lariat, for his role in *Under the Pampas Moon* (1935) and learned to play the Basque game of pelota for the character he portrayed in *Their Mad Moment* (1931). This acting philosophy and careful attention to detail had a powerful impact on his love scenes by giving them added realism. In *Under the Pampas Moon*, for example, he used his ability with the boleodoro to harness the leading lady into a kiss. In *Their Mad Moment*, his leading lady was first attracted to Baxter's character because of his skill at the game of pelota.

Baxter's screen kisses, in particular, seem remarkably realistic. He had a reputation for passionate on-screen kisses and his film performances give every appearance of "real" rather than "stage" kisses. For example, different actresses in different films all react with the same look of surprise when coming out of Baxter's embrace. Ruby Keeler in *42nd Street*, Myrna Loy in *Penthouse*, and Joan Bennett in *Vogues of 1938* (1937) all register the same visceral reaction during their kissing scenes. Actress Marjorie Weaver, having been kissed by Baxter in *I'll Give a Million* (1938), confirmed this by saying:

> He really makes you believe him, whatever role he is playing. Because some actors, even when they are kissing you in a scene, seem to be just acting. You know—just thinking of camera angles and whether or not you are going to get lipstick on them and whether or not the part in their hair is straight. But when it's Warner, you forget there is a camera about. (qtd. in Rhea 67)

Much like his lovemaking system, this acting philosophy of naturalness and verisimilitude was a constant factor in all of Baxter's performances throughout his career.

## Alternating Career Plan

From early in his career, the movie studios for whom Baxter worked recognized the commodity value of his characteristics as a "great lover" and used a variety of marketing techniques to promote them. By inscribing his romantic image in advertising and press releases, they capitalized on his lovemaking appeal. However, as will be discussed later, these commodity strategies created a certain tension between his "great lover" image and his changing career goals. Publicity materials of the period focused on Baxter's popularity at the box office and pairings with female stars.

Jim Tully, in his syndicated *Boston Herald* column, described the formula for Baxter's unique appeal:

> He is one of the most valuable, dependable assets any studio could have. His personality is the kind that grows on audiences; his popularity is the kind that goes never backward, always forward. And the reason? He is a man's man who has never failed to interest the women in the audience. (n. pag.)

For example, a Fox Films press book for *Romance of the Rio Grande* (1929) depicted Baxter as a "romantic lover" who is both "hard fighting" and "hot loving" and highlighted his universal appeal to both women and men as being "at home in saddle or in boudoir."

It was his pairing with other stars, particularly actresses, that proved to be mutually beneficial. Columnist Bland Johaneson called Baxter "Hollywood's leading man deluxe," and some of his most enduring films featured the following female co-stars: Joan Bennett (two films), Alice Faye (two films), Janet Gaynor (three films), Myrna Loy (four films), and Helen Vinson (three films). Conversely, teaming him with an unknown actress often provided a boost to her career. According to Johaneson, "Playing with Baxter is a sure shove to stardom for any fortunate young lady who tries it" (n. pag.). Hedda Hopper stated, "There's a kind of superstition about him. If you begin with Warner, you're on your way" (n. pag.). Hollis Wood agreed:

> Warner Baxter has been at the head of the cast a number of times when various ladies, who subsequently became stars, were getting their sea legs in pictures. However, because it has happened so frequently, Hollywood is getting to think there is really something to the Baxter-to-stardom sequence. (n. pag.)

For example, actress Myrna Loy signed her first long-term contract after she appeared with Baxter in *Renegades* (1930). Janet Gaynor, already on her way to stardom, became an even greater star after their work together in *Daddy Long Legs* (1931). Others whose careers benefited from their collaboration with Baxter included Alice Faye, Rochelle Hudson, Ruby Keeler, June Lang, Marian Nixon, Marjorie Weaver, and Arleen Whelan.

By the mid-1930s, Baxter had began to age and, tiring of lovemaking roles, remarked, "It's difficult for me to play opposite a youngster under twenty. By contrast they make me look a bit grand-fatherish for my own good" (qtd. in Rhea 26). Also, having seen other "great lovers" come and go, he concluded that a romantic lead had a definite limit to the length of his career:

> There are two courses open to a player at my stage of a career. He may continue on with romantic leads until there comes that awful day when he finds roles no longer available. Or he may anticipate that event by several years, and seek other forms of dramatic expression in which to mold a new career against the day when his earlier type of role is no longer open to him. ("Alternate" n. pag.)

The time to build the foundation for that kind of career, he believed, was while the actor was at the height of his popularity so that his bargaining power would not be reduced by any loss of prestige. Therefore, in 1934, when his Fox contract was coming up for renewal, Baxter devised a unique mid-career plan that would allow him to alternate romantic leads with character roles. He explained:

> And so it was that I specifically asked Darryl F. Zanuck, after he had renewed my contract with Twentieth Century Fox, to place me in strong character parts. I expect to continue this alternation between the two general classes of roles until

the time comes when I confine myself entirely to character. (qtd. in Sobol 6)

At the time, this was a daring decision. Having infused his performances with his realistic lovemaking system, coupled with the studio's commodity packaging of his romantic image, the question remained as to whether the public would accept Baxter as a character actor. In 1936, he starred in *The Prisoner of Shark Island*, in which he portrayed the doctor wrongly accused of aiding Abraham Lincoln's assassin. Its critical and popular success signaled the beginning of a new career in character roles. This interesting and novel handling of Baxter's career set a precedent as he became the first major star of his generation to make a smooth and uninterrupted transition from romantic lead to character actor.

This alternating career plan had a direct effect on the love scenes in Baxter's films, most notably with regard to the diminishing of kissing scenes and declarations of love. For example, he played a happily married man in *To Mary With Love* (1936). Here the focus was on domestic life and other issues rather than ardent lovemaking. In other, romantic films of the period in which Baxter won a lady's love, there were fewer kisses and her character, not his, became the one to say "I love you." For example, in *Slave Ship* (1937), much of the love scene is performed with Baxter's back to the camera, his female romantic interest has all of the love dialogue, and there is only one kiss. In *Kidnapped* (1938), the woman performs the declaration of love without a kiss. In *Barricade* (1939), the woman rests her head on Baxter's shoulder, but there is no spoken declaration of love nor a kiss.

Baxter's career transition was complete when *Adam Had Four Sons* (1941) premiered at Radio City Music Hall and the program notes announced, "It brings Warner Baxter's departure from the 'glamour boy' roles for which he has long been known" (5). This acceptance of the former romantic star as a character actor was echoed by the reviewer for the *Richmond News Leader*, who stated, "Warner Baxter finds much better field for his talents in a character part than in trying to be the romantic leading man" ("Film Adapted" n. pag.). In addition, with Baxter's performances in the 1940s *Crime Doctor* series, the burden of romantic lovemaking was lifted from his shoulders and placed, instead, upon the supporting actors.

## The Production Code Influence

The "Code to Govern the Making of Talking, Synchronized, and Silent Motion Pictures" (hereafter referred to as the Code) was a document adopted in 1930 by the Association of Motion Picture Producers, Inc., in response to public protest over violent and immoral movies. Serving as a means of self-censorship, it offered the film industry a set of rigid guidelines that were incorporated into a system and enforced by the Production Code Administration beginning in 1934. With the overriding theme that no film should lower the moral standards of those who see it, the Code dictated how movie plots should depict crime, sex, and religion; had certain strictures on costume and dancing; and defined what was obscene and vulgar. This system remained in effect for several decades, "patrolling the diegesis" of every movie produced in Hollywood (Doherty 3).

Of the twelve "Particular Applications" outlined by the Code, the sections on "Sex" and "Costume" had the strongest implications for lovemaking in Baxter's films. Prior to 1934, his film love scenes were characterized by intensity, complexity, variety, and duration. Following the enforcement of the Code in 1934, many of these characteristics were altered or eliminated entirely from his subsequent films. The overall effect was one of diminishing and compacting various elements, resulting in a watered-down version of his former lovemaking style. As Thomas Doherty has stated, "Erotic sparks still flew but less visibly, with lower voltage" (3).

"Application II—Sex" of the Code stated that "scenes of passion should so be treated that these scenes do not stimulate the lower and baser element" (qtd. in Leff and Simmons 285). The resulting effect was fewer, shorter, and more restrained love scenes in Baxter's movies. Typically, the earlier films feature two or more extended love scenes of up to ten minutes each in duration, with multiple kisses. For example, the couples in *Linda* (1929) and *Penthouse* continue their lovemaking by moving from room to room, while those in *Behind That Curtain* and *Doctors' Wives* (1931) engage in extended sexual foreplay. The passion is so savage in *Renegades* and *Paddy the Next Best Thing* (1933) that the women are forced to endure physical pain. In contrast, later films such as *Grand Canary*, *Under the Pampas Moon*, *Vogues of 1938*, and *Slave Ship* feature only one or two kisses with love scenes of under two minutes.

One example of such diminishing and compacting of elements occurs between two of the Latin-themed westerns, *In Old Arizona* and *Under the Pampas Moon*. The earlier film is dense with "scenes of passion" including foreplay, three extended love scenes, multiple kisses, infidelity, heavy drinking, and innuendo. The latter film distills this activity down into the lyrics of a song, which addresses the gaucho dancing, kissing, and making love with various young women in the hours after the cattle have been put to sleep, with the pampas moon above. Consequently, the "scenes of passion" of the first film are reduced to a "song of passion" in the second.

Similarly, "Application VI—Costume" of the Code stated that "indecent or undue exposure is forbidden" and "undressing scenes should be avoided" (qtd.

in Leff and Simmons 285). Here, the resulting effect was more conservative costuming and the elimination of clothes-changing scenes. Because Baxter was attractive and well built, his earlier films featured him in daring, revealing, or exotic attire. Some of his costumes included tight pants, jodhpurs, high boots, boleros, cummerbunds, burnooses, trench coats, open-necked tunics with no undershirt, and centered holsters with pistols pointing to his crotch. In addition, early films typically featured him changing clothes with the help of a servant or a loved one. For example, in *Romance of the Rio Grande* (1929), the young woman who rescues him helps him out of his clothes. In *Doctors' Wives*, his estranged wife/nurse changes him into his surgical garb. In *The Squaw Man* (1931), the native woman opens and closes his shirt while dressing his wound. In *Man About Town* (1932), his valet, through a point-of-view shot, dresses him in his scarf and coat. In his later films, though well costumed, Baxter's clothes are less exotic, more modest, and looser fitting. The dressing scenes are entirely eliminated.

## Conclusion

Warner Baxter was a popular silent film star whose image as a romantic leading man intensified with the coming of sound. After winning the Academy Award for best actor, he maintained his popularity as a romantic actor and made a seamless switch to character parts in his later years. As a star whose body of work coincided with the advent of the Motion Picture Production Code, the love scenes in his films offer interesting areas for an analysis of sexual politics.

The development and changes in lovemaking in Baxter's films were caused by an interplay of three forces. First, Baxter's philosophy of acting and dramatic-lovemaking formula remained a constant throughout all of his love scenes. Second, Baxter's alternating career plan created a tension between the commodity exploitation of his romantic image and his desire for artistic development. Third, the enforcement of the Motion Picture Production Code diminished and compacted Baxter's on-screen lovemaking, altered the appearance of his costuming, and abolished the intimacy of dressing and undressing that had been part of his early performance style.

## Works Cited

"Alternate Film Types, Baxter Says." *New York Post* 22 Aug. 1936. New York
    Public Library Theatre Collection (MFL+ n.c. 2236).
Baxter, Warner. "Warner Baxter on the Rules of Screen Productions."
    *Pittsburgh Press* 22 Feb. 1924. New York Public Library Theatre Collection

(*ZAN *T213 #40).

Doherty, Thomas. *Pre-Code Hollywood: Sex, Immorality, and Insurrection in American Cinema, 1930-1934.* New York: Columbia University Press, 1999.

Everson, William K. *A Pictorial History of the Western Film.* Secaucus, NJ: Citadel Press, 1969.

"Film Adapted from 'Legacy.'" *Richmond News Leader* 9 May 1941. New York Public Library Theatre Collection (Clippings File, *Adam Had Four Sons*).

Fox Films. *Romance of the Rio Grande Press Book.* 1929. New York Public Library Theatre Collection (*ZAN *T23).

Greene, Alice Craig. "Gentleman in the Dark." *Motion Picture* 12 Apr. 1943. New York Public Library Theatre Collection (MFL+ n.c. 2236).

Hopper, Hedda. "Warner Baxter Given 'Great Guy' Rating." 1938. New York Public Library Theatre Collection (Clippings File, Warner Baxter).

Hughes, Elinor. *Famous Stars of Filmdom: Men.* Freeport, NY: Books for Libraries Press, 1931.

Johaneson, Bland. "His Newest Lead is Marjorie Weaver." *New York Daily Mirror* 12 July 1938. New York Public Library Theatre Collection (MFL+ n.c. 2236).

Leff, Leonard J., and Jerold L. Simmons. *The Dame in the Kimono: Hollywood, Censorship, and the Production Code from the 1920s to the 1960s.* New York: Grove, 1990.

"Radio City Music Hall." *Showplace Magazine* 27 Mar. 1941: 5, 13.

Rhea, Marian. "How Does Warner Baxter Do It?" *Motion Picture* 3 Apr. 1938: 26, 67-68.

Sobol, Louis. "The Voice of Broadway: Down Memory Lane with Warner Baxter." *New York Evening Journal* 10 Apr. 1937: 3, 6.

Stuart, Ray. *Immortals of the Screen.* New York: Bonanza Books, 1965.

Tully, Jim. "Warner Baxter and Women." *Boston Herald: Magazine Section* 12 June 1936. New York Public Library Theatre Collection (*ZAN *T213 #23).

Wood, Hollis. "Baxter-to-Stardom Sequence Becoming Traditional in Hollywood." *Richmond News Leader* 18 July 1938. New York Public Library Theatre Collection (MFL+ n.c. 2236).

# CHAPTER THREE

## QUEERING *CITIZEN KANE*

## DAVID M. LUGOWSKI

Considerable work within feminist, gay, and queer theory and analysis has focused on readings of well-known, often canonical media texts in order to explore the implications of style, narrative, and performance for the cultures within which these texts circulate. The ambition is to open up the workings of a heterocentric, (white) raced patriarchy: to map histories, consider contradictions, reappropriate canonical cultural texts for political and cultural gain, and indeed understand the diverse pleasures that readings of these texts produce (Doty, *Making*, xii). Surely, few media texts within U.S. (and international) culture have given more pleasure and can be considered more canonical than Orson Welles' film *Citizen Kane* (1941). And yet, this film has been strangely overlooked (if not entirely, then at least considerably) in studies of gender and sexuality. But consider the time period during which the film emerged. Lesbian, gay, and otherwise queer imagery proliferated in U.S. film as never before in the 1930s and for some time thereafter, given the lively gay culture of the 1920s, the coming of sound (and risqué dialogue) to Hollywood film, and the emergence of artists and genres (e.g., the musical, the horror film) central to the development of lesbian, gay, and queer cultures. When box-office receipts began to decline during the early years of the Great Depression, filmmakers responded in various ways, trying to step up titillating sex and violence in ways that might get around the workings of the conservative Motion Picture Production Code guidelines for film content (Lugowski 3). Coming at the very end of the Great Depression—this singular economic downturn, this immense cultural upheaval—*Citizen Kane* is at once a typical product of its time, a major work of film art, a remarkable summation of its era, and a fascinating commentary upon it, as scholars including André Bazin, Robert Carringer, James Naremore, and William Simon have demonstrated. And thus it is perhaps not surprising that *Citizen Kane* is so very queer.

Work done elsewhere by myself, George Chauncey, and other researchers has demonstrated that homosexuality, open gayness in public life, and queer representation in cinema were quite common and yet socially and politically charged matters during the Great Depression. The country moved in an increasingly conservative direction after the perceived excesses of the 1920s, and the unemployment of so many male providers—coupled with the perceived threat of so many working women—engendered a crisis in masculinity during this era. As Robert McElvaine explains:

> The Depression can be seen as having effected a "feminization" of American society. The self-centered, aggressive, competitive "male" ethic of the 1920s was discredited. Men who lost their jobs became dependent in ways that women had been thought to be. (340)

Men "experienced their inability to provide adequate family support as a failure of masculinity," and they became less interested in seeing seemingly weak, effeminate men and ambitious, "mannish" working women (McFadden 119). Cities such as New York and Los Angeles, familiar with nightclub "pansy" humor and other visible markers of gay culture, enjoyed such "sophisticated" (and usually humorous) representations, and these cities were disproportionately important to the box-office success of many films (Shindler 143). On the other hand, more rural and conservative areas, if they understood the codings involved in queer representation, complained bitterly about these sorts of representations.

The Production Code that had been written in 1930, which included the line that "sexual perversion or any inference of it is forbidden," had been rather loosely enforced during the Depression's early years. But when the Catholic Legion of Decency threatened to boycott theaters, Hollywood began, in mid-1934, to regulate its own content rather more firmly, empowering the highly conservative and bigoted Joseph Breen to head up the Production Code Administration (PCA) (Black 21). The content regulation files of the PCA, held by the Margaret Herrick Library of the Academy of Motion Picture Arts and Sciences, illustrate Hollywood's attempts to "censor" its own films rather than have the federal government or local boards ban films or ruin films' continuity by making their own cuts. Among dozens of films about which PCA files at the Academy library feature content regulators warning studios about "pansy humor," "lesbianism," or other forms of "sexual perversion," one could cite *Just Imagine* and *Charley's Aunt* (both 1930); *The Front Page* (1931); *Blessed Event, Hell's Highway, The Kid from Spain*, and *Lawyer Man* (all 1932); *Blood Money, Design for Living, Diplomaniacs, Fast Workers, International House, Little Giant, Only Yesterday, Our Betters, Queen Christina, Son of a Sailor*, and *So This Is Africa* (all 1933); *Circus Clown, Dr. Monica, The Gay Divorcee, One More River*, and *Wonder Bar* (all 1934); *Barbary Coast, The Flame Within, Roberta*, and *Top Hat* (all 1935); *The Big Noise, The Bold Caballero, Dracula's Daughter, Follow the Fleet, Swing Time*, and *Sylvia Scarlett* (all 1936); *Hollywood Hotel* and *The Life of Emile Zola* (both 1937); *Vivacious Lady* and

*Up the River* (both 1938); *The Bank Dick* and *Turnabout* (both 1940); and *In the Navy* and *Love Crazy* (both 1941). These files (and other sources from the era, such as film reviews and even studio publicity materials) prove that queerness existed in the eyes of readers (in this case, censors) back then, and not only in our readings of these films today.

To take a particularly good example, the file on Cecil B. DeMille's epic of ancient Rome, *The Sign of the Cross* (1932), features memorable letters from angry religious ministers and others who took offense at a scene in which a dancing bisexual woman attempts a lesbian seduction of the film's virtuous Christian heroine. Later queer representation during the Depression, however, while often somewhat less overt than in the 1930-34 period, could not fully be eradicated, because it both provided so much entertainment value and was a necessary ideological prop for "straightness."

The lesbian and gay life that had been so open in certain major cities, as documented by George Chauncey, Lillian Faderman, and others, was clamped down upon as the Depression progressed. Queer representation, in fact, received the scorn of both the left and the right. Many communists and liberals perceived queerness as a sign of the decadence of capitalism, while conservatives generally read queerness as communist in nature, or as part of the "sinfulness" of the 1920s for which the country was now paying the price. The Depression in the United States really did not end fully until it entered World War II. Given that Charles Foster Kane's (played by Orson Welles) politics shift in various ways during *Citizen Kane*, that his political sympathies and personal motivations are read so diversely by others, and that he is readable as quite queer, my goal is to explore issues of sexual representation and film style within the context of these shifts in relation to American sociopolitical history and culture.

While quite a number of films from the Depression era feature prominent supporting characters and even leads who perform queerness, the majority of the figures that I have been focusing upon in my research are cameo-appearance "bit part" queers. Some might contend that the brevity of these cameos renders their function within the text and the culture at large as insignificant, that all one can really read from these figures is that gays, lesbians, and other queers were stereotyped as much as other minorities during this time, and were less visible than most. And yet the hundreds of examples, as well as the level of objections to them, suggest that such representations are highly significant. I want to suggest that these visible but usually overlooked traces of queerness in films are not only quite common but can indexically or metonymically signal larger contradictions or ruptures in America's cinematic discourses and its cultural politics. Let us consider just such a cameo.

Given the widely prevalent cultural codes of the era, the librarian of the Walter Parks Thatcher Memorial Library in *Citizen Kane* evokes the "mythical mannish lesbian," especially in its sexless professional woman and spinster incarnations. Her dress and demeanor send signals that can elude the reader, or that readers can ignore, but which, given some focus, are hard to mistake. Laura Mulvey seems to make this point when she describes the librarian as lacking "the slightest vestige of femininity, dressed in a severe suit and with an equally severe, repressive manner" (48). Her brusque, businesslike and curt manner in dealing with the reporter Thompson (played by William Alland), the aggressive, muscular swing to her arms as she walks toward the reading room, her extremely short hair and tailored suit—sporting a trademarked signifier of lesbianism in this period, a man's necktie—code her as queer. This widely known stereotype was one of the most prevalent representations of lesbianism during this era. Jennings (played by Joe Manz), the male guard, meanwhile, has much less to do and say, and he is dressed in a fairly neutral uniform. Yet, as I have demonstrated elsewhere, gay and lesbian types are frequently teamed up in films of this period, such that if the lesbian librarian is coded more overtly, Jennings is still queer by association.

> When patriarchy admits to only two genders, feminizing a man seems to require the masculinizing of a woman, and vice versa. A heterocentric system of oppression relies on queerness to establish normalcy, yet that queerness only breeds other queernesses, further undermining the system it was meant to bolster. (Lugowski 17-18)

Beyond this, however, even Jennings' tiny bit invokes two queer types: the vague, ineffectual sissy and the comically ridiculed servant figure. When Thompson closes Thatcher's memoir in frustration at not finding out what "Rosebud" means, Jennings, with just a hint of sashaying in his walk, asks, "I beg your pardon, sir. What did you say?" with a touch of the gentle propriety so common in the queerly coded butlers and other "men's men" of the era.

Of vital importance, too, is that queerness exists in coded language and in the readings of other characters within films. In offering a thinly disguised take on real-life newspaper tycoon William Randolph Hearst, Welles and company even dared to use "Rosebud," Hearst's term of endearment for the vagina of his mistress, the woman he tried to make into a movie star, Marion Davies (Brady 287). That said, the term "rosebud" also has more queer connotations. Thompson, still wondering about the meaning of Kane's mysterious last word, addresses the portrait of Thatcher with a flip, cynical wisecrack, "You're not Rosebud, are you?" He then tries the librarian, and finally asks the guard, "And your name's Jennings?" Even the suddenly intrusive, sarcastic wail of the muted brass in the film's score, sounding like mocking laughter, suggests a campy tone to Thompson's wisecracks. Considering two men, and a mannish woman, as possibly being "Rosebud" operates queerly on two levels. One is that the term is a gay slang expression for the anus (Carroll 61). Another, though, would have been known much more widely in U.S. culture at this time, namely that calling men by the names of flowers, or speaking of flowers even indirectly in connection with men, was enough to suggest that they might be effeminate queers. A virtual florist's shop full of species is used in this manner in U.S. films of the Depression era; effeminate male characters are linked with, or called, pansies most commonly, but also violets, gardenias, lilies of the valley, and geraniums. The *tres gai* Cowardly Lion in *The Wizard of Oz* (1939) even refers to himself as a "dandelion" (thus not only evoking a flower but also outing himself as a "dandy," a figure with queer connotations). In terms of the characters' signifiers of dress and performance, then, along with the film's score and the comical readings of characters within the diegesis, Jennings and the librarian are queer.

Given that queerness at first glance resides in these "traces" from *Citizen Kane*, what import might they have for the larger textual system of the film and its meanings? What does it mean that the librarian and Jennings are the caretakers of the legacy of Walter Parks Thatcher, who is considered, even if sarcastically, as a candidate for "Rosebud" by Thompson? Our reading of the bit part characters thus could extend to Thatcher, who plays a fussbudget in the film. He has a somewhat effete and overly precise manner, and we never see or hear anything about any wife or family he might have. He is identified with the potentially decadent forces of wealth (and also conservatism) often read as queer in Depression-era culture, and he is the embodiment of the force of "good fortune" that takes Charles away from his family (even if it is a case of his mother sending him away) into a fairy-tale world of luxury. Thus, Thatcher has a queerness about him as the replacement for the heterosexual family, and insofar as he is a failure as a heterosexual father (or mother) figure. The story of young Kane, then, is that of a boy who is sent away from his parents to live with an apparently single, wealthy, older man, to be kept in some kind of strange (dare I say queer?) alternative family arrangement.

Even Charles' "natural" family and the actions of his mother in sending him off with the queer Thatcher read queerly. The film suggests that Mrs. Kane (played by Agnes Moorehead) has made a wrong decision in choosing for her son the "American dream" of material wealth and status over that of a more traditional and humble family existence, but this connotes a certain queerness to her as well as to the American dream itself. Furthermore, another of her reasons for sending Charles away—the sometimes abusive nature of Mr. Kane (played by Harry Shannon)—presents one of the film's many representations of dysfunctional heterosexual families. Also, Agnes Moorehead, in her film debut already giving one of her memorable portraits of waspish neurosis and sporting a somewhat harsh, spinsterish look, has important connections as both performer and persona to queer readings and queer culture (White 181-193).

Besides featuring Orson Welles as director, co-writer, and star, *Citizen Kane* is an unusual film for its overtly leftist-liberal political stance amid the workings of often (though not always) conservative Hollywood. Michael Denning has identified the film as part of late Popular Front discourse, and Welles' works in media including theater, radio, and film are key examples of Denning's rich metaphor of the "laboring" of "the cultural front" that he shows began during the Depression (362-402). Perhaps my primary use of Denning, or my contribution to his ideas, is to suggest that queer codings and implicit debates over queer discourses are at work amid these larger political struggles. Thus, insofar as we may read Thatcher as queer, the film is also typical of its time as an indication of how the political left (as well as the right) stigmatized queerness. At one point in the film, Thatcher disparagingly attempts to label Kane a communist. The film's subtle casting of Thatcher as queer thus connects with the American left's attempts to stigmatize potentially fascistic conservatives as queer. In the famous film-within-the-film newsreel we also see a man speaking at an open-air public rally. Contrasted with the forum of the press conference, the costuming, and other facets of how we have seen Thatcher denounce Kane, this man can be read as working-class, perhaps as a union leader, or even a communist rally organizer. To suggest that Kane is not only complex but also ultimately unknowable, that all figures, especially those as public as Kane, are constructed discursively, Welles contrasts Thatcher's charge with this man angrily accusing Kane of being a fascist. Thus, the film represents the scorn of the right and the left, each using the same figure for its own political ends. While queer representation was not the only site of contestation, it too, like Kane, received the scorn of both ends of the political spectrum. And, as we shall see, no matter how we read the politics of Charles Foster Kane, or see how they change over the course of the film, he too is readable as queer in his many incarnations.

Once we become inclined to read queerness in *Citizen Kane* in terms of representation operating as part of the film's larger discursive and ideological systems, we find that it inheres, in different ways and to varying degrees, throughout the film. As the film progresses, Kane's closest and in many ways most enduring and successful relationships are with other men, especially his best friend Jed Leland (played by Joseph Cotten) and his loyal sidekick Bernstein (played by Everett Sloane). Bernstein, a rare character in this period to have a name that is so "openly" Jewish (which has connections with queerness itself at this time, as we shall see), does have a brief but lovely and memorable monologue about never forgetting a woman he once saw wearing a white dress and sporting a parasol. His reverie, though, seems as much a romanticizing of his youth and a sweetly nostalgic memory, queerly based at least partly on the fineries of female fashion and accessories as much as on the drives of heterosexual attraction. Even such tropes as dance, which are vital to gender performance and queer readings in this period (e.g., the RKO musicals starring Ginger Rogers and Fred Astaire), come into play in the film. Jed Leland remembers being the partner of Emily (played by Ruth Warrick), the first Mrs. Kane, at a dancing school, but he does not suggest that he had any romantic inclinations. Instead, he notes a bit narcissistically, "I was very graceful."

Alexander Doty argues that the relationship between Leland and Kane, or at least the feelings that Leland has for Kane, are "the major queer element" in the film (*Flaming*, 17). Doty observes that when Kane is kicked out of one school after another, Leland follows him around with a bad case of hero worship, eventually insisting on becoming the queerly coded drama critic for Kane's newspaper. Even the nature of Leland's narration is queer: In telling of Kane's relationships with Emily and Susan, the second Mrs. Kane (played by Dorothy Comingore), Leland narrates "the romantic and sexual parts of the story—the parts that would be most interesting to a queer guy who is himself in love with his friend," at least until Kane's obsession with Susan and their dispute over her operatic debut push Leland away (Doty, *Flaming*, 17).

Indeed, throughout the film, neither Leland nor Bernstein are fleshed out as characters by means of any representation of heterosexuality. Of course, for this film's narrative this is not necessary; the central character is Kane, and Leland and Bernstein are important largely insofar as they relate to him. Nevertheless, as these men move from the playful homosocial hijinks of college to their later crises and breakups, Kane's relationships with Bernstein and Leland take on a resonance that not all friendships among men in Hollywood narratives duplicate. Friendships among men are not, of course, necessarily homosexual (in terms of sex and sexuality) or queer (in terms of cultural identity). I would not be inclined to read Leland and Bernstein as either the openly effeminate pansy types or the fussy, henpecked sissies of the era because the subtlety of specificity would be lost. Yet within a binary dynamic in which heterosexuality and homosexuality in our culture are opposed, an absence of one does admit the presence of the other.

Beyond that, *Citizen Kane* shows an awareness of strong same-sex feelings that can compete with heterosexual family structures. Kane, for example, spends more time playing with the boys in the masculine realm of the office—Emily's "only co-respondent" as she describes her rival for Kane's love, the newspaper—than he does with her, and not of course for the patriarchal reason that he needs the money. He and Emily also quarrel over Bernstein's apparently flamboyant (queer?) gift to their child, one that meets with her disapproval.

(This battle also highlights differences between Emily's upper-class WASP tastes and those of the Jewish middle-class Bernstein; class and ethnicity impact queer readings as well.) Kane's concern for Bernstein's feelings over those of his wife is on some level an inherently queer part of the loyalties within the world of same-sex friendship.

The characters of the queer librarian and queer security guard led us to a queer reading of Thatcher and, through him, to one of Kane and his friends. As I have noted, Kane's queerness might relate to his having been raised from an early age by a queer man. But Kane's queer roots go back even further. In a vaguely Freudian sense, Charles is forever Oedipally tied to the dominating mother who takes him away from an overly aggressive (read: masculine) father and sends him to be raised by a queer man, thus feminizing the boy. Or, alternately, the mother, empowered by the money left in her name and not her husband's, becomes a dominantly "mannish" figure who then has a queer effect upon her son. (The "mama's boy" figure is also readable as queer during this time.) In other words, seen in terms of Depression-era culture, both the fancy manners and effete wealth of Thatcher, and the emasculating wealth and assertiveness of the mother, are queer forces at work. No wonder they occupy the same side of the frame (the right) while the overruled father (on the left) watches his wife sign away his son as the boy, framed in the middle, plays with his Rosebud in the white snow of innocence. Either way, Kane develops into a man whose wealth and power lead to an over-investment in the performance of masculinity, one that leads to marital infidelity, sexual transgression, and the beginnings of his downfall. Indeed, much of *Citizen Kane* operates queerly insofar as it details Kane's failures at maintaining and developing heterosexual relationships with Emily and Susan. Kane is queer because, as Susan notes late in the film, he is ultimately incapable of (heterosexual) love.

Once we see Kane's life as queer, even characters the film picks up along the way, especially those relating to his private life, can be read as queer, too. The best example is the opera coach Matiste (played by Fortunio Bonanova). Via his "backstage" occupation in the world of theater, his spiffy costuming and grooming, and especially his seething yet comically used emotionalism, Matiste relates to the theatrical sissy types of the era. He is also a flamboyant Italian queer who exemplifies the links between various ethnicities and queer male representations that were fairly common during this time. Italians, Frenchmen, Latinos, and Russians were often portrayed as excessively florid and demonstrative; Jews were seen as the unmanly urban outsiders who, like gays, could pass for what they were not; Asians and Asian Americans were often linked with perversity and exoticism; and African-American characters were commonly servile and cowardly. Thus it was that "Aryan" types were less stigmatized in terms of portraying a more "suitable" masculinity. The opera connection, meanwhile, even makes Susan's performance of gender and sexuality a bit suspect: Unable to manage the excessively feminine trappings of garb and melodrama that opera requires, she traipses about the stage (under Matiste's watchful queer gaze) like an under-rehearsed drag queen. Reading Matiste as queer also leads us back to Kane's own obsession with status through the theatrical world of opera, and his own compulsive collecting of fine art, which takes us back full circle to Noël Carroll's reading of Rosebud as a sign of Kane's anal-retentiveness.

Thus, the presence of queerness near the beginning of *Citizen Kane*, once worked through the text, signals the film as a late Depression-era study of the failures of apparently masculine heterosexuality in a world of undisciplined and unsteady capitalism. If the film does somewhat use its queerness as part of its condemnation of certain characters and discourses, that is perhaps only to be expected. As other readings of the film have suggested in vastly different ways, *Citizen Kane* is an exceptional film for the thorough and subtle ways it utilizes motifs, style, and discursive tropes to construct its complex narrative and pointed political critique. It is, however, also a film very much of its time in its borrowings from the trappings of mass culture: newspaper headlines, pulp fiction, Hollywood, gossip about Hearst and Davies, widespread leftist rumblings, the "dollar-book Freud" Welles claimed for it, and, as I have suggested, conventional attitudes toward queerness, however artfully used (Giannetti 499).

Maybe the way I can redeem some of the film's use of queerness is akin to what my work (and that of many others) has been pursuing for years: suggesting that the contradictions of queer representation, and the very visibility of queerness as spectacle and entertainment as a destabilizing force in this period, demand a more flexible awareness of how it operates than that available through an "images of" analysis of stereotypes. Maybe, too, *Citizen Kane* is a good signpost of how queerness functions structurally as well as locally. If Charles Foster Kane is ultimately unknowable, perhaps it is because he is so queer but represented through a system one would think was designed to represent and promote only heterosexuality. One might argue that some of the brilliance of the film lies in pointing this out. Kane is at once closeted by the conventions and politics of American culture and refracted as queer by the distorting mirrors of that culture; as in near the film's end, what we have are an infinite series of images. Among those images, what I am choosing to view as one of the film's basic scenarios—a study of troubled masculinity in a time of economic and political crisis as indexed by traces of queer representation—makes *Citizen Kane* an important summation of Depression-era queer discourse. I would contend that this queer reading and historical contextualization of *Citizen Kane* is of ongoing relevance, not only because the film itself has played such an immense role in our popular culture, but also because our culture and our world are still dealing with the points of contact that emerge among money, masculinity, war, economic ups and downs, the "American success" story, fame, and politics—especially as these are played out through the prism of sexuality within the realm of media representation.

## Works Cited

Bazin, Andre. *Orson Welles*. New York: Harper & Row, 1978.

Black, Gregory D. *Hollywood Censored: Morality Codes, Catholics and the Movies*. New York: Cambridge University Press, 1994.

Brady, Frank. *Citizen Welles*. New York: Charles Scribner's Sons, 1989.

Carringer, Robert. *The Making of Citizen Kane*. Berkeley: University of California Press, 1985.

Carroll, Noël. "Interpreting *Citizen Kane*," *Persistence of Vision* 7 (1989): 51-62.

Chauncey, George. *Gay New York: Gender, Urban Culture, and the Making of the Gay Male World, 1890-1940*. New York: Basic Books, 1994.

Denning, Michael. *The Cultural Front: The Laboring of American Culture in the Twentieth Century*. New York: Verso, 1996.

Doty, Alexander. *Making Things Perfectly Queer: Interpreting Mass Culture*. Minneapolis: University of Minnesota Press, 1993.

—. *Flaming Classics: Queering the Film Canon*. New York: Routledge, 2000.

Faderman, Lillian. *Odd Girls and Twilight Lovers: A History of Lesbian Life in Twentieth-Century America*. New York: Columbia University Press, 1991.

Giannetti, Louis. *Understanding Movies*. 8th ed. Upper Saddle River, NJ: Prentice-Hall, 1999.

Lugowski, David M. "Queering the (New) Deal: Lesbian and Gay Representation and the Depression-Era Cultural Politics of Hollywood's Production Code." *Cinema Journal* 38.2 (1999): 3-35.

McElvaine, Robert. *The Great Depression: America, 1929-1941*. New York: Times Books, 1984.

McFadden, Margaret. "'America's Boy Friend Who Couldn't Get a Date': Gender, Race, and the Cultural Work of the *Jack Benny Program*, 1932-1946." *Journal of American History* 80.1 (1993): 113-134.

Mulvey, Laura. *Citizen Kane*. London: British Film Institute, 1992.

Naremore, James. *The Magic World of Orson Welles*. New York: Oxford, 1978.

Shindler, Colin. *Hollywood in Crisis: Cinema and American Society, 1929-1939*. New York: Routledge, 1996.

Simon, William G. "Introduction." *Persistence of Vision* 7 (1989): 1-7.

White, Patricia. *Uninvited: Classical Hollywood Cinema and Lesbian Representability*. Indiana: Bloomington University Press, 1999.

Part II
Film and Sexual Politics in the Postwar Era

# CHAPTER FOUR

# THE LOVE BETWEEN WARDEN AND PREW THAT DARE NOT SPEAK ITS NAME: CONTAINING HOMOSEXUALITY AS SUBTEXT IN *FROM HERE TO ETERNITY*

## KYLO-PATRICK R. HART

> Hollywood, despite its history of censorship and its pretense to heterocentrism, is one of the queerest institutions ever invented.
> —Ellis Hanson (7)

In the years following World War II, many fears circulated in U.S. society pertaining to the "reconversion" of veterans to life in postwar America. Common among these was the concern that the soldiers returning home would not be able to successfully resume their expected role as "family men," because they had typically been exposed to various forms of "perversion" and homosexual acts during their years of military life (May 88). The first Kinsey report on men raised eyebrows when it was published in 1948, in large part because it revealed that a high percentage of U.S. men had engaged in homosexual sexual activities, and many also had sex outside of presumed monogamous relationships. It is perhaps unsurprising, therefore, that all forms of sexual behavior outside of marriage became a national obsession in the late 1940s and early 1950s, and that government officials led a campaign of homophobia in the postwar years (May 94).

As it had in earlier decades, the Production Code Administration (PCA) in the 1950s continued to operate as the primary censor of the U.S. film industry, enforcing the provisions of the Motion Picture Production Code. Without official approval from the PCA, confirming that a specific project did not contain Code violations, no studio could shoot a script or release a specific film (Simmons 70). In addition to taboos such as the depiction of prostitution, narcotics addiction, and venereal disease, the Code prohibited explicit references to homosexuality in all U.S. cinematic offerings, even those set in locations that were regarded as potential hotbeds for homosexual activity, such as prisons and military bases. This means that creative filmmakers and audience members were forced to foreground particular images, gestures, character behaviors, plot developments, narrative ambiguities, and related components of any film in order to encode and/or decode any homosexual subtext it might (need to) contain (LaValley 60-61).

Because it was based on a novel filled with obscenities and "shady ladies," the 1953 film *From Here to Eternity*, directed by Fred Zinnemann, was scrutinized closely by the PCA at various stages of its production (Mitgang 5). The members of this censoring organization required two primary changes from the novel to the film: (1) a more unhappy outcome for the first sergeant and the captain's wife, who partake in an illicit affair; and (2) conversion of the New Congress Club from a house of prostitution to a social club without any connotation of being a brothel, a "sort of primitive U.S.O. [and] a place of well-worn merriment" (Mitgang 5). In addition, PCA officials initially requested that either Sergeant Milton Warden (played by Burt Lancaster) or Karen Holmes (played by Deborah Karr) wear a bathrobe in their famous lovemaking scene at the beach, and that Warden not use a broken bottle as a weapon during a barroom confrontation, but they backed off of these additional concerns once their primary concerns had adequately been addressed (Simmons 75).

What the PCA censors appear to have overlooked entirely, however, is that this film contains a substantial homosexual subtext, which to the careful viewer reveals itself to be a homosexual love story between Warden, a man's man who is respected both by his superiors and the G.I.'s he leads, and Pvt. Robert E. Lee Prewitt (played by Montgomery Clift), a skilled bugler and former boxer who intends, like Warden, to be a "thirty-year man" in the army. This oversight seems particularly surprising in an era that so vigilantly and virulently sought to repress homosexuality in all aspects of American life.

## Homosexuality and Homophobia in the Postwar Era

"Sex was seen as perhaps the most important thing in life in fifties America," Richard Dyer has explained, convincingly citing publishing events including the release of the Kinsey reports on men and women (in 1948 and 1953, respectively), best-selling novels such as *From Here to Eternity* (1951) and *Peyton Place* (1956), and the premiere issue of *Playboy* (1953) as evidence of this claim (24). The topic of homosexuality figured prominently within discussions of 1950s sexuality. Gay men of that era were presumed to be sexual "perverts," with "no masculine backbone" and lacking in emotional stability, who would readily fall prey to communists and members of other subversive organizations because they were believed to lack the moral stamina necessary to resist being seduced or blackmailed (May 94-95). Bachelors over the age of 30 were typically presumed to be gay and deserving of psychotherapy to help "cure" their deviance (Lundberg and Farnham 370). The weak and effeminate appearance of many men of the era, whether gay or otherwise, was presumed to be the deleterious end result of uncontrolled "momism" (Wylie 210).

As Steven Cohan notes in his book *Masked Men: Masculinity and the Movies in the Fifties*, America was experiencing a perceived postwar masculinity crisis during the 1950s. The launch of the cold war was accompanied by a decreasing confidence in the ability of American men, who appeared to be suffering from an imperiled state of national manhood, to adequately defend the nation's borders from outside threats (Cohan x). During the period from June 1948 to June 1955, for example, more than half of all U.S. men between the ages of 18 and 25 who were registered for the draft and called for pre-induction physicals were rejected by military officials on physical and/or mental grounds ("Are We" 35). In addition, tests conducted on U.S. and European children found that, at every age from 6 to 16, American young people were far less muscular than their European counterparts ("Are We" 35).

The postwar masculinity crisis—along with the inherent homophobia it promoted—was triggered, to a substantial degree, by growing evidence that many U.S. veterans had engaged in sexual activities with other men during the war, often with implicit approval from military leaders. As Cohan explains:

> Officially, the military pathologized homosexuality, defining it as the inversion of heterosexual masculinity (the "sissy") and basing the diagnosis on the outward effeminacy of potential soldiers; but at the same time, the military permitted camp entertainments featuring men in drag, officially endorsed the close, passionate bonding of men in buddy relations, and tended to look the other way when men engaged in homosexual activity in the barracks or on ship. Men who had same-sex encounters to relieve sexual deprivation, moreover, did not necessarily have trouble thinking of themselves as "normal" or "heterosexual" afterward. (xiv)

It is clear that World War II placed U.S. soldiers into circumstances containing new sexual possibilities, at ages before many of them had ever considered marriage (D'Emilio and Freedman 260). Accordingly, as historian John D'Emilio has posited, the war represented a vital turning point in the prevalence of homosexuality's social expression, because wartime conditions freed millions of men from environments in which heterosexual sexual expression was regarded as being the acceptable norm (233-234). Numerous World War II veterans have, to date, revealed details of their wartime homosexual acts, or what Cohan has referred to as their "wartime bisexuality" (86). He goes on to demonstrate that the 1943 army manual *Psychology for the*

*Fighting Man* did not condemn homosexual activity as long as it served as a "substitute" for a man's "preferred form of sexual gratification" and its participants did not maintain too much intimacy with other men once they returned home after the war (Cohan 86, 88). This officially endorsed attitude toward homosexual encounters in the all-male military environment of the war years is somewhat surprising, especially given the levels of intolerance and homophobia that began to dominate U.S. military policy as soon as the war ended (Cohan 86).

## The Homosexual Subtext of *From Here to Eternity*

Given these various social realities, by the time *From Here to Eternity* premiered in August 1953, a widespread fear of homosexuality permeated U.S. culture, the U.S. military had begun to unilaterally oppose homosexual activity in all its forms, and the Motion Picture Production Code continued to prohibit any overtly homosexual characters or homosexual storylines from appearing on screen. As such, it was impossible for this film, or any other, to contain an explicit gay storyline, explicit instances of any form of homosexual activity, or explicitly gay characters, even if its screenwriter or director had wanted it to. Nevertheless, whether intentionally or unintentionally, *From Here to Eternity* contains a readily identifiable homosexual subtext that infuses the film with an added degree of textual flexibility to viewers who choose to read it "against the grain" and reject the "preferred" or dominant (i.e., heterocentric) decoding of the work in favor of a more narratively satisfying, homoerotic one (Doty 2; Hall 128-138).

Reviews of the film from the week it premiered contain substantial doses of critical praise. The review from *The New York Times*, for example, reads in part:

> Although it naturally lacks the depth and fullness of the 430,000 words and 850 pages of the book,...the team of scenarist, director, producer and cast has managed to transfer convincingly the muscularity of the basically male society with which the book dealt; the poignance and futility of the love lives of the professional soldiers involved, as well as the indictment of commanding officers whose selfishness can break men devoted to soldiering. They are trapped in a world they made and one that defeats them. Above all, it is a portrait etched in truth. ("Screen in Review" 16)

Similarly, the *Newsweek* review states:

> The result is one of the most absorbing and thoroughly honest movies to cross a national screen in years. Produced at a time when Hollywood is preoccupied with escapism, and even busier escaping from itself with 3-D gadgetry, *From Here to*

*Eternity* is a grown-up movie for anybody who can afford a babysitter. ("New Films" 82)

The *Time* magazine review concludes:

This is what Hollywood calls "a big picture," loaded with "production values." And yet, *From Here to Eternity* also tries to be something more.... The picture does succeed, perhaps without quite intending to, in saying something important about America. ("New Pictures" 96)

Although these reviews, and many like them, comment at length about various romantic and homosocial relationships of note in the film, none of the reviewers in 1953 whose writings I have encountered comment explicitly on the burgeoning romantic and sexually charged relationship between Warden and Prewitt that also exists in the cinematic version of *From Here to Eternity*. Like the PCA censors before them, these reviewers appear not to have detected the film's substantial homosexual subtext that seems so glaringly apparent today.

From the moment Warden and Prewitt first meet in the film, there is a queer chemistry between them. This is instantly evident in their admissions that each has already heard about the other, and far more importantly in the intensity of the eye contact and eyeline matches between the two men as they interact. In all of their subsequent scenes together in the film—with the exception of Warden's viewing of Prewitt's dead body at the end—this extreme degree of eye contact between the two men continues unabated, and it becomes intensified further by increasing degrees of physical contact between them. What initially begins as a homosocial pat on the shoulder after Warden offers to arrange a weekend pass, against his captain's wishes, that will enable Prewitt some relief from the brutal "treatment" he has been experiencing soon blossoms into homoerotic drunken groping of Prewitt by Warden during the scene in which they drink together while sitting in the middle of a road. As soon as Prewitt sits down next to him, Warden begins massaging Prewitt's shoulder. "I've got the biggest troubles in the world," Warden confides in Prewitt during this encounter, as he runs his hand down Prewitt's forearm and his fingers through Prewitt's hair. "Take love. Did you personally ever see any of this love?" he asks Prewitt, which suggests that Warden has not personally experienced fulfilling love with the captain's wife or any other woman. Careful attention to this scene's on-screen actions and dialogue readily reveals that Warden may be interested in a romantic, or at least a sexual, relationship with Prewitt, instead. At the moment when Warden is on the brink of exceeding the limits of homosocial behavior and proceeding into the realm of homosexual behavior, however, he catches himself and redirects the conversation, apparently in an attempt to not come on too strong. "How's your girl?" he abruptly asks Prewitt, as he retains his grip on the man's bicep and continues to run his fingers through Prewitt's hair. Seconds later, their interaction is unexpectedly curtailed when one of their colleagues almost runs them both over with a fast-moving Jeep; the colleague seems shocked when Warden suddenly refers to "my friend Prewitt" and claims that Prewitt is "the best stinkin' soldier in the whole army."

The seeds of a potential sexual attraction between Warden and Prewitt are planted early in the film as Warden, wearing only a towel around his waist, walks past Prewitt in his bunk. Prewitt is clearly intrigued by this action, as it immediately prompts him to ask a fellow soldier, "What's the deal with him, anyway, with Warden? I don't figure him." Shortly thereafter, it becomes evident that Warden feels some sort of extra affection for Prewitt and does not want to risk having him removed from his company, as Warden talks his superior, Captain Dana Holmes (played by Philip Ober), out of having Prewitt court-martialed for insubordination. It is noteworthy that Warden breathes a huge sigh of relief, in recognition that his efforts have been successful, the moment the captain exits the room. Days later, a drunken Warden admires Prewitt's physique as Prewitt plays the bugle across a smoke-filled barroom and, after breaking up the barroom altercation between Prewitt's close friend Angelo Maggio (played by Frank Sinatra) and a sadistic stockade guard (played by Ernest Borgnine), he glances in Prewitt's direction before walking past Prewitt to step outside for a breath of fresh air, realizing that Prewitt will likely follow. He does. It is during their outdoor conversation that Warden reveals he has been keeping close tabs on Prewitt's love life. "I've heard you've gone dippy over some dame at the New Congress Club," Warden tells Prewitt, before walking back inside, alone. Later in the film, even though it is certainly not in the best interest of his military career, Warden repeatedly covers for the AWOL Prewitt, reporting him as being present even though he has been missing from the barracks for several days. "Maybe I do [like him]," Warden ambiguously explains to a fellow soldier, as his deep caring for Prewitt becomes increasingly obvious in the narrative as it unfolds.

What allows the homosexual subtext of Warden and Prewitt's burgeoning relationship to emerge so blatantly (albeit latently) on the screen, yet to simultaneously go undetected by so many of the film's viewers, is the reality that both of these men are, at least to some degree, manifestly pursuing female love interests during the course of the narrative. Warden has been cuddling up with the captain's wife (Deborah Karr), and Prewitt has become emotionally involved with Lorene (played by Donna Reed) from the New Congress Club, who is clearly a prostitute but yet explicitly presented in the film as being a hostess from that social establishment, which promises only "dancing, snack bar, soft drink bar, and gentlemanly relaxation with the opposite gender so long as they are gentlemen, and no liquor is permitted." Explicit incorporation of

female characters such as these, as potential heterosexual love interests for male
characters who appear to be "bonding" in unique ways, has historically been a
common technique for undermining the hegemonic threat that the two men
together can pose, deflecting attention from the presence of homoeroticism and
homosexual subtextual elements in the film (LaValley 69).

Immediately after its premiere, *From Here to Eternity* was hailed by a *New
York Times* critic for its noteworthy depictions of "its basic admiration and
respect for the unlettered enlistee passionately devoted to his calling" as well as
"its ill-fated romances" (Weiler 1). Two questions immediately arise after
reading those assessments: (1) Why does Prewitt remain so devoted to the army,
despite the fact that he is being treated so badly in his military life? and (2) Why
are Warden's and Prewitt's relationships with the women they claim to love,
and say they wish to marry, ultimately doomed to failure?

The first question has puzzled many of the film's viewers, past and present.
Several weeks after *From Here to Eternity* was released in 1953, a different
*New York Times* writer questioned Prewitt's professed devotion to the army,
finding it to be ultimately unconvincing. Critic Bosley Crowther expressed
concern over "the stubborn character of the youthful soldier-hero of the picture,
who seems slightly ambiguous to our view. We found it a little hard to figure
how a fellow could be constituted so that he loved the authority of the Army and
yet refused to fight on his company's boxing team. To us, this seemed vaguely
inconsistent" (1). Crowther's point is an important one. In addition, at key
moments in the film, Prewitt informs Lorene that he loves the army and plans to
devote his entire career to it—despite the fact that his life there recently has
been anything but enjoyable—and he ultimately insists on getting back to his
company at all costs, even if it means that his stomach wounds may reopen in
the process or that he will lose Lorene's affection and companionship forever.
"A man loves a thing, that doesn't mean it's gotta love him back," Prewitt tells
her, adding that, when he enlisted at age 17, "I didn't belong no place, 'til I
entered the army." To prevent Prewitt from leaving her in the wake of the
Japanese attack on Pearl Harbor, Lorene asks him repeatedly why he wants to
go back to the army. "What do I want to go back to the army for? I'm a soldier,"
he replies. Beyond that tautological declaration, no truly rational explanation is
ever provided.

The second question, pertaining to why Warden's and Prewitt's relationships
with the women they claim to love and want to marry are ultimately doomed to
failure, is equally puzzling. All Warden needed to do to secure a married life
with Karen, once she divorced her philandering husband, was to complete a new
extension course and become a commissioned officer, but he didn't want that
badly enough to even sign and submit the necessary paperwork. Similarly, all
Prewitt needed to do to secure a married life with Lorene, and help to make her

the more "proper" woman she wished to become, was to relinquish his total allegiance to the army, but he readily favored his allegiance to the military, rather than to the woman he claimed to want to marry so badly, in the end. Just what is so appealing about military life that both of these men prefer to devote their whole lives to serving in the army, rather than pursuing other life options they claim repeatedly to desire?

Clearly, a subtextual reading of *From Here to Eternity* provides more fulfilling answers to both of these questions, which otherwise remain entirely ambiguous in the narrative's manifest contents. It appears that, unlike their surrounding colleagues, Warden and Prewitt will never experience the "reenlistment blues" that are constantly being sung about by their peers because they possess latent homosexual tendencies that they are, either consciously or unconsciously, beginning to wrestle with. The burgeoning attraction between them, which is so readily apparent in the film's subtext, far outweighs the hegemonic pressures they feel to establish long-term romantic and sexual relationships with the women they pursue more blatantly as the narrative unfolds. When all is said and done, it appears that both of these characters are simply performing the expected "masculine masquerade," with its emphasis on heteronormativity, of the time period and setting in which they lived, within a film that was expressly prohibited from explicitly revealing that anything more than typical buddy relations might be developing between them (Cohan 26).

Prewitt's motto in *From Here to Eternity*—"If a man don't go his own way, he's nothin'"—can apply equally well to either his hardheaded nature in general or to the film's subtext of exploring homosexual romantic and sexual desires. Without a doubt, the significance of the continuous eroticized looks and instances of physical contact between Warden and Prewitt throughout *From Here to Eternity*, along with the ambiguous plot developments that can effectively be read "against the hegemonic grain," are impossible to dismiss once they have been identified, as is the impact of Warden's sad, sentimental reaction to the sight of Prewitt's lifeless body at the film's end, which comes after both men have chosen to abandon the women they supposedly loved. Warden grieves over the discovery of the man's corpse and speaks to it quietly and solemnly, in the presence of several of his company's men. Apparently realizing that the men may be catching on to the true depths of his affection for Prewitt, however, Warden abruptly snaps himself out of the tenderness of the moment and begins to snap verbal commands to his surrounding soldiers: "What's the matter with you guys? Ain't you ever seen a dead man? Let's get this body out of here! We ain't got all night!"

## Concluding Remarks

Within weeks of its initial release, *From Here to Eternity* was banned by the U.S. Navy—which concluded that the film was "derogatory to a brother service"—despite the fact that the Army-Air Force Motion Picture Service had already given the work its own seal of approval ("From Somewhere" 20). It is unclear what criteria the Navy used to reach its decision that Army officials may, or may not, have overlooked (Crowther 1). What is more clear, however, is that the film's overall contents produced anxiety in at least a subset of its viewers, whether or not they were able to accurately articulate the causes of their concerns. The homosexual subtext of the film likely accounts, at least in part, for such anxiety.

Upon his arrival at Schofield Barracks, Prewitt is reunited with his friend Maggio, and a close bond reemerges between the two soldiers that ultimately results in Prewitt avenging Maggio's death from injuries instilled by the abusive stockade guard. In the wake of playing a moving "Taps" on his bugle in Maggio's honor, with tears streaming down his face, Prewitt seeks out and stabs the stockade guard, killing him. In relation to the topic of a subtextual reading of *From Here to Eternity*, a handful of contemporary critics have focused on the relationship between Prewitt and Maggio as a prime example of homosexual sexual desire. I remain unconvinced by such claims. Although a good deal of love is evident between those two men, little compelling evidence can be found to viably suggest that their relationship, even at the level of subtext, is anything more than simply loyal, devoted friends.

In contrast, the less obvious, burgeoning homoerotic relationship between Warden and Prewitt in the film offers a far more compelling example of subtextual homosexual desire. While adapting James Jones' novel for the screen, writer Daniel Taradash intentionally intercut the romantic escapades of Warden with the captain's wife, and Prewitt with the hostess from the New Congress Club, in order to provide a "feeling of the unconscious interrelation of [the two men's] lives" (Mitgang 5). Ultimately, a careful subtextual reading of *From Here to Eternity*, as provided in this chapter, reveals that the lives of these two attractive, masculine men were likely far more intimately interrelated than the film's manifest contents suggest. By restraining the homoerotic aspects and plot developments of Warden and Prewitt's relationship primarily to the latent level of cinematic subtext, this film thereby effectively contained male homosexuality, once again, as a kind of love that dare not speak its name in U.S. society during the 1950s.

# Works Cited

"Are We Becoming 'Soft'?" *Newsweek* 26 Sept. 1955: 35-36.

Cohan, Steven. *Masked Men: Masculinity and the Movies in the Fifties.* Bloomington: Indiana University Press, 1997.

Crowther, Bosley. "The Readers React: Comment and Rebuttal on the Film 'From Here to Eternity.'" *New York Times* 20 Sept. 1953, sec. 2: 1.

D'Emilio, John. "The Homosexual Menace: The Politics of Sexuality in Cold War America." *Passion and Power: Sexuality in History.* Ed. Kathy Peiss and Christina Simmons. Philadelphia: Temple University Press, 1989. 225-240.

—, and Estelle Freedman. *Intimate Matters: A History of Sexuality in America.* New York: Harper, 1988.

Doty, Alexander. *Flaming Classics: Queering the Film Canon.* New York: Routledge, 2000.

Dyer, Richard. *Heavenly Bodies: Film Stars and Society.* London: British Film Institute, 1986.

"From Somewhere to Fraternity." *Time* 7 Sept. 1953: 20.

Hall, Stuart. "Encoding/Decoding." *Culture, Media, Language.* Eds. Stuart Hall and D. Hobson. London: Unwin Hyman, 1980. 128-138.

Hanson, Ellis, ed. *Out Takes: Essays on Queer Theory and Film.* Durham, NC: Duke University Press, 1999.

LaValley, Al. "The Great Escape." *Out in Culture: Gay, Lesbian, and Queer Essays on Popular Culture.* Eds. Corey K. Creekmur and Alexander Doty. Durham: Duke University Press, 1995. 60-70.

Lundberg, Ferdinand, and Marynia Farnham. *Modern Woman: The Lost Sex.* New York: Harper and Brothers Publishers, 1947.

May, Elaine Tyler. *Homeward Bound: American Families in the Cold War Era.* New York: Basic Books, 1988.

Mitgang, Herbert. "Transmuting a Touchy, Topical Tome." *New York Times* 14 June 1953, sec. 2: 5.

"New Films: From Here to Eternity." *Newsweek* 10 Aug. 1953: 82-83.

"The New Pictures: From Here to Eternity." *Time* 10 Aug. 1953: 94, 96.

"The Screen in Review: 'From Here to Eternity' Bows at Capitol With Huge Cast, Five Starring Roles." *New York Times* 6 Aug. 1953, sec. 1: 16.

Simmons, Jerold. "The Production Code and Precedent." *Journal of Popular Film and Television* 20.3 (1992): 70-81.

Weiler, A. H. "Rich Dividend: 'From Here to Eternity' Triumphs Over Problems Presented by the Novel." *New York Times* 9 Aug. 1953, sec. 2: 1.

Wylie, Philip. *Generation of Vipers.* Normal, IL: Dalkey Archive Press, 1996.

# CHAPTER FIVE

# "TO GOD THERE IS NO ZERO": THE INCREDIBLE SHRINKING MAN AND ALLEGORIES OF MALE ANXIETY IN POSTWAR AMERICA

## NATE BRENNAN

> The Organization Man seeks a redefinition of his place on earth—a faith that will satisfy him that what he must endure has a deeper meaning than appears on the surface.
> —William H. Whyte (6)

> If we do discover a complete theory of the universe, it should in time be understandable in broad principle by everyone, not just a few scientists. Then we shall all, philosophers, scientists, and just ordinary people, be able to take part in the discussion of the question of why it is that we and the universe exist. If we find the answer to that, it would be the ultimate triumph of human reason—for then we would know the mind of God.
> —Stephen Hawking (qtd. in Rosenheim 19)

*The Incredible Shrinking Man* (1957) marks a pivotal moment for the American science fiction film in the 1950s. Critical reaction was varied: while *Newsweek* summed up the film as "a perfect illusion," most other contemporary reviewers were either indifferent or not so kind ("Playing Tricks" 106). In an overview of the science fiction genre, the higher brow *Film Quarterly* looked down on the film as "irrational and antiscientific," concluding that it began a "minor series of increasingly poor films about people who are too small or too big" (Hodgens 35). Although the film was received indifferently by critics, it was a commercial success with audiences. Made for $70,000, the film returned a healthy profit of $4 million for Universal-International ("Huge Props" 143).

Released twelve years after the end of World War II, *The Incredible Shrinking Man* encapsulates many popular themes (e.g., atomic anxiety, gigantism, the "unknown") that had developed in the genre as early in the postwar years as 1949. In many ways, Jack Arnold's film adaptation of the Richard Matheson novel of the same name represents the intellectual zenith for a genre generally disdained and dismissed as schlocky camp. Its release near the end of the decade is also important, because its thoughtful and probing narrative may only have been possible after the new collective work ethic had been given time to sink in. Also of note is the fact that, of all of Arnold's films, *The Incredible Shrinking Man* has garnered the most critical attention from a variety of viewpoints such as feminism, folklore, and comparisons with survivalist fiction, Pee-Wee Herman, and Stephen Hawking's *A Brief History of Time*.

Thought of today, the science fiction film of the 1950s conjures up images of histrionic actors running in terror from an absurd monster, in offerings produced cheaply and on the quick. While there are many such films, they tend to overshadow other, more thoughtful offerings, such as *The Incredible Shrinking Man*, that tend to be lumped in as being "just as bad." This, however, is not the case.

Many of these science fiction films fit into one of several recurring narrative motifs, such as the invasion narrative, featured in Arnold's *It Came From Outer Space* (1953); the monster-on-the-loose narrative, as in *Creature From the Black Lagoon* (1954); the apocalyptic/final warning narrative, as in *The Day the Earth Stood Still* (1951) and *The Space Children* (1958); or the atomic-anxiety narrative, in which an insect, animal, man, or woman grows to monstrous proportions after being exposed to or awakened by radioactivity (Tudor 90). Most 1950s science fiction films fit easily into one or more of these categories. Like offerings in all genres, these films generally adhere to their own conventions and expectations. Prevalent conflicts include pressure on the individual from the group, a sharp division between the military/protectors of social order and members of the scientific community, and the need to formulate/reform the heterosexual couple and destroy the monstrous threat by the end of the film.

What makes *The Incredible Shrinking Man* so interesting is that it doesn't adhere to any one of the established science fiction narratives, nor does it follow the genre's narrative conventions. Its narrative concerns Scott Carey (played by Grant Williams), a young ad agency employee, who lives in the suburbs with his wife, Louise (played by Randy Stuart), and their cat, Butch. Scott is the typical Organization Man of the postwar period. His job ensures a steady paycheck, enough to finance life in the suburbs. However, it does not ensure upward mobility, or necessarily any mobility at all.

The film unfolds in three acts. The first act follows Scott after he becomes coated with a mysterious radioactive mist, to some months later when he begins to decrease in size. The narrative features Scott shrinking from a normal height of approximately six feet to a mere six inches. Along the way, Scott attempts to rationalize his illness while trying to maintain his flagging masculinity. The second act takes place after Scott, smaller than six inches, has been knocked into the cellar by the family housecat. In the cellar world, Scott finds that household objects of convenience, now magnified hundreds of times, become obstacles making up a surreal landscape of man-made mountains, cliffs, canyons, and caves. Smaller objects acquire new use-value: a sewing pin becomes a sword and a grappling hook, thread becomes rope, and a matchbox becomes Scott's shelter. In addition to a new world of the (un)familiar, Scott faces his nemesis, a large spider that stands between him and his only potential source of sustenance: a moldy piece of cake. The final act, only several minutes long, details Scott's acceptance of his fate as he rejects the symbolic and embraces/becomes the vast nothingness of infinite space.

In his influential book *The Organization Man*, William H. Whyte writes that, following World War II, white middle-class Protestant men and women began flocking to work for large corporate organizations. This dramatic shift created many changes in the American work ethic and placed strain on the traditional family unit. Whyte says that the so-called "Organization Man" builds upon the fundamental national ideal of the "American dream." That is, he retains his individual freedom while also allowing himself to be part of the larger organizational machine. Whyte refers to this ideal as the social ethic, which rationalizes organizational demands for cooperation while still providing a sense of dedication in its workers. He writes that the social ethic converts a "bill of no rights" into a "restatement" of individualism that "makes morally legitimate the pressures of society against the individual" (6).

In order to climb the organizational ladder, the Organization Man must make necessary sacrifices both at home and in the workplace. He begins to lose his sense of identity as he confronts the reality that he must conform in order to move ahead. In a way, he has been emasculated and also, so to speak, "put in his place." Whyte clearly sums up the Organization Man's sentiment in the following passage:

> No longer can he console himself with the thought that hard work never hurt anybody and that neuroses don't come from anything but worry. He knows that he has committed himself to a long and perhaps bitter battle. Psychologically, he can never go back or stand still, and he senses well that the climb from here on is going to involve him in increasing tensions. (157)

According to Whyte, the Organization Man's willing denial of the self for the good of the organizational group caused an identity crisis for the young men of the postwar generation. The traditional model of American masculinity, self-made and independent, clashed with the organizational work ethic that stressed values inherently feminine in American culture: dependency and cooperation. No longer were these men masters and controllers of their own lives; instead, they had to forgo their identities (and, by extension, their sexuality as dominant males as well) and allow themselves to be controlled by the infinitely larger organization. The image that plays behind the opening title sequence best represents Scott's plight as well as the underlying fears of the working man in the 1950s: the white silhouette of the iconic man in the gray flannel suit, slowly getting smaller until he disappears into the blackness of the screen.

Scott is the archetypal Organization Man: He lives in the suburbs with his wife, and he has a job working for an advertising firm. He is the dominant member of the household because he provides money and a home; in turn, his wife is expected to depend to him. Scott is, however, also financially dependant on his brother, an issue that comes up almost immediately.

The film economically sets up the expectations and rules of a marital relationship within the first scene. Scott and Louise are vacationing on a small boat. The establishing shot introduces the couple lying idly on the bow of the boat. In the composition, the couple appear as equals. Scott doesn't necessarily dominate his wife, and Louise doesn't exactly seem to "live" to serve her husband. Scott leans over and asks his wife to get him a beer from below deck. She playfully refuses, noting that they are *both* on vacation. In return, Scott mock-orders her to fetch him a "flagon" of alcohol; he seeks to reassert his masculine control by reverting to terms and language symbolic of a more masculine-oriented time period, the Middle Ages (Jancovich 192). Eventually, Scott wins out in this argument by saying, "I provide the boat, you provide the beer." It is Scott's job to provide for his wife so that she can be comfortable; in turn, it is her job to reciprocate by taking care of him. Louise, however, reminds him that it is his *brother's* boat; they're just borrowing it. As Louise goes below deck, the boat approaches a mysterious cloud and Scott, alone on deck, is coated with a shiny substance.

When Scott encounters this mist, he does so half-naked and alone. The vast expanse of the sea as well the mysterious cloud are gendered feminine as the Archaic Mother, a "formless...totalizing, oceanic presence" that consumes and incorporates all around it (Creed 61). The cloud consumes Scott, wrenching him away from the symbolic order of patriarchal society within which he has become so comfortable. His absent wife has been temporarily replaced by a mysterious, all-encompassing Mother: the infinite unknown, something the film will return to again and again.

When Louise rejoins Scott above deck and he explains what happened, she notes a clear sign of his new difference: his half-naked torso is covered with a sparkling substance. Scott tries to brush it away with his hand, but it does not come off. The substance marks Scott's difference in a way that undermines his masculinity: in popular ideology men don't "glow," women do. What follows will remind Scott of this initial anti-masculine difference, as he slowly regresses to embrace the unknown.

In the next scene, some time later, the couple is at home. Here the film sets up, once again, each character's particular role in regard to the other. Louise moves through the kitchen and dining room, denoting the home (and especially the kitchen) as a feminine space. In contrast, Scott is in the bedroom, which is associated with male power and sexual dominance. In these first two scenes, therefore, the couple's marital relationship is set up as being unmistakably suburban. Scott works in the organization, while Louise runs the household.

Months later in the film, after he has accidentally come into contact with a pesticide that triggers a biological reaction, Scott realizes he is getting smaller. His worst fears are confirmed after he undergoes a battery of medical tests. The doctors inform him that what is happening to his body is a sort of "anti-cancer" that is causing all of the organs in his body to decrease proportionately in size.

The circumstances surrounding Scott's infection—the mysterious cloud, the pesticide—are only ways of justifying the story. The pseudoscience of "anti-cancer" doesn't really mean much. It is merely a way of propelling the story along. What is most interesting is *not* the pseudoscientific rationalization of man's impermanence and fear of death, but rather the way such a dramatic change will force Scott to see his world from a different perspective and may ultimately free him from a world of material goods and human limitations.

Scott's transition from a normal six-foot-tall man to a child-size man only increases his reliance on things and others. His wife and brother become surrogate parents to him after he is no longer able to work. Scott's masculinity, undermined even before the film began, is now reduced to total dependence upon a woman who previously depended primarily on him. Over time, Scott's behavior becomes increasingly more belligerent toward his wife as he struggles to find ways of reasserting his masculinity within the domestic sphere that has become his prison.

The doctors, the media, and even his brother take control for Scott when he can no longer take care of himself in his ever-diminishing state. In order to assert his rapidly deteriorating male dominance, Scott begins to act increasingly more irritably. In his voice-over narration, he explains, "Every day I became more tyrannical, more monstrous in my domination of Louise." His inability to take care of himself in a world that is becoming increasingly alien to him means that he must come under the care of his concerned and faithful wife. Scott resents this reality because their proscribed roles have been reversed: his wife now acts as the caretaker and protector, while the continued reduction in his size renders Scott virtually impotent in all aspects of his life.

In another striking scene, Scott, at three feet tall, accuses his wife of not working hard enough to secure their privacy from the outside world. After she fails to obtain an unlisted telephone line, Scott berates her by saying, "Use your influence, Louise. I'm a big man; I'm famous!" After a moment of frustration, Scott apologizes to his wife. "Lou...I'm sorry. I must be losing my mind, talking to you like this." To this she replies, with one of the film's most interesting and overlooked lines, "No, it's all right. I know what you must be suffering." Scott indignantly replies, "Can you?" Indeed, Louise probably knows full well what Scott is suffering. Her needs have most likely fallen on deaf ears in the past, and she too would know what it feels like to be confined to a house all day. The house becomes Scott's prison, just as it had once been Louise's. Their proscribed roles, both social and gendered, have been reversed. Scott can no longer work, so Louise must take care of him and make ends meet.

Eventually, Scott determines that he must leave the house and venture out into the world to clear his mind. He finds himself outside a traveling carnival and overhears the barker drawing people in to see the side show. The barker yells, "Tiny Tina...36-and-a-half inches of feminine fortitude." The camera immediately cuts away to Scott, who after hearing the barker covers his ears and runs away from the carnival. The carnival's display of the unnatural and the abject feminine (the "unnaturally" small woman) reminds Scott of the emasculating effect of his illness. Like the members of the sideshow, Scott's affliction marks him as an object to be looked at. Scott calls himself "the Shrinking Freak" because he no longer controls the active gaze; he is now on the receiving end, that which connotes, to use Laura Mulvey's term, "to-be-looked-at-ness." Indeed, in the transition shots of Scott walking to and from home, several passersby pause to stare at the normally proportioned three-foot-tall man.

An interesting aspect of both the film and the novel is the ambiguous nature of the characters' names. For example, Scott affectionately refers to Louise as Lou, which would otherwise be considered a masculine name. The housecat, Butch, is in many scenes associated with Louise. Cats are traditionally gendered feminine, yet Butch's name connotes not only masculinity, but also a more masculine-oriented femininity, as well. Even Scott's name implies gender confusion: the first name, Scott, suggests male-ness, while the last name, Carey, suggests female-ness. Scott's feminine qualities are inherent, although to him they only become apparent after he begins to shrink.

In a fitting metaphor, Scott, at less than three inches tall, is forced to take up residence in a dollhouse. The only suitable habitat for a shrinking man is a girl's plaything with which she learns the rules of feminine domesticity. The suburban home that will eventually become the prison of the domestic housewife is now modeled as a dollhouse, the domestic prison of the shrinking man. The film draws an analogy with Scott that maps his feelings of helplessness and loss of self onto the feelings of his wife. Gender boundaries collapse as man becomes analogous with woman and vice versa, a fear not unknown in 1950s America. In a *New York Times* article aptly titled "Trousered Moms and Dishwashing Dads," Dorothy Barclay reflects the sentiments of *The Incredible Shrinking Man* when she writes:

> [Specialists] find dad's current position hopelessly ill-defined. How can a boy learn what it means to be a man...when mother and father in so many homes carry out identical tasks in relation to home and children? Changes in women's rights and responsibilities inevitably have created changes in men's. (SM25)

In contrast to Barclay's neutral take on shifting gender roles is Robert Coughlan's hysterical screed against the feminist movement and its purported effects on the American home. In a 1956 *Life* article, "Changing Roles in Modern Marriage," Coughlan describes, with little more than veiled misogyny, an unsettling epidemic of masculinized women and feminized men. For Coughlan, the source of trouble lies in what he calls the "suburban syndrome." He writes:

> The wife, having worked before marriage, or at least having been educated and socially conditioned toward the idea that work...carries prestige, finds herself in the lamentable position of being "just a housewife".... In her disgruntlement she can work as much damage on the lives of her husband and children (and her own life) as if she were a career woman, and indeed sometimes more. (111)

In Coughlan's view, the fault lies almost solely with the woman and, more specifically, with the feminist movement. He writes of this new career woman as though she had more sinister motives lurking just below the surface:

> As she moves ahead in her career she would of necessity develop those sides of herself that were most aggressive. She might as well mask these under a feminine manner. But one way or another she would acquire aggression, exploitation, and dominance, and to that degree would become masculine. (110)

Likewise, male emasculation is the fault of just such a woman, one the male may have found in his own mother and from the absence of a strong, masculine father figure. Ultimately, Couglan suggests that this newfound sexually dysfunctional couple arises as a result of mutually contradictory wishes. The female wishes to dominate yet retain her femininity. Likewise, the male wishes to be passive, accepting his wife as his mother figure, yet also to act aggressively in order to dominate the relationship (111). Coughlan's epidemic of feminine husbands and masculine wives goes hand in hand with Whyte's Organization Man. Both respond to a particular problem of identification felt during the postwar 1950s, and both incorporate a common element: the fear of feminine intrusion, not only into the masculine world (of business, politics, etc.), but also of the male body itself.

As with most science fiction and horror narratives, the monstrous Other represents an eruption of the id, a walking/crawling/slithering manifestation of latent fears. In *The Incredible Shrinking Man*, Scott's latent fears of femininity and castration come to light in two monstrous incarnations: the now-gargantuan housecat, Butch, and the ultimate signifier of what Barbara Creed terms the monstrous-feminine, the spider.

If a man's home is his castle, Scott constantly finds that his home is under attack. First, the public attempts continually to catch a glimpse of "the Shrinking Man." Then, Scott is attacked by something familiar to him, the family cat, who does all she can to get to Scott inside the dollhouse. (This motif of home invasion will be repeated later in the film, after Scott is forced to take shelter inside a matchbox. The spider crawls around on top of the box, sticking its legs into the opening, in much the same way that Butch paws through the windows of the dollhouse.) Butch's attack represents Scott's first encounter with the monstrous-feminine that poses a physical threat of injury or death. Scott hears a noise and opens the door to see Butch's hissing mouth, a *vagina dentate* of sharp teeth that threatens to devour the three-inch man. He quickly shuts the door, hoping that what exists in the outside world cannot invade the comfort and familiarity of home. The cat, however, is not so easily dissuaded. She forces her way into the home, expelling Scott into a world of the (un)familiar. His former home—complete with living room, kitchen, and foyer—has now become a vast expanse that offers nowhere to hide from a monstrous (albeit slightly humorous) cat. The extended battle and flight from the cat result in Scott's banishment to the cellar world and the assumption of his death by his wife and brother.

In the cellar, Scott is truly a stranger in an alien land. Looking out at the scenery, he remarks, "The cellar floor stretched out before me like some primeval plain, littered with the relics of a vanished race." In the basement world, things that were once ordinary and familiar now make up an alien landscape of unfamiliar obstacles. For instance, a mousetrap holds the only available sustenance but simultaneously threatens to kill Scott. The stairs leading to the basement become an impossibly large and unscaleable mountain. Other ordinary objects offer relief: an empty matchbox becomes a shelter, and a box of sewing implements provides Scott with a makeshift rope and grappling hook. As with the dollhouse, Scott's tools are invariably gendered feminine. The sewing implements, the matchbox, and even the mousetrap are all aspects of a traditionally feminine domestic responsibility (Hendershot 329).

The place of Scott's banishment is also of particular interest. Tania Modleski writes that the basement was a "quintessential '50s space where Dad could escape the routine of family life to pursue the solitary hobbies which would bolster his flagging masculinity" (Modleski 58). Indeed, if Scott is trapped in a place that is gendered masculine while still encountering objects gendered feminine, then he does his best to reconfigure those objects to a masculine ideal. A sewing needle, for example, becomes a weapon with which he battles his nemesis, a grossly disproportionate spider that stalks him. "With these bits of metal," he says in narration, "I was a man again." In this case, as in suburban culture, the possession makes the man. Another object Scott finds is an old nail, which he uses to rip and shape his tunic. He even sits on the ground, his legs splayed out in a V with the nail sitting between his legs as an exaggerated phallus.

In the cellar, however, Scott makes a dramatic shift from invalid to survivalist. He no longer struggles for dominance in a world in which he continues to lose relevance; now he exists as a new creature in a completely alien world. He relies on his masculinity to keep him alive. As he says in one of his voice-over monologues, "I had only to exist."

Residue still remains of his previous life. Upon coming to the cellar window screen, Scott scares off a sparrow just to prove to himself that he still has control over *something*. This desperate act proves hollow, however. Scott sinks to the ground, grasping the prison bars of the window screen. He says, "My prison, almost as far as I could see.... A gray, friendless area of space and time. And I resolved, as man had dominated the world of the sun, I would dominate my world."

In the cellar world, Scott's primal masculinity begins to emerge and his physical features change dramatically. For example, in the "domestic sphere" as husband and then as abnormal child, his looks are feminine. In the cellar world, however, Scott is quite different: He's unkempt, rugged, and dirty. A five o'clock shadow masks much of what might previously have been regarded as marks of feminine beauty. He is now clothed in a rough tunic and resembles a medieval hero of legend.

The guardian of the cellar world and Scott's nemesis is the spider, in the book a black widow, and in the film (because it photographed better) a tarantula. The spider is a fascinating monster because its very physiognomy (the hair, the egg-shaped body, the pulsating mouth) so closely ties in with Creed's monstrous-feminine. Creed writes that revulsion from the spider, on Scott's part as well as the viewer's, comes not from an emphasis on castration, but rather from the "gestating, all-devouring womb of the archaic mother" (63). This serves to explain the dramatic close-up shots of the spider's hairy mouth that threatens to devour Scott.

Although there is no doubt that the spider is a signifier of monstrous femininity, precisely where the source of that monstrousness lies for Scott or for the viewer (does it represent Louise? all women in general?) has spawned considerable critical debate. In his book *The Bosom Serpent*, Harold Schechter writes that the spider is meant to be an analogue for Scott's wife. He argues that both *Shrinking Man* texts should be read as allegories of economic strain and not of sexual dysfunction and/or anxiety. In Schechter's view:

> Scott's struggle to vanquish the [spider] represents his effort to free himself from the clutches of a devouring female creature whose only purpose, as far as he is concerned, is to snare him in a web and keep him trapped there forever as a permanent source of sustenance. (80)

Although the spider is certainly a feminine signifier, Schechter's take on the spider as an out-of-control consumer seems very narrow. Carol Clover, in her review of *The Bosom Serpent*, for example, writes that *The Incredible Shrinking Man* "could hardly be more sexually blatant and that, whatever the movie's other valences, there is no avoiding the 'impotence' associations of the plot in general and the 'vagina' associations of the spider episode in particular" (Clover 49).

Instead, the film may also be read as a story about terminal illness and the dramatic impact such a tragedy could have on the afflicted as well as their loved ones. In at least one occasion in Matheson's novel, Scott mentions—to his wife's protests—that she and their daughter will have to make arrangements after he dies/disappears into nothingness. In the film, Lou is faithful and caring to the end, only moving away when she presumes her husband to be dead. The spider clearly represents a fear of castration and becoming feminine, though not necessarily a fear (and hatred) of Lou.

To Scott, the spider represents a necessary obstacle to be overcome in order to survive: He must kill it before it kills him. In a latent sense, however, the spider represents something deeper to Scott: a femininity that threatens to consume him. The spider, after all, has much that identifies it with the feminine abject. It appears as a giant, hairy, crawling eight-legged mass. All close-ups of the spider are low-angle shots of its pulsing, hairy mouth, the all-devouring *vagina dentate*, or the "female genitalia which threatens to give birth to equally horrific offspring as well as threatening to incorporate everything in its path" (Creed 63). The spider abstractly represents the revulsion that is triggered in response to the female body (in all of its functions and representations) in a patriarchal society. To Scott, the spider/feminine threatens to not only castrate, but to devour him as well. In addition, the spider is associated with the maternal. Scott must defeat the spider to obtain food that is located just underneath its vast web. The web, therefore, acts as a reverse womb; it holds the key to Scott's survival, yet it threatens death if penetrated.

Scott's conflict with the spider is not only an act to assert dominance and ensure survival. It also represents a battle between patriarchy (Scott) and matriarchy (the spider). Scott wishes to build his new world in much the same image of his previous life. In order for the system of masculine control to work, the feminine must be repressed at all costs.

When Scott prepares to do battle with the spider, he does so by taking up another phallic signifier: an enlarged sewing pin that becomes a sword. Pulling the pin out of a giant cushion, Scott remarks in voice-over, "With these bits of metal, *I was a man again*. If I was to die, it wouldn't be as a helpless insect in the jaws of a spider." With the phallic pin, Scott is endowed with masculine power. Significantly, when Scott finally does come to blows with the spider, he delivers the death wound while underneath the spider. When the pin penetrates the spider's abdomen, its blood and guts run down the sword, past his arm, and onto Scott's chest.

The spider's blood serves two purposes that reinforce patriarchal ideology. One refers, again, to the abject feminine. The spider's blood references menstrual blood. Secondly, like the space of cellar itself, a sublevel below the civilized world, it serves to further the regressive process that has consumed Scott. Like a mini-Siegfried, Scott bathes in the blood of his fallen enemy to assume her power and domain.

The film's finale ultimately questions the premise that Scott's masculinity has been reasserted by vanquishing a deadly foe with the implements at his disposal. Quite the opposite, after killing the spider, Scott gains his prize—the moldy piece of cake—but no longer feels hungry. Now small enough to fit through the wire mesh of the window screen, Scott finds his exit from the house that has contained him for the majority of the film. He stands at the cusp of a brave new world, realizing that the finite reasoning of man and the attachments to material things and others were merely limitations. For example, in a transitory scene prior to the spider's death, Scott walks by an empty can with the words "use less for best results" written on the side (Yacowar 280). Using less for better results is ultimately a lesson for Scott: he has to let go of the life which he cannot live anymore to understand that there may be more beyond what he cannot comprehend.

After killing the spider, Scott walks out of the basement window, looking up at the vastness of space. Diminishing into nothingness, he accepts his fate. Staring at the cosmos, he says in voice-over:

> I looked up as if, somehow, I would grasp the heavens. The universe. Worlds without numbers; God's silver tapestry spread across the night. And in that

moment I knew the answer to the riddle of the infinite. I had thought in terms of man's own limited dimension. I had presumed on nature. That existence begins and ends is man's conception, not nature's.... All this vast majesty of creation, it had to mean something. And then I meant something, too.

The ending of the film is particularly problematic. On one hand, it seems to presage the next step for human evolution, that is, the rejection of material objectification and the rejection of human limitation as an entry way into the unknowable. Implicitly phallocentric, the film implies that Scott's acceptance of his fate allows him to shed the skin of conformity and deny the world of material things, in his words, the world of "man's limited dimensions." Scott "use[s] less for best results" because he no longer needs to use anything at all. All boundaries for Scott collapse and, in the nexus between the finite and the infinite, gender gaps, bureaucratic organization, and difference disappear.

On the other hand, the film, via voice-over, still implies Scott's subjectivity: If he dwindles away into nothingness, how can he narrate his own story? Tania Modleski writes that the convention of the voice-over in this film "confer[s] a kind of godlike (i.e., phallic) authority on the male protagonist who remains firmly in control" (59). Although in some ways Scott has become extra-human (or, perhaps more appropriately, "man after-man"), and freed from the constraints of the male body and now enlightened, the film nonetheless undeniably reasserts his masculinity, as Modleski suggests.

Far from being a perfect text, the film does, despite its shortcomings, have a unique twist when compared to other films of its period. That is, though Scott may retain his masculinity *in absentia* of his body, the narrative unravels rather than resolving all conflicts and returning to normalcy. Thus, the heterosexual couple is not reunited and normalcy does not return. Instead, Scott disappears into nothingness and Louise must move on without him (Wood 80).

Though the film remains staunchly masculine-oriented from beginning to end, it is important not to downplay the importance of the feminine to the narrative, in both its negative and positive connotations. In one sense, the film is a reaction against feminine invasion and the threat of emasculation. In another, the film does not necessarily hard-line Scott's masculinity, and in many ways it blurs the boundaries between masculine and feminine. The film's final shot echoes the title sequence and first shot; the vast expanse of the ocean is here replaced by the infinity of space, each instance ripe with feminine signifiers. As Scott stands at the threshold of human knowledge and experience, he looks to the cosmos above. "To God," he says, "there is no zero." He diminishes beyond the limitations of the human body to worlds infinitely smaller than our own. Returning to the beginning, he inhabits a space between male and female. For Scott, he is no longer zero, but one.

# Works Cited

Barclay, Dorothy. "Trousered Moms and Dishwashing Dads." *New York Times* 28 Apr. 1957: SM25.

Clover, Carol J. Rev. of The *Bosom Serpent: Folklore and Popular Art*, by Harold Schechter. *Film Quarterly* 43.2 (1990): 46-50.

Coughlan, Robert. "Changing Roles in Modern Marriage." *Life* 24 Dec. 1956: 109-116.

Creed, Barbara. "Horror and the Monstrous-Feminine—An Imaginary Abjection." *Screen* 27.1 (1986): 44-70.

Hendershot, Cyndy. "Darwin and the Atom: Evolution/Devolution Fantasies in *The Beast From 20,000 Fathoms, Them!,* and *The Incredible Shrinking Man.*" *Science Fiction Studies* 25.2 (1998): 319-335.

Hodgens, Richard. "A Brief, Tragical History of the Science Fiction Film." *Film Quarterly* 13.2 (1959): 30-39.

"Huge Props to Shrink a Man." *Life* 13 May 1957: 143.

Jancovich, Mark. *Rational Fears: American Horror in the 1950s.* New York: Manchester University Press, 1996.

Modleski, Tania. "The Incredible Shrinking He(r)man: Male Regression, the Male Body and Film." *Differences* 2.2 (1990): 55-75.

"Playing Tricks." Rev. of *The Incredible Shrinking Man. Newsweek* 11 Mar. 1957: 106.

Rosenheim, Shawn. "Extraterrestrial: Science Fictions in *A Brief History of Time* and *The Incredible Shrinking Man.*" *Film Quarterly* 48.4 (1995): 15-21.

Schechter, Harold. *The Bosom Serpent: Folklore and Popular Art.* Iowa City: University of Iowa Press, 1988.

Tudor, Andrew. *Monsters and Mad Scientists: A Cultural History of the Horror Movie.* Cambridge, MA: Basil Blackwell, 1989.

Whyte, William H. *The Organization Man.* New York: Simon and Schuster, 1956.

Wood, Robin. *Hollywood from Vietnam to Reagan and Beyond.* New York: Columbia University Press, 2003.

Yacowar, Maurice. "The Bug in the Rug: Notes on the Disaster Genre." *Film Genre Reader III.* Ed. Barry Keith Grant. Austin, TX: University of Texas Press, 2003. 277-295.

# CHAPTER SIX

# VISIBLE VIRGINS: HOW HOLLYWOOD SHOWED THE UNSHOWABLE IN LATE 1950S FILMS

## TAMAR JEFFERS MCDONALD

It has been traditional to look at the American 1950s as a time of consensus and conformity, as scholars such as Alan Nadel, David Sterritt and Gary Gore, and William O'Neill have demonstrated. The stereotype of this period is one of stasis in contrast to the political and social upheavals of the following decade's sexual and political revolutions. The contemporary scene was never so monolithic, however. Careful examination of popular media offerings of this era, including films, reveals a society awash with doubts and anxieties. Many of these tensions were prompted by the figure of the woman, especially after the publication, in 1953, of Alfred Kinsey's *Sexual Behaviour in the Human Female*. Kinsey's main revelation was that half of his sample of unmarried thirty-year-old women were not virgins. Therefore, if his sample were in any way representative, half the single women in America might similarly be expected to be sexually "experienced." This finding defied prevailing sexual mores, which assumed that women would be virgins on their wedding nights whereas men would not. The presumption of pre-marital chastity in women and sexual experience in their men was the contemporary "double standard" in sexual behavior, and what Kinsey's report suggested was that it was being ignored by many more women than had previously been assumed.

The mid-century popular media became fixated with this new persona of the single woman who was not willing to postpone her sexual feelings, one who was tempted and might fall; devoting popular attention to this figure, however, did little to assuage the many anxieties she set circulating. For example, in dealing with the fallout from the "K bomb," as Kinsey's report was known, many of the counter-blasts attempted to ameliorate the nebulous worries it unleashed through the establishment of clear-cut distinctions, such as virgin/post-virgin, girl/woman, and not doing it/doing it, as well as virginity being externally representable/virginity not being externally representable, not showing it/showing and suggesting it, and signs helping/signs being deceptive.

In addition to uncertainties over which side of these dichotomies was "right," there was concern that the lines between such areas might not be so easy to draw. While many contemporary responses to Kinsey's *Sexual Behavior in the Human Female*, in various media, were involved in the endeavor to binarize women over their sexual status, it might be expected that films, since they could visually depict women and their stories, would be prominent in such attempts to establish clear boundaries. Indeed, a number of films put into production after Kinsey released the 1953 report can be understood as Hollywood's response to the contemporary apprehensions set circulating by its disclosures because they make central this figure: the new, desirous young woman who provoked a mixture of anxiety, desire, and prurience by being prepared to flout the double standard.

Therefore, a short cycle of films can, I believe, be detected, appearing in cinemas from approximately 1957 onwards, that feature this new desiring virgin; I call these the "virginity-dilemma films," since they put center stage, for the first time, the conflicting reasons both against *and for* premarital sex. These films are interestingly cross-generic; they include both comic and dramatic narratives dramatizing the "will she or won't she?" story in this short cycle. It seems somewhat surprising that the seriousness of the problem of virginity at this time—which reinforced the habitual societal attachment of importance to a girl's chastity with a new anxiety that it might be, unseen, disappearing—would not prevent mainstream cinema from making light of this topic in comedies. The audience could be certain, however, with comic treatments that something would occur just in the nick of time to prevent the virgin from yielding to whatever temptations came her way; Hollywood was not at this point prepared to make comedy out of virginity and then let it be sacrificed. Thus, in the majority of the comic entries in the virginity-dilemma cycle, while the inevitable final-reel marriage assures the audience that her chastity will soon be relinquished, the female hero nevertheless reaches the end of the film intact.

What I am interested in considering here is *how*, at a time when mainstream film could not show the sexual act itself, these films could indicate the change in sexual status. While script references could now be included as a result of the slackening of the Motion Picture Production Code in the mid-1950s, as the research of Leonard Leff and Jerold Simmonds shows, mainstream films were still somewhat shy about presenting such stark information in plain language. Instead, I maintain that the bodies of the actors playing the tempted virgins visibly externalize their sexual categorization for audiences to read.

I am primarily concerned with two specific ideas here: (1) the fact that, at this time, the outcome of the virgin's story correlates with genre-based rules, associating loss with the melodramatic, and the maintenance of virginity with the comic genre; and (2) that these different outcomes correlate visibly with the performances in the films. I contend that the different burdens of virginity and experience are carried by the bodies of the female actors within these texts, put on and worn like outfits. In the comic films, virginity is indicated by a buoyant physicality, an unruly, uncontrolled energy. In contrast, in the more serious offerings which narrativize virginity's loss, the maiden is marked by an identifiable stillness and passivity.

This split in the methods of performance interests me not only because the difference between the physical styles of acting in the comic and serious films is both so marked and so uniform across offerings of the virginity-dilemma cycle, but also because of its over-determination. As noted, these films post-date the mid-1950s relaxing of the Production Code, which means that storylines built around sexual initiation could now be used, as well as dialogue that boldly included the word "virginity" alongside such euphemisms as "purity" and "immaturity." While mainstream American films (unlike their European counterparts) still felt uneasy about *showing* the sexual act itself, a certain overtness about sex was now permissible. Why, then, did the virginity-dilemma films feel impelled to have their actors enact sexual inexperience physically in these buoyant/static ways?

Perhaps the invisibility of virginity caused no more anxiety for contemporary society than it did for film; the late-1950s culture alarmed by Kinsey and the figure of the transgressive desirous female which his report had conjured up needed clear externalization of the virgin, but so did cinema, a medium predicated on *showing*. In this way, it can be posited that the very visuality of film demanded a way that sexual status could be shown without recourse to signposts in the script or plot machinations. Thus, the intensity of the anxieties aroused by this new virgin required her physical manifestation. By asserting that sexual status could be rendered externally, both film and society attempted to remove worrisome ambiguities and ambivalences that threatened their discrete traditional structures. The films of this era can therefore be seen as attempting to manage two competing forces by encouraging the actors' visible somatic performance of virginity: on the one hand, the urge to see some clear sign of sexual status, and on the other, the impossibility of representing an internal nothingness.

## Visible Virginity

The different types of virginity-dilemma films organize themselves around different attitudes toward the sexual moment. The comic ones are able to laugh at virginity and desire because nothing, in the end, will actually be sacrificed. The more serious films take a graver view of the status shift between virgin and post-virgin because their narratives include the moment of change.

Because of the different generic allegiances these films obey, there seems to be a very real dialectic operating in the physical performance styles of the female actors. This range of dichotomies can be mapped as follows:

| | |
|---|---|
| Comedy | Melodrama |
| Kinesis | Stasis |
| Constant | Fluctuating |
| Pratfalls | Moment of trial |
| Maintenance | Loss |

In the comic treatments of the virgin dilemma, the maiden's body is seen in unruly motion. Her enactment of virginity in this way is constant and marked by archetypical slapstick moments such as when, her arms windmilling frantically, she tips off her spindly heels or rends the jacket of an admirer by pulling away too fast. In the more serious, melodramatic treatments of virginity, set up to deliver its actual loss rather than simply tease over its possibility, the virgin body is generally marked by its stasis, its composure. This may fluctuate, increasing and decreasing from one scene to the next, but it will become critically ruptured during the virgin's moment of trial, when her desires war with her conscience, and win.

Obviously, even the swiftest glance across various film periods and performers indicates that energetic physicality has always been the cause of humor; from the Keystone Kops to Jerry Lewis to Jim Carrey, physical comedy involving accidents, pratfalls, and body torsion has historically been employed to provoke laughter. Furthermore, such comedy is not gender specific, although there are noticeably fewer female performers who make a career out of this style (perhaps Lucille Ball in her later, TV-show incarnation might be the best example).

However, the prevalence of both this performance style in the comic entries in the cycle, and that of its opposite, the enactment of virginity through a still and static demeanour, appear to tap into contemporary discourses about the appropriateness of female agency. I am thinking here of conduct literature, that strand of popular culture that attempts to provide guidelines pertaining to proper behavior and polite manners, whether through the sporadic information offered in newspaper and magazine advice columns or entire volumes such as, most notably, Emily Post's *Etiquette*. Post's book was first published in 1922 and has regularly been revised and reissued ever since; between the 1950 and 1960 issues alone, there were two other revisions, in 1955 and 1958. The stated intention of this book is to educate the reader in the tenets of polite society and thus inculcate in her or him a habit of perpetual and generous courtesy to all. This said, there were distinct differences mandated in the recommended ways for treating a social superior or an inferior and, significantly for this study, radical shifts in behavior and demeanor necessitated depending on one's gender. Two brief, illustrative narratives from Post's book indicate the necessary etiquette for young women who are to be considered polite. In the first, a girl becomes separated from her friends at a baseball game. Naturally, because she is well-bred, she cannot raise her voice to call to them. Instead, she cannily removes her large hat and holds it at arm's length above her head so that they can recognize it and make their way through the masses to her. The second, longer story furthers the notion that proper women cannot manifest themselves in public:

> At the country club, or perhaps at a mountain resort, at the dance on a Saturday night, John Towne is introduced to Mary Lovely. They dance several dances and they sit out several more. She likes him more than anyone she has met—so much so that she walks over to the hotel the next day with the definite hope that he may be there and that he will single her out again. (Post 180)

When Mary arrives, there is no sign of John and she (again being well-bred) instantly realizes the dilemma she has created for herself: if he comes into the hotel lobby where she is sitting and does not see her, she can neither call out nor go over to him. She must sit there, either on her own or with friends, until he comes to her because, as Post succinctly states in an earlier section, "The man must take the initiative" (80). As such, the woman has no voice nor agency in the public spaces of the hotel lobby or stadium but can only position herself intelligently and hope that her needs are recognized, and met, by men.

In this particular societal context, in which cultural assumptions enjoin the young lady at all times to be still, silent, passive, and waiting if she wants to be thought "polite," it can be seen just how transgressive the noisy, clumsy, and energetic figure of the comic virgin is. Being "polite" is very close in cultural terms to being "good," as the desirous virgins of the dilemma films are always asserting they are and should remain. The comic virgin's energies, however, exceed the bounds of contemporary politeness—the appropriate female behavior—just as her desires exceed what had, before Kinsey, commonly been assumed to be appropriately post-nuptial female desire.

The comic virgin's classic film moment has her tearing or breaking something, or falling over, or sometimes both. She is typically clumsy, physically unruly and unguarded, and given to slapstick and the tearing or misplacing of her clothes. Thus, in *Ask Any Girl* (1959), Meg (played by Shirley MacLaine) is constantly (though innocently) left without, or uncomfortable in, her clothes, whether as the result of having them stolen, confiscated, or drenched. Similarly, in *Sunday in New York* (1963), comic virgin Eileen (played by Jane Fonda) breaks the handle of a door in her physical zeal at opening it and misplaces her clothes when surprised by her ex-boyfriend.

Furthermore, while the destructive power of the comic virgin's energies is
seen to impact on the world at large, it rebounds especially on the man who will
eventually win her. For example, Meg accidentally squirts ink onto her future
husband's tie upon first meeting him, while Eileen gets her jacket caught on that
of her partner-to-be, eventually wrenching his entire pocket off. Such incidents
go beyond traditional romantic comedy conventions to indicate the force of the
virgin's destructive capabilities. Marrying the girl is then, for the hero, not so
much a matter of being the only way he can bed her, but rather the only way he
can hope to survive. The life-threatening power of the virgin in these comic
offerings reaches its peak in the 1964 virginity-dilemma film *Sex and the Single
Girl* when Dr. Helen Brown (played by Natalie Wood), trying to prevent her
patient's bogus suicide attempt beside the East River, ends up pushing him in.

In these films, the female protagonist's body—unruly, generous in
movement—is meant to provoke humor through its erratic, knockabout flailing.
These signs are the constant banner of her virgin state: she is possessed of an
excess of motion indicating excessive emotion not yet channelled into sex.
Against these comic pratfalls, the melodramatic virgin is marked by her static
quality: she is more poised, self-contained, dignified. In this generic strand,
inexperience is rendered visible through a usually upright deportment, an
overarching stillness. The habitual stillness and passivity of the serious virgin is,
significantly, at its most visible when even her chastity becomes subject to trial,
before being suddenly ruptured in a physical outburst that indicates, though it
need not necessarily coincide with, capitulation to passion. For example, in
*Marjorie Morningstar* (1957), the heroine arrives at her decision at a friend's
wedding, when her future lover is not there; alone, as the camera tracks nearer
and nearer to her still form, its stasis enforced by its framing next to a marble
pillar, Marjorie (played by Natalie Wood) appears ill at ease, lost in thought, as
only her eyes dart about. The next scene presents the sound of her footsteps
running to the man's apartment where she appears and halts, totally still in the
symbolically laden doorway, before rushing into the room and her lover's arms
as the scene fades out. This sudden kinetic eruption anticipates the imminent
sexual act and can perhaps be read as a forecast of its climax.

Another melodramatic virgin, April Morrison (played by Diane Baker) in
*The Best of Everything* (1959), similarly presents the fluctuating stillness/motion
pattern found in films obeying the rubric of less comic films. As her would-be
lover, Dexter (played by Robert Evans), cajoles and threatens her to yield, April
listens crouched at his feet, still, passive; this stasis is suddenly and crucially
fractured with a close-up shot of April's hand reaching out to grasp Dexter's
wrist, the explosion of movement marking her surrender.

## Sandra Dee and the "Absolute Ultimate!"

Those various brief sketches show the way that the actors were physically performing virginity, according to a genre-derived rubric that aligns comedy with physicality and maintained chastity, and melodrama with stasis and virginity's loss. I want now to examine this performance dichotomy in more detail, examining two films featuring the same performer, from the same year, that clearly illustrate this generically determined performance-style split. Both 1959 films star Sandra Dee: *Gidget* (directed by Paul Wendkos) and *A Summer Place* (directed by Delbert Daves).

Frances "Gidget" Lawrence is narratively destined to remain a "good girl," despite the twin temptations of Moondoggie (played by James Darren) and the Big Kahuna (played by Cliff Robertson). For a time, she entertains the notion of relinquishing her virginity to the Big Kahuna in order to spite Moondoggie, but the film assures the audience that she is never really in jeopardy, both through bouncy musical cues on its soundtrack and, quite significantly, through the buoyancy of her performance.

In her role as Gidget, Sandra Dee presents a comic kinetic body, swinging her arms, bouncing on her toes, throwing herself about, wrinkling her nose, and fixing her hair even while surfing. Notably, her voice, too, is subject to many more modulations as she talks, giggles, growls, and—against the warnings of Emily Post—raises both her voice and her arms on the beach to attract Moondoggie's attention.

In *Gidget*, the comic virgin's usual pratfalls are rather neatly narrativized as tumbles from the girl's surfboard. Such dilemma films suggest that the comic virgin's many physical mishaps are caused by an excess of energy not yet channelled into sex, at the same time they impose narratives that ensure this sexual energy cannot be released until after the final fade-out. Because Gidget, at 17, is the youngest of the comic virgins, the film realistically realizes that it cannot hope to marry her off at the end of its narrative, even though the theme song does indicate her suitability as bride material with its line "although she's not kingsize, her finger is ring-size." So for Gidget, however much she may desire Moondoggie—and this film does take pains to show the physical effects the boy has on the girl, the sensuous reality of her sexual desires—the "absolute ultimate" she keeps saying she seeks must be gained through surfing, rather than sex.

The film provides many moments that illustrate the traits of this performance style. For example, we see Gidget practicing surfing on her bed, then surfing at the beach. Constant motion is at the heart of Dee's performance. In contrast, Dee abandons comic kinesis for her portrayal of Molly Jorgensen in *A Summer Place*, presenting the viewer instead the static body found in the melodramatic treatments of the virginity dilemma. For unlike Gidget, Molly *does* succumb to sensual temptation and relinquish her virginity. Before the kinetic outburst that symbolizes the moment of yielding, Dee's performance style is very much that of the still and passive maiden. Significantly, when an accident befalls her, it is used for sexualized purposes, rather than slapstick. Molly catches her stocking on a thorn in the rose garden; this snagging is the kind of accident that often befalls the comic virgin but, if Dee were performing that trope here, she would pull away and somehow her whole skirt would be ripped off. Instead, she waits, absolutely still, for both the camera and Johnny (played by Troy Donahue) to fetishize her leg and stocking.

When, soon afterwards, Johnny kisses her for the first time, Molly's immobility is emphasized by the fact that it is he who initiates the kiss; while the urgent gestures of his physical performance bespeak active desire and the pursuit of satisfaction, her stasis symbolizes quiescence. Johnny has to take her hands to place them around his neck—Molly does not actively embrace him herself. The film is not hinting that she does not desire Johnny; on the contrary, it shows in detail the external physical effects—panting, sighing, eyes closed in ecstasy during kisses—aroused in Molly by Johnny. The acting mode visually emphasizes the character's appropriately maiden passivity, which her voice further bears out, being this time far flatter and less given to modulation than the vocal style Dee exhibited as Gidget.

The thorn incident works to bring the future lovers literally, tantalizingly, closer together, but it also has symbolic connotations—the penetrative thorn, the hymeneal blood, the pains of love. Molly's catching on the thorn may suggest her ripeness for further penetration but does not, here, indicate any clumsiness arising from an excess of unchannelled energy: the melodramatic virgin keeps her energies bottled up until the moment of narratively crucial outburst, rather than dissipating them through frantic windmillings of the arms and teetering on her heels.

Molly's crisis of virginity occurs in a scene during which the would-be lovers talk on the beach about how difficult it is to be good (i.e., to *be* good rather than doing what *feels* good). Molly's habitual stillness here is broken by the sudden explosion of energy that indicates her capitulation to Johnny's desires: when he gets up and walks away from their conversation, agreeing sardonically that they must stop thinking of consummating their relationship, she suddenly runs to join him. This kinetic outburst both signifies her yielding and breaks the passivity that marked her maidenhood.

## Conclusion

In considering such visible virginity performances as those enacted by Dee, with kinesis for Gidget and stasis for Molly acting as external indicators of the characters' chaste states and pointing forward to the eventual narrative conclusion, one further question arises: By comparison to whom does the comic virgin appear uncontrolled and the dramatic virgin appear poised? With regard to the former, comic virgin, there is no "before and after" in the comic treatments of the dilemma; there is only "before," because "after" is not only after *sex* but after the end of the *film*, after the inevitable marriage that marks the conclusion of the narrative. Instead, the comic virgins have other post-virginal characters around them with whom to contrast their excessive energies: Meg and Eileen, in the two comic virginity-dilemma narratives mentioned earlier, both have a counterpart overtly marked as sexually experienced, women whose poise and confidence around men tell the viewer as much as their diaphanous outfits and libidinous one-liners. With the much younger girls who make up Gidget's friends, such levels of sophistication would seem dangerously out of place, but Francie too is marked as innocent because of the greater maturity (both emotional and, as the film takes pains to demonstrate, physical) of her girl friends, who go to the beach to show off their bodies in bikinis to boys, rather than to surf.

With regard to the maiden characters from the more melodramatic offerings in the cycle, since the loss of virginity is actively narrativized, there could be an opportunity to study the "before and after" of the virgin's somatic portrayal, comparing her virginal self with the postlapsarian. Significantly, however, it appears that the habitual stillness is present *before* the sexual act. It is thus not a question of before and after, with the maiden displaying unruly energies that are dissipated in the unseen consummation; the poised virgin is not made calm by sex but has already always been calm. In this way, with regard to Molly, there is a temporal before and after her succumbing, but this is not married to a physical difference, a transformation of somatic display aligning itself with the divide of sexual experience. The maidens who will fall are still and passive *before* they have sex—they are marked from the film's beginning as the ones who are going to leave "the continent of girls for another world" (Jaffe 98).

This association of poise with a postlapsarian state is an interesting one; the post-virginal woman seems physically to be more in control of herself, more contained. Significantly, while this composure contrasts with the kinesis of the comic slapstick virgins and, in seeming to comply with the dictates of contemporary conduct literature such as Emily Post's *Etiquette*, appears less transgressive than the comic virgin's unruly motion, this stillness is found in the melodramatic heroines *before* they succumb to temptation. In this way, it seems as if the possession of poise marks the girl who is out for premarital sex.

What prompts the associations at the heart of this performance dichotomy, however? Why are the girls who are destined to remain good "bouncy," and the soon-to-be-bad "still"? Perhaps in endeavouring to answer these questions we can return to the anxieties caused by the idea of the desirous virgin prepared to flout the double standard. This figure's decision to engage in premarital sex might then be viewed as being worrisome enough without showing her *active* body, too.

With the comic virgin, whose loss of maidenhood is positioned after the final curtain, her innate bounciness and her evident expenditure of energy are permissible because she is never going to be allowed to have sex within the diegesis: the destructive energies that cause so many accidents are due to her not yet directing them into the bedroom, and the films that employ her as a character choose to keep this so, inventing plot exigencies that ensure she is married before her unruly energies can achieve their ultimate end. In contrast, the virginity-dilemma films do not allow the same physicality to those virgins who are narratively destined to succumb to temptation, because energy and agency together would be too threatening. The female characters who are going to yield make their doomed virginity visible through stasis and stillness, then, not only to reveal the momentous nature of the step they eventually take, but also to keep within the bounds of at least one ruling of normativity endorsed by contemporary society: the idea prevalent at the time that even sexually active women should still be sexually *passive*. Coupling Gidget's bouncy buoyancy with Molly's intent to fall would be too transgressive for an American audience at this time. As such, Sandra Dee was left surfing towards an "absolute ultimate" because this immature tomboy goal threatened only her own equilibrium, rather than that of society as a whole.

## Works Cited

Jaffe, Rona. *The Best of Everything*. New York: Simon and Schuster, 1958.

Kinsey, Alfred C., Wardell B. Pomeroy, Clyde E. Martin, and Paul H. Gebhard. *Sexual Behavior In The Human Female*. London: W. B. Saunders, 1953.

Leff, Leonard J., and Jerold L. Simmonds. *The Dame in the Kimono: Hollywood, Censorship and the Production Code*. Revised ed. Lexington: University Press of Kentucky, 2001.

Nadel, Alan. *Containment Culture: American Narratives, Postmodernism and the Atomic Age*. Durham, NC: Duke University Press, 1995.

O'Neill, William L. *American High: The Years of Confidence, 1945-1960*. New York: Simon and Schuster, 1990.

Post, Emily. *Etiquette: The Blue Book of Social Usage.* New York: Funk and Wagnalls, 1922.

Sterritt, David, and Gary Gore. *Mad to be Saved: The Beats, the 50s and Film.* Carbondale, IL: Southern Illinois University Press, 1998.

# CHAPTER SEVEN

# VICE'S DEVICES: THE SEXUAL POLITICS OF OBSCENITY IN POSTWAR LOS ANGELES

## WHITNEY STRUB

Defending his office from accusations of "smut laxity" in 1964, Los Angeles City Attorney Roger Arnebergh touted his 80 percent conviction rate over the course of the preceding three years and, in an attempt to distance himself from *actual* smut laxity, declared, "My standards aren't those of the Supreme Court" (*Westwood Hills Citizen*, 1 Oct. 1964).

He was right: they were not. But while Arnebergh intended his comment to reassure concerned Angelenos that their neighborhoods remained secure from the influx of "smut" seemingly invited in by recent liberal Supreme Court decisions, a contemporary reading invites more sinister conclusions. For while the standards used to determine the legal obscenity of smut in postwar Los Angeles may not have been those of the Supreme Court, they were those of a conservative law enforcement bureaucracy far less influenced by Supreme Court mandates than by a homophobic moral panic engulfing Los Angeles. The result was a discursive conflation of homosexuality and obscenity that generated not just a renegade local regime of obscenity unable to withstand appellate court review, but also an apparent effort to destroy the public-community formation of local gays via strategic obscenity charges. In short, "gay" equaled "obscene" in the eyes of the local power structure in Los Angeles, and this chapter seeks to trace the contours of that equivalence's construction.

In many ways, the history of obscenity in the postwar United States followed two divergent trajectories. At the national level, Supreme Court decisions distilled obscenity down to its core component, "hardcore pornography," while at the local level, Court rulings operated only through the mediating lens of local culture. Historians have been slow to recognize this disjunction, perhaps because existing narratives of obscenity fall largely into two groups: legal histories privileging court decisions, particularly those of the Supreme Court; and intellectual histories tracing the conceptual construction of obscenity (or its twin, pornography) at the abstract discursive level (see the works of Ira Carmen, Edward de Grazia and Roger Newman, Max Ernst and Alan Schwartz, Richard Hixson, Walter Kendrick, Richard Kuh, and Andrew Ross). In recent years, scholars such as R. Bruce Brassell, G. Wayne Dowdy, Pat Murdock, Brian O'Leary, and Elaine Sharp have begun to recognize and explore the distorted feedback loop that runs between courtroom convictions and cultural convictions, but despite exciting work on obscenity in early modern France (by Joan DeJean), nineteenth-century England (by Lisa Sigel), and early twentieth-century New York City (by Andrea Friedman), very little scholarship exists on local obscenity standards and policies in the postwar United States.

An examination of postwar Los Angeles, then, proves revealing in that it shows the construction of obscenity as a process governed less by the legal dictates of the Supreme Court than by the imperatives of local social and cultural concerns. Scholar Moira Rachel Kenney has called Los Angeles "the greatest hidden chapter in American gay and lesbian history" (7). This chapter is not a history of queer L.A., but rather an examination of one social construction officially welded to homosexuality: obscenity. If Los Angeles was indeed the "landscape of desire" that its artists and boosters contended, then this work looks at the attempts to keep the topography of that landscape flat (McClung 3). It also points to Los Angeles' law enforcers, as well as their anti-gay allies in the local media and general populace, as "perverse spectators."

"Contextual factors, more than textual ones, account for the experiences that spectators have in watching films and television and for the uses to which those experiences are put," explains Janet Staiger in her formulation of the perverse spectator, a category that "can imply a willful turn away from the norm" (1-2). In Los Angeles, the context of newfound visibility for the gay community clearly outweighed the textual content of the works prosecuted as obscene, which uniformly won First Amendment protection after several protracted court battles. But while legally futile, these obscenity charges proved effective in stifling the worrisome public gay presence in Los Angeles. Local courtroom convictions met with subsequent reversals. But the cultural convictions regarding the equivalence of "deviant" gay sexuality and obscenity proved far more difficult to reverse.

Los Angeles was hardly unique in erupting into an anti-gay panic in the years following World War II. The dislocations of wartime quickly gave way to reassertions of the sexual status quo, and homosexuality provided a useful demonized term against which the domestic ideal could be pitted. From Idaho to Iowa to Florida, gay men were branded as deviants, deviates, sexual psychopaths, and perverts, and they were blamed for everything from moral decay to gruesome murders to diminished property values, as scholars Fred Fejes, John Gerassi, and Neil Miller have demonstrated. But the "lavender menace," to use David Johnson's term, held a special pertinence in Los Angeles. As the research of Allan Berube reveals, World War II had functioned as a catalyst for thousands of gay men and women to recognize their sexual identities and structure their lifestyles around them. These newly self-identified homosexuals often opted for urban living rather than a return to their hometowns after the war, and Los Angeles saw a dramatic increase in the visibility of their presence. Awareness that "the number of 'queers' and degenerates are increasing in this city" was noted by an LAPD Vice Squad Officer in 1943, and the numbers continued to bear out his observation into the postwar years: arrests for sodomy jumped from 19 in 1940 to 90 in 1947, while "sex perversion" arrests accelerated even more rapidly, leaping from 22 to 437 during the same period (Wellpott n.pag.; LAPD Annual Reports). Gay enclaves (such as Silver Lake) and cruising grounds (such as Pershing Square and Griffith Park) were well known and, by the end of 1950, the city was home to the nation's first homophile activist group, the Mattachine Society, which vocally called for gay legal rights (D'Emilio 57-74; Timmons 95-171).

Civic leaders responded to this newfound visibility with a campaign to rid the city of "deviance." In late 1947, the Los Angeles City Council adopted a resolution calling upon the LAPD to "use every latitude in its power" to close bars operating as "rendezvous headquarters for homosexuals." The resolution "conceded" that the status of the bars' liquor licenses was "beyond the jurisdiction of the police," but nonetheless asked them to act "on the basis of the violation of public morals." Suggesting that even more sweeping gestures might be required, the resolution stated that "additional legislation might have to be so restrictive as to make a normal act of shaking the hand of a friend an overt act in order to reach these homosexuals" (Council File 30874).

Local newspapers played a role, too, in fomenting fear. The *Daily News* ran a four-part series in late 1948 on the "alarming increase" in sex crimes and followed it up with sensationalistic headlines such as "Hunt Pervert Who Lured Two Boys" and "Hunt Pervert as 2 Boys Return" (13 Dec. 1948; 10 Sept. 1949; 8 Sept. 1949). The sexual panic sustained itself far beyond the initial shock; a decade later, the *Los Angeles Times* printed a story on the "cancer-like spread of vice" threatening the "L.A. way of life." It explained that a recent rise in venereal disease, "according to health officials, is accounted for largely by the activity of homosexuals!" Unstinting in its use of exclamation marks, the article went on to note that while 4 percent of the national male population was homosexual, experts on L.A. "boost the estimate to 10 percent—about 140,000!" (29 Jan. 1961).

Well into the early 1960s, local newspapers made regular pleas for additional vice squad members to "curb homosexuals" so that Los Angeles could "stop being a mecca for queers," as the *Hollywood Citizen-News* put it in its January 23, 1962 edition. This extended wave of anti-gay reaction coincided with the institutionalization of the professionalism model by the Los Angeles Police Department, by which the LAPD established itself as an autonomous body free from political influence with a "war on crime" mentality, as Joseph Woods has shown. Though much scholarship (by Edward Escobar, Gerald Horne, and others) has focused on the racial policies of the LAPD toward Latino and African-American citizens, less has been written about the aggressive "masculinization" of police work that accompanied professionalism, or its corollary sexual politics (Appier 139-66). But William Parker, chief of police from 1950 until his 1966 death, eagerly enlisted his troops in the battle against gay culture, assuring the City Council in 1951 that the LAPD would continue its activities pertaining to homosexual offenses. These activities would come to include the branding of gay-themed print and screen media as "obscene."

Probably the first victim of this obscenity regime, Bob Mizer, founded the Athletic Model Guild (AMG) with two associates in 1945. Selling 5x7-inch and 8x10-inch black-and-white photographs of barely clad men, either alone or in accepted scenarios such as wrestling matches, AMG took off immediately. When men's magazines refused to carry AMG's advertisements, Mizer began binding pictures together and selling them as a magazine. *Physique Pictorial* debuted in 1951, and by 1952 it had attracted a global subscription list by appealing to the emerging homosexual niche market (Leyland 1; Waugh 215-283).

It also attracted the attention of Paul Coates, a columnist for the *Los Angeles Mirror*, who began a campaign against it in 1954. After presenting "an unpleasant fact—the fact of homosexuality in Los Angeles" on his television program *Confidential File* in late April, Coates used his newspaper column to zero in on *Physique Pictorial*. "Sooner or later, almost every teenage kid will have some contact with the homosexual," Coates warned, listing the possible contact places as movie theaters, public restrooms, and parks, "or maybe the homosexual will be the man who stops his car to offer your boy a ride home from school." Having reinforced this already widely perceived threat, Coates went on to note "the existence in Los Angeles of certain magazines dedicated to the unique interests of the homosexual," including *ONE* and *Physique Pictorial*. While *ONE*, discussed below, later faced its own obscenity problems, Coates rested content with singling out Mizer's publication for particular scorn. Calling it "thinly veiled pornography," he tied it back to his original scare tactics in his column of May 4, 1954 by claiming, without evidence, that "it finds its largest audience among the most brutal, horrifying sex criminal—the sadist."

Coates returned to this topic two weeks later, again emphasizing that the appeal of *Physique Pictorial*, "whether intended or not, is really to the sick, half-world of homosexuals, sadists, and masochists." Musing in his *Los Angeles Mirror* column of May 18, 1954 that "perhaps the harm wouldn't be too great, if perverts limited their practice to their own small circle," Coates followed with an ominous sentence masquerading as a paragraph: "But they don't." This time, Coates exercised a tangible influence; the next morning's *Mirror* carried a brief front-page notice that Bob Mizer had been arrested and charged with "possession and sale of indecent literature" for his magazine, which appealed "to those having an artistic appreciation of the male physique."

Coates celebrated his victory in his column of May 21, 1954 by reiterating his earlier charges in even more hyperbolic language and adding that a photographer who advertised in *Physique Pictorial* had a studio "located right next to a playground and less than 250 yards from an elementary school building." A few months later, Mizer was convicted by a jury on the basis of one witness for the prosecution (the arresting officer) and nine exhibits of photographs entered as evidence, many of which his lawyer claimed had not come from *Physique Pictorial* and portrayed fully naked men (People v. Mizer).

In his appeal, Mizer's lawyer observed that his client had neither photographed nor possessed the nude photos presented as evidence; he also took a more sweeping gesture in arguing that "the concept underlying obscenity is cultural rather than rational so that the definition of obscenity is something which changes even more than drifting sand." Their own argument drifting like sand, the City Attorney's office retreated to a brief dropping the unaccounted-for nudes and pleading that "surely photographs of males showing the body in a nearly nude state, many showing the uncovered rump," constituted obscenity. Openly scoffing at the city's "dependence on the 'uncovered rump' character of the pictures," a subsequent appellant's brief helpfully informed them that "to an athlete and artist the rump is an essential muscle, the gluteus maximus."

Mizer won his appeal on January 31, 1955. But what might otherwise seem a significant moment in gay legal history had a muted impact, for several reasons. The local newspapers, including the *Mirror*, neglected the

Los Angeles Superior Court reversal, and because the case was local and went unreported, it failed to set a precedent. Mizer himself, relieved but extremely cognizant of his precarious position, took a self-described "timid" stance thereafter; as other gay magazines began including full-frontal nudity in the 1960s, he withheld that level of explicitness from *Physique Pictorial* for an extra five years, still intimidated by the threat of additional obscenity charges. By the time of Mizer's appellate victory, another local gay publication had already been deemed obscene.

Though Paul Coates had mentioned *ONE* in his attack on *Physique Pictorial*, he begrudgingly admitted in his column of May 4, 1954 that the former magazine "makes an editorial effort, at least, not to be more lurid than necessary." His reluctant distinction stemmed from the fact that *ONE* included none of *Physique Pictorial*'s racy photographs, but was rather a text-based publication. Founded by members of the groundbreaking homophile group the Mattachine Society (which Coates had also pulled into his spotlight in 1953), *ONE* addressed the pressing gay issues of the day, from police entrapment to psychoanalytic misdiagnoses, in straightforward prose (D'Emilio 57-91). But while *ONE* managed to pass Coates' sneering muster, it failed to clear that of Los Angeles Postmaster Otto Oleson.

Alarmed by the outspoken gay presence announced in *ONE*, Oleson detained its August 1953 issue from the mail just months after the magazine had been founded. When the Solicitor General in Washington found no basis for the obscenity charges necessary to withhold it from the mail, a reluctant Oleson allowed it to circulate. *ONE* recounted this story in its October 1954 issue, along with a short lesbian story and a poem with lines including, "Some peers are seers but some are queers/And some boys WILL be girls" (Gundy, 18). Ironically, as *ONE* gleefully celebrated its right to publish, Oleson initiated a new round of charges directed at it, withholding the October issue as obscene. This time, the charges stuck.

Initially optimistic, the publishers of *ONE* soon saw Oleson's edict upheld by a federal district court, then by the Ninth Circuit Court of Appeals. Though the ACLU promised to give "serious consideration" to assisting in the case, it ultimately declined to become involved (Watts n. pag.). As the trials progressed, *ONE* ran humorous covers such as a picture of a blinded Lady Liberty next to the headline "'Cheap pornography…Vulgar & Indecent'—says the Court!," but it also noted, more seriously, that "homosexual literary themes, compared to heterosexual, are not judged with an equal degree of candor and realism," recognizing that its demarcation as obscene had less to do with its barely ribald content than with the mere fact of the sexual orientation espoused by its authors (Reid 4).

Like Mizer, *ONE* eventually won its case, climbing the judicial ladder all the way to the top. But when the U.S. Supreme Court unanimously reversed the Court of Appeals on January 13, 1958, it did so without a written decision. So again, as in the Mizer case, a would-be precedent went unheeded. The next day, the *Los Angeles Times* carried front-page news of President Eisenhower's new budget and the Dodgers' quest for a field, while the *Herald-Express* made the rescue of John Wayne's baby from a fire its top story. Neither paper, nor the *Examiner*, nor the *Mirror*, made any mention of the groundbreaking ruling by the nation's highest court that indisputably, albeit silently, mandated a separation of homosexuality and obscenity. As a result, the two remained intertwined in Los Angeles.

While *ONE* remained in legal limbo, the LAPD Vice Squad infiltrated the Coronet theater to arrest operator Raymond Rohauer in October 1957. In a confusing charge, the police leveled one count of obscenity at Rohauer, even though he had screened four films, and they had singled out two of them as obscene. Less confusing was the understanding of obscenity conveyed by the charge. *Voices*, an avant-garde story of a neurotic man strolling while listening to the voices in his head, featured a brief glimpse of a naked woman seen through an open window. But *Fireworks* drew the true fury of the vice squad. The Kenneth Anger film, made in 1947 and screened frequently across the nation during the intervening decade, was easily the most openly queer film to precede the late 1960s. Filled with homoerotic scenes of sailors, public bathrooms, and phallic imagery, it contains no actual nudity or literal sex, only impressionism. The prosecution attempted to collapse the difference, referring to "somebody set[ting] fire to his penis" in the climactic scene, though in fact the film depicted only a symbolically phallic firecracker (People v. Rohauer Transcript 165). The arresting officer admitted the substantive thrust of the charges at Rohauer's trial: *Voices* inspired "no particular feeling" in him, but *Fireworks* he found "sickening." Pressed to define obscenity, he grew frustrated, muttering, "I don't have my dictionary with me," but he finally explained, "Obscene is something that isn't general practice by the public" (People v. Rohauer Transcript 83-87).

The trial focused largely on *Fireworks*, as city prosecutors called in a series of teenage boys to testify as to their presence at the Coronet. When defense attorney Stanley Fleishman questioned the relevance of their testimony (as well as the convoluted and vague obscenity charge, not even filed under the most appropriate city ordinance) and called for a dismissal, Judge Harold Shepherd admitted, "I think you have a good argument, counsel" (People v. Rohauer Transcript 38). Despite this, he denied Fleishman's call, ignored the psychoanalyst and the former Guggenheim winner brought in to testify as to the redeeming metaphoric and aesthetic value of *Fireworks*, and found Rohauer guilty of exhibiting obscene material.

Yet again, the conviction failed to withstand appellate review, and the Los Angeles Superior Court reversed Shepherd, citing the *ONE* case (decided by the time of the appeal in 1959) and definitively declaring that while homosexuality "may be regarded as a cruel trick which nature has played on its victims" and "is not a condition to be approved," it is "nonetheless not obscene, in and of itself" (People v. Rohauer Opinion n. pag.). Dissenting Judge Leon David, however, reflected the prevailing cultural beliefs of the time, hearkening back to Paul Coates in describing *Fireworks* as "abnormal stimuli" for the "lascivious thoughts, lustful desires, and sadistic satisfactions" of "sexual psychopaths" (People v. Rohauer Opinion n. pag.).

While the ruling this time was incontrovertible, perspectives such as David's refused to adhere to it. The conflation of obscenity and homosexuality was by now so firmly established that the two concepts became inseparable. *Los Angeles Daily Journal* reporter Edsel Newton, in a lengthy report on pornography, even discursively reconfigured key terms by describing as "harmless stuff" the "unwholesome literature encountered on the whole by postal authorities," in contrast to "hardcore" publications, photographs, and films that "cater to the 200,000 homosexuals that are said to exist in the Los Angeles area" (n. pag.). Newton added "morbidly curious youths and adults" to the groups held in thrall to "hardcore" pornography, but the redefinition of terms was obvious; a sanitized vision of "unwholesome" heterosexual porn made its potential effects appear negligible when pitted against the gay "hardcore," which would cause "a breeder of domestic animals" to "look around for new stock if he observed among his herds such deviations as are encountered" in such hardcore material (n. pag.). Homosexuality, despite the courts, had already been rendered culturally obscene, and Newton created a symmetry by queering pornography itself.

Equivalences such as this made for an easy semantic slide from representation to behavior, making the discourse of homosexuality and that of obscenity nearly interchangeable. Rohauer's trial had revealed LAPD motives to relate as much to context as to content; local film societies had screened *Fireworks* sporadically for a decade without interference, but the Coronet was a fairly well-known gay haven. Arresting officer Donald Shaidell's awareness of this reality came through clearly in his testimony. When Shaidell said the films had no meaning, Rohauer's lawyer asked if other viewers might find meanings in them. Shaidell answered affirmatively, "because there was [*sic*] so many known homosexuals whom I recognized in the audience of this theater" (People v. Rohauer Transcript 96).

The LAPD was able to conceal its attack on the gay community at the Coronet in the legal language of obscenity, effectively destroying it as Rohauer went into debt and out of business as a result of his trials. But the disabling of that legal language made for a less smooth, yet no less effective, discursive slide from obscenity to homosexuality five miles south of downtown Los Angeles in Huntington Park, when community protests against the Lyric Theater began just over a year after Rohauer's appellate acquittal (Siebenand 14).

When residents of Huntington Park began protesting the Lyric Theater in late 1960, Los Angeles County Supervisor Frank Bonelli ordered its license revoked. But because Bonelli lacked the power to simply revoke the Lyric's license, the Board of Supervisors called a referee, M. B. Dickson, to hold official public hearings in the matter. In March 1961, Dickson recommended revocation of the Lyric's license, citing such films as *Hideout in the Sun*, *Isle of Levant*, and *The Nude Set* as especially problematic and noting that "concern was felt for the effect of such pictures on the minds of children passing the theater" (1). The case for closing the Lyric, then, was officially presented as being based on its nudist films and the invasion of Huntington Park's public space by their intrusive promotional posters.

The actual concerns of community protestors, however, were largely unreported or downplayed in Dickson's correspondence to the Board of Supervisors, which briefly mentioned that "several witnesses mentioned the presence of teenage patrons as well as undesirable-appearing adult patrons in the theater" but otherwise remained focused on the films themselves. A transcript of the hearings, though, reveals a near-singular emphasis on such "undesirables." The first question County Counsel Alfred Deflon asked Lyric manager George Munton was, "Do you ever cause your [male] ushers to wear bathing suits for the purpose of their work in the theater?" Growing more bold, Deflon continued, "Have you ever touched the private parts of any usher or person who is applying to be an usher?" When Munton denied this, Deflon inquired about charges brought against Munton in November 1960. "I really don't know," Munton responded. "To be very frank with you, that is something of another case" (In the Matter of Lyric Theatre Transcript 9).

It *was* another case, but only in a legal sense, not in the eyes of the Lyric's opponents. Munton's arrest had been on charges of molesting two male teenage ushers at the Lyric, and the hearings reflected far more community concern over the Lyric's perceived role as a magnet for gay audiences than for the nudist films it presented. Witnesses and speakers repeatedly admitted that the Lyric's films were not obscene. A sergeant in the County Sheriff's Office noted the abundance of nudity in one movie, but also stated that "so far as any lewdness of the film or any suggestiveness, there was none" (In the Matter of Lyric Theatre Transcript 16). A concerned local woman admitted, "I really couldn't say under oath that they were obscene.... I really am not up here to say that the pictures were objectionable" (48). Perhaps the closest anyone came to actual charges of obscenity was the accusation by a Knights of Columbus member that *Isle of Levant* contained a diving sequence in which "the penis was exposed for a fleeting moment" (77). Eager to emphasize his point, the man added, "The testicles could also be seen in diving" (77).

Instead, the opposition to the Lyric emerged as being concerned more directly with the theater's perceived homosexual character. The sergeant who found nothing lewd in the films noted "some pretty slovenly looking characters coming in there" (16), while another witness saw "several younger men attending with older men. What appeared to be teenage boys with older men" (32-33). A member of the Jaycees saw nothing "lewd" occurring in the seats during a screening, but did suggestively describe encountering "a very offensive odor which I cannot describe" (61) in the theater, an aroma also described as "very offensive" by another witness (52).

Referee Dickson attempted to keep the hearings focused on the alleged obscenity of the films. When one woman noted seeing an "undesirable class of people" not just in the theater but even "on the streets of our Florence Avenue especially," Dickson followed immediately with, "Well, let's talk about the amount of exposure in *Isle of Levant*" (48). It was to no avail. The community members present clearly wanted to use the umbrella charge of obscenity to express their actual fears of a homosexual invasion hitting Huntington Park, led by the smelly Trojan horse of the Lyric. Their fear was palpable; as another woman testified, she and two friends had decided to investigate the Lyric, but when the lights went down and a lone male patron chose a seat only one removed from them, "it frightened [us] so much that the three of us felt we couldn't stay any longer so we left" (41).

As noted, Dickson couched their fears in the language of nudist films and their harmful effects on children, and the Board of Supervisors accepted the referee's recommendation, revoking the Lyric's license to operate. But by 1961, nudist films had established a ubiquitous presence in Los Angeles, and a Superior Court judge ordered the revocation annulled. Only then did the officials who were opposed to the Lyric resort to open articulation of their real fears, citing the now-convicted Munton and the "acts of sexual perversion being committed or attempted to be committed in the Lyric Theater" (Bonelli n. pag.). This time, instead of revoking the Lyric's license, the County Supervisors simply voted against renewing it when it expired, effectively forcing a change in ownership and format.

The quick discursive slide from obscenity to homosexuality, and the use of the former as a codeword for the latter in the Lyric case, exemplify the deep intertwining of the two concepts in postwar Los Angeles. That the issue was framed in terms of film content rather than attendee behavior suggests that the officials who translated the community concerns into official policy recognized the legal flaws of their aims. Other Angelenos, however, proved more brazen in their prescriptions. "Other large cities in America have managed to run them out of town, so why can't we?" wrote a female resident to the *Citizen-News*, upping the vitriol quotient in response to an already vitriolic editorial seeking to transform Los Angeles' status as "a mecca for queers" (30 Jan. 1962). It was sentiments such as that letter-writer's feelings of "nausea and anger and also a burning desire to make my hometown of Hollywood clean again" that led to yet another cinematic obscenity trial, directed at *Scorpio Rising*, in 1964.

Like *Fireworks*, *Scorpio Rising* was directed by Kenneth Anger, and it features a typically obtuse underground semi-narrative, with scenes of bikers riding their motorcycles and modeling themselves on James Dean and Marlon Brando juxtaposed against shots of Hitler and Jesus. It culminates in a drunken party with rowdy homoerotic activity. The courtroom drama surrounding the film virtually replayed the *Fireworks* trial. Again, city prosecutors emphasized the nature of the audience, asking the arresting officer, "Were most of the patrons in the theatre that evening male?" (People v. Getz Transcript, Vol. I, 72). Once again, defense attorney Stanley Fleishman delivered an impassioned plea for dismissal, and again the judge, Bernard Selber, acknowledged, "People's case at this point I will say is very weak" (People v. Getz Transcript, Vol. II, 354). Nevertheless, the film was ultimately found to be obscene, and although Selber characterized it as "hardcore pornography which is not redeemed by any social importance" to fit the mandates of the Supreme Court, he simultaneously recognized that "it may well be that an appellate court may overrule me" (People v. Getz Transcript, Vol. III, 18).

By the time of the *Scorpio Rising* case, the Supreme Court had reiterated its *ONE* stance in another case, this time more clearly pronouncing that "portrayals of the male nude cannot fairly be regarded as more objectionable than many portrayals of the female nude that society tolerates" in exonerating a set of nude male physique magazines (Manual Enterprises v. Day). Combined with the standing local *Fireworks* precedent, this created something of a roadblock for *Scorpio Rising*'s prosecutors, who convolutedly explained, "The People's position is this: the problem is not the idea of homosexuality...but it is the depiction of the idea which is the problem" (People v. Getz Transcript, Vol. I, 83). This "depiction" largely amounted to a few hotly contested shots of exposed penises, lasting mere frames, and sufficiently unclear as to allow one witness to testify, "I cannot even identify it as a penis by magnification.... I see a blob of something there" which he suggested "might be a potato" (People v. Getz Transcript, Vol. III, 626). When the film's content proved to be more ambiguous than prosecutor Warren Wolfe had hoped, he fell back on repeated references to the "degeneracy" of the film's makers, characters, and audiences, despite multiple sustained objections by the defense that "degeneracy" was a loaded and "emotionally-laden" term (People v. Getz Transcript, Vol. III, 580).

Getz's conviction clearly held little legal standing, given its open flaunting of obvious precedent; that it was reversed on appeal six months later came as a virtual inevitability. But that it even came to trial in the first place offers abundant evidence that the cultural construction of obscenity based on homophobia in Los Angeles superseded the legal construction of obscenity based on court rulings well into the 1960s.

The localized regime of obscenity that allowed Los Angeles to render homosexuality obscene reflected a broader trend of community disregard for Supreme Court mandates. When prudish Ohio censors banned Louis Malle's *Les Amants* (1958), an exasperated Supreme Court attempted to clarify its position in 1964. "It has been suggested," read Justice William Brennan's opinion, that the basis for determining obscenity was "the standards of the particular local community from which the case arises." Leaving no room for ambiguity, Brennan bluntly averred, "This is an incorrect reading" of the Court's position. Instead, he insisted on a national standard: "It is, after all, a national Constitution we are expounding" (Jacobellis v. Ohio).

This forceful ruling, followed by subsequent decisions further restricting the realm of obscenity, expanded free speech to the point that author Charles Rembar soon declared an arrival at "the end of obscenity" in his book with those words in its title. And, indeed, prosecutions became increasingly futile as the Court threw out one conviction after another, often without bothering to add written opinions. This did not prevent Los Angeles officials from continuing to deploy obscenity charges in their attempts to criminalize gay public spaces. A contest over the legality of the Vista Theater near Silver Lake, for example, virtually replayed the earlier Lyric controversy. LAPD vice squad agents began observing the patrons of the Vista in 1965, noting "unusual" and "unorthodox sexual practices" in the theater and its men's room. When the Vista showed the heterosexual-themed film *The Raw Ones* in 1966, its manager was charged with obscenity, even though the film was no more explicit than numerous others playing around town in theaters with more "acceptable" clientele; rather than contest the charge, he simply pleaded guilty and paid a small fine. Later that year, the Board of Supervisors attempted to revoke the Vista's license to exhibit motion pictures. When the Vista's owners challenged the action in Los Angeles Superior Court, they lost, on the grounds that the theater had been convicted of "displaying lewd films." While manager Stuart Burton appealed the decision, the LAPD subjected him to repeated arrests, charging him with unlawful exhibition on August 8, 10, 11, 15, 16, 17, and 19, 1967. This pattern of harassment went well beyond protocol, and the California Supreme Court eventually ruled in Burton's favor, striking down the Los Angeles film-exhibition ordinance. Though again unsuccessful, the LAPD had once more attempted to harness obscenity charges in the service of its anti-gay efforts (Sawyer Theatres File n. pag.).

One result of late-1960s Supreme Court rulings was a bolder level of explicitness in pornography as "hardcore" porn, graphically depicting unsimulated sex acts, entered the market. As this transition occurred during the early 1970s, the LAPD continued to devote a disproportionate amount of time to using obscenity pretenses to harass members of the gay community. In April 1972, a vice obscenity sweep involved twenty businesses—at least five of them gay-oriented—and the underground newspaper *Gay Sunshine* was seized along with hardcore heterosexual publications, despite eyewitness accounts of officers examining the paper and saying, "This is nothing" ("Gay Paper Seized" 2). The following year, when an undercover vice squad member investigated the Boulevard Book Store in Hollywood, he bypassed the straight porn nearest the door and headed directly for the "far south wall of [the] premises," where books and magazines depicting "nude males in various acts of oral copulation" were located (LAPD Complaint Application n. pag.).

When the Supreme Court issued the 1973 Miller v. California ruling, returning obscenity regulation to the states rather than the federal government, law enforcers widely understood the decision as conferring permission to resume or accelerate their obscenity arrests. The Paris Theatre on Santa Monica Boulevard bore the brunt of this policy shift, as its staff was charged with obscenity at least six separate times during 1973 and 1974. The Century, another gay movie theater, routinely faced obscenity charges for its hardcore films even as the "porno chic" phenomenon heralded by *Deep Throat* (1972) saw celebrity luminaries regularly and openly attending straight hardcore films. Again, the homosexuality rather than the obscenity clearly guided law-enforcement decisions. As gay filmmaker Fred Halsted explained of LAPD Chief Ed Davis, "Davis doesn't like gay porn, doesn't like gays period" (Siebenand 204).

Halsted was accurate in his assessment. Because gay sex remained illegal in California until consenting-adults legislation was introduced in 1976, Davis' ability to collapse the distinction between representation and reality went unimpeded, and in 1974 the LAPD arrested a group of gay pornographic filmmakers, including the owner of the Century theater, on charges of obscenity and conspiracy to violate state sodomy laws. That police fervor was driven by moral panic, rather than evidence, was made clear when the basis of their search warrant was revealed to be allegations so obviously faulty that the district attorney recommended immediate dismissal of the charges.

Perhaps the most egregious example of the discursive conflation of homosexuality and obscenity, however, came in 1977, as LAPD investigator Lloyd Martin began a campaign against child molestation that functioned as a thinly veiled (if veiled at all) attack on homosexuality. "Save our children from pornography or homosexuality," read a flyer for a talk by Martin, which called the threats, in a conspicuous use of the singular, "The Menacing Disease Attacking Our Children" (Broome n. pag.). Martin's allegations that "70 percent of the sexual exploitation of children is homosexual" inspired Reverend Donald Pederson of the Metropolitan Community Church to write to the LAPD for precise statistics. Of 1,879 reported child-molestation cases with male suspects in 1976, the department admitted that only 414, or fewer than 20 percent, involved male victims. Using his fabricated statistics, however, Martin went on to achieve national prominence with spurious allegations of widespread child pornography in the 1980s (Nathan and Snedecker 39-42). With its entrenched history of "obscene" homosexuality, Los Angeles continued its moral panic unabated.

Such constructions of obscenity in Los Angeles gradually faded by the end of the 1970s, for a nexus of reasons too complex to fully unravel here. Influential factors certainly included the growing prominence of the New Right's sexual politics, in which abortion, homosexuality, pornography, sex education, and feminism all melded into a generalized discourse of opposition to all threats to the sanctity of the nuclear family, thereby diminishing the significance of "obscenity" as a controlling trope, as well as the declining visibility of the pornography market as home videos for private consumption replaced the public consumption and corollary activities of theaters. New tropes of disease and apocalypse launched at the gay community with the onset of the AIDS crisis also served to retire the need for obscenity as a mechanism of articulating moral panic, particularly in major urban areas such as Los Angeles.

Not everything was bleak for gay L.A., of course. Especially after the 1969 Stonewall rebellion, the public gay presence in Los Angeles attained new levels of mainstream acceptance. City Attorney candidate Burt Pines was even successfully able to win election in 1973 by recognizing and reinterpreting the discursive overlap between homosexuality and obscenity, reframing them as related "victimless crimes" that diverted limited police resources from attention to more important crimes, the *Los Angeles Times* reported on February 23, 1973. Incumbent Roger Arnebergh attempted to rouse an anti-gay panic by claiming Pines would appoint gays to prominent positions in the city legal bureaucracy and even introduce homosexuality into school classrooms as an acceptable "alternative lifestyle," but his efforts failed, as Pines won the election with nearly 60 percent of the vote (*Los Angeles Times*, 25 Apr. 1973). Pines lived up to his promises, scaling back obscenity efforts and refusing to press charges when the LAPD continued to infiltrate gay bathhouses on various pretenses.

But if Pines, the Supreme Court, and gay liberation effectively split the conflation of homosexuality and obscenity, they hardly ended homophobia in Los Angeles: Arnebergh's anti-gay campaign did, after all, attract approximately 40 percent of the vote. And while West Hollywood subverted the "mecca for queers" label by embracing it, the LAPD stubbornly extended its perverse spectatorship beyond print or screen media by applying it directly to gay community activities. When the Mark IV Health Club held a charity "slave auction" in 1976 to raise money for venereal disease treatment by "selling" men in leather S/M gear, the LAPD chose to "read" the auction as real, arresting forty men on felony involuntary servitude charges. The context of a homophobic police force clearly outweighed the actual content of the auction in the LAPD's decision-making process, and widespread outrage, condemnation, and dropped charges followed, but not before the police released a sensationalistic press release emphasizing sex toys, nipple clamps, and cups of Crisco in an attempt to justify their intrusion.

Ultimately, the perverse spectatorship required to maintain the gay/obscene equivalence became legally untenable, but its cultural relevance outlived its legal viability. As our current government escalates obscenity prosecutions after years of semi-lax enforcement, it is more imperative than ever that individuals understand the ways in which obscenity's cultural construction has consistently overstepped its legally defined bounds in the interest of silencing marginalized sexualities and catering to backward-looking desires for a homogeneity that has never existed.

# Works Cited

Appier, Janis. *Policing Women: The Sexual Politics of Law Enforcement and the LAPD.* Philadelphia: Temple University Press, 1999.

Berube, Allan. *Coming Out Under Fire: The History of Gay Men and Women in World War Two.* New York: Free Press, 1990.

Bonelli, Frank. Los Angeles Board of Supervisors. Motion (unanimously adopted). 29 Aug. 1961. Stanley Fleishman Papers. UCLA Special Collections.

Brassell, R. Bruce. "'A Dangerous Experiment to Try': Film Censorship During the Twentieth Century in Mobile, Alabama." *Film History* 15 (2003): 81-102.

Broome, H.F. Letter to Donald Pederson, with photocopied flyer attached. 14 Feb. 1977. Joel Wachs Papers. Los Angeles City Archives.

Carmen, Ira. *Movies, Censorship, and the Law.* Ann Arbor: University of Michigan Press, 1966.

de Grazia, Edward. *Girls Lean Back Everywhere: The Law of Obscenity and the Assault on Genius.* New York: Random House, 1992.

—, and Roger Newman. *Banned Films: Movies, Censors and the First Amendment.* New York: R.R. Bowker, 1982.

DeJean, Joan. *The Reinvention of Obscenity: Sex, Lies, and Tabloids in Early Modern France.* Chicago: University of Chicago Press, 2002.

D'Emilio, John. *Sexual Politics, Sexual Communities: The Making of a Homosexual Minority in the United States, 1940-1970.* Chicago: University of Chicago Press, 1983.

Dickson, M. B. Letter to Board of Supervisors. 20 March 1961. Stanley Fleishman Papers. UCLA Special Collections.

Dowdy, G. Wayne. "Censoring Popular Culture: Political and Social Control in Segregated Memphis." *West Tennessee Historical Society Papers* 55 (2001): 98-117.

Ernst, Max, and Alan Schwartz. *Censorship: The Search for the Obscene.* New York: Macmillan, 1964.

Escobar, Edward. *Race, Police, and the Making of a Political Identity: Mexican Americans and the Los Angeles Police Department, 1900-1945.* Berkeley: University of California Press, 1999.

Fejes, Fred. "Murder, Perversion, and Moral Panic: The 1954 Media Campaign Against Miami's Homosexuals and the Discourse of Civic Betterment." *Journal of the History of Sexuality* 9 (2000): 305-47.

Friedman, Andrea. *Prurient Interests: Gender, Democracy, and Obscenity in New York City, 1909-1945.* New York: Columbia University Press, 2000.

"Gay Paper Seized in Porn War." *Advocate* 24 May 1972: 2.

Gerassi, John. *The Boys of Boise: Furor, Vice, and Folly in an American City.* New York: Macmillan, 1966.

Gundy, Brother. "Lord Samuel and Lord Montagu." *ONE* Oct. 1954: 18-19.

Hixson, Richard. *Pornography and the Justices: The Supreme Court and the Intractable Obscenity Problem.* Carbondale, IL: Southern Illinois University Press, 1996.

Horne, Gerald. *Fire This Time: The Watts Uprising and the 1960s.* Charlottesville: University of Virginia Press, 1995.

In the Matter of Lyric Theatre. License Hearing Board Transcript. 23 Jan. 1961. Stanley Fleishman Papers. UCLA Special Collections.

Jacobellis v. Ohio. 378 U.S. 184. 1964.

Johnson, David. *The Lavender Menace: The Cold War Persecution of Gay Men and Lesbians in the Federal Government.* Chicago: University of Chicago Press, 2004.

Kendrick, Walter. *The Secret Museum: Pornography in Modern Culture.* Berkeley: University of California Press, 1987.

Kenney, Moira Rachel. *Mapping Gay L.A.: The Intersection of Place and Politics.* Philadelphia: Temple University Press, 2001.

Kuh, Richard. *Foolish Figleaves? Pornography In and Out of Court.* New York: Macmillan, 1967.

Leyland, Winston, ed., with photography by Bob Mizer. *Physique: A Pictorial History of the Athletic Model Guild.* San Francisco: Gay Sunshine Press, 1982.

Los Angeles City Council Files. Los Angeles City Archives.

Los Angeles Police Department. *Annual Reports.* 1940-1947.

—. Complaint Application. 25 Sept. 1973. Stanley Fleishman Papers. UCLA Special Collections.

—. Press Release. No date (1976). Joel Wachs Papers. Los Angeles City Archives.

Manual Enterprises v. Day. 370 U.S. 478. 1962.

McClung, William Alexander. *Landscapes of Desire: Anglo Mythologies of Los Angeles.* Berkeley: University of California Press, 2000.

Miller, Neil. *Sex-Crime Panic: A Journey to the Paranoid Heart of the 1950s.* Los Angeles: Alyson, 2002.

Miller v. California. 413 U.S. 15. 1973.

Murdock, Pat. "The Lone 'Lady Censor': Christine Smith Gilliam and the Demise of Film Censorship in Atlanta." *Atlanta History* 43.2 (1999): 68-82.

Nathan, Debbie, and Michael Snedecker. *Satan's Silence: Ritual Abuse and the Making of a Modern American Witch Hunt.* New York: Basic Books, 1995.

Newton, Edsel. "Report on Pornography." Booklet reprint of *Daily Journal* articles. 1958. Southern California ACLU Papers. UCLA Special Collections.

O'Leary, Brian. "Local Government Regulation of the Movies: The Dallas System, 1966-93." *Journal of Film and Video* 48 (1996): 46-57.

ONE, Incorporated v. Olesen. 355 U.S. 371. 1958.

Parker, W. H. Letter to Board of Police Commissioners. 22 May 1951. City Council File 48346. Los Angeles City Archives.

People v. Getz. Los Angeles Municipal Court Case No. 207224. Reporter's Transcript. Stanley Fleishman Papers. UCLA Special Collection.

People v. Mizer. Municipal Court Case File CR A 3216. Los Angeles County Record Center.

People v. Rohauer. Memorandum Opinion. Los Angeles Superior Court. Printed in *Los Angeles Daily Journal Report Section.* 13 July 1959.

—. Reporter's Transcript. Los Angeles Municipal Court. 13 Jan 1958. Stanley Fleishman Papers. UCLA Special Collections.

Randall, Richard. *Censorship of the Movies: The Social and Political Control of a Mass Medium.* Madison: University of Wisconsin Press, 1968.

Reid, Ann Carroll. "Editorial." *ONE* March 1957: 4.

Rembar, Charles. *The End of Obscenity.* New York: Random House, 1968.

Ross, Andrew. *No Respect: Intellectuals and Popular Culture.* New York: Routledge, 1989.

Sawyer Theatres File. Stanley Fleishman Papers. UCLA Special Collections.

Sharp, Elaine. "Culture Wars and City Politics: Local Government's Role in Social Conflict." *Urban Affairs Review* 31 (1996): 738-58.

Siebenand, Paul. "The Beginnings of Gay Cinema in Los Angeles: The Industry and the Audience." Diss. University of Southern California, 1975.

Sigel, Lisa. *Governing Pleasures: Pornography and Social Change in England, 1815-1914.* New Brunswick, NJ: Rutgers University Press, 2002.

Staiger, Janet. *Perverse Spectators: The Practices of Film Reception.* New York: New York University Press, 2000.

Timmons, Stuart. *The Trouble With Harry Hay: Founder of the Modern Gay Movement.* Boston: Alyson, 1990.

Watts, Rowland. Letter to William Lambert. 17 July 1957. Southern California ACLU Papers. UCLA Special Collections.

Waugh, Thomas. *Hard to Imagine: Gay Male Eroticism in Photography and Film from Their Beginnings to Stonewall.* New York: Columbia University Press, 1996.

Wellpott, P.A. Memorandum. 8 Aug. 1943. Griffith Family Papers. UCLA Special Collections.

Woods, Joseph. "The Progressives and the Police: Urban Reform and the Professionalization of the Los Angeles Police." Diss. UCLA, 1973.

Part III
Controversial Cinematic Representations

# Chapter Eight

# The Good, the Bad, and the Unborn: The Abortion Issue in U.S. Cinema

## Heather MacGibbon

This is how we picture the angel of history. His face turned toward the past. Where we perceive a chain of events, he sees one single catastrophe, which keeps piling wreckage upon wreckage and hurls it in front of his feet. The angel would like to stay, awaken the dead, and make whole what has been smashed. But the storm is blowing from Paradise; it has got caught in his wings with such violence that the angel can no longer close them. This storm irresistibly propels him into the future to which he is turned, while the pile of debris before him grows skyward. This storm is what we call progress.
—Walter Benjamin (257-258)

When dealing with the reflection of social issues in the cultural products of society, particularly the arts, I find myself thinking about the above passage by Walter Benjamin. As scholars interested in social issues that are historically loaded with meaning and relevance for our society, we cannot help but to feel certain identifications with this image, especially when we consider the history of sexuality on the cinema screen. It is important to keep in mind that we, today, have the unique perspective that time and distance lends us when reflecting on the problems of censorship and sexuality in film. I state this as a warning for readers and for myself as we begin to examine the history of cinematic representations of the abortion issue in U.S. cinema. What are some of the problems that such a sexually charged, taboo subject faces in this public and very influential medium? For the purposes of this chapter, I focus on representations of abortion during the first half of the last century—particularly at the beginning of the film industry—because that is where many of the narrative structures and themes that form and inform the debate between the current pro-choice and pro-life movements in the twenty-first century took hold.

When I began my study of the abortion issue in U.S. cinema, I thought I would have difficulty finding adequate material for analysis in pre-Roe v. Wade times. Surely, I believed, filmmakers during the early part of U.S. history and in the early years of cinema would have shied away from something so charged: bringing together conflicting sets of strongly held American values such as community, religion, and family as opposed to independence, self-determination, and freedom. I knew that I would find sex in early cinema, since sex has always been a part of film content. Many of the first moving-picture shows that exposed naked bodies for public view produced the need for continual work on the part of this budding industry to constantly legitimize cinema as an art form. Interestingly, this need for legitimization is responsible, at least in part, for a surge of films dealing with the topic of abortion that were released between 1916 and 1928.

The turn of the twentieth century was a time of popular progressive movements that attempted to replace the religious and moral approach to life with a new belief in science. These movements embraced the motion-picture industry as a new, exciting, and powerful vehicle for the promotion of their ideas, because of the mass circulation of silent films as well as the unique attributes of the filmic medium. Science had brought about the ability to recreate reality before people's very own eyes. What could be more persuasive about the virtues of science itself? By this time, the American medical establishment had begun the process of positioning itself in distinct opposition to "folk practitioners," who had prevailed in the early years of U.S. history. I borrow the term "folk practitioners" from the work of James Mohr to refer to all medical workers who were not trained in the new medical-school establishment and often relied on herbal remedies passed down from generation to generation (Pernick 27).

Abortion, along with eugenics and euthanasia, was one of the defining issues of modern medicine because it transformed doctors into moral leaders as well as guardians of public health, and the media played a major role in popularizing this view. Professional campaigns organized by doctors such as Horatio Robinson Storer were praised as physicians attempted to educate the public about various medical issues, using film as their medium of propaganda. Storer was, of course, very well known as the man who helped fund the American Medical Association through his personal influence and letter-writing expressing the urgent need for scientifically trained doctors to take the moral and medical issue of abortion away from folk practitioners, with claims that doing so was in the best interests of the moral and physical well-being of American citizens. Films about public health helped to create a public environment that was both open and susceptible to his ideas. As Martin Pernick has revealed:

The new level of public faith in scientific expertise was in large measure a mass-media creation. By 1915, only a decade after the first movie theaters had opened, the silent screen was filled with films on every aspect of medicine, from how to bathe a baby to how to avoid venereal disease; all [were] part of an intense campaign to disseminate the discoveries of scientific public health and to promote the power and expertise of the scientific physician. (119)

Thus, abortion became one of many important health-related topics to hit the silent screen in the form of medical/moral drama. Such dramas not only presented the value and morality of science when applied properly by "good" physicians for the "right" purposes, but they also allowed for reaffirmation and inculcation of audiences with the traditional American values of the time. As E. P. Christian, a member of the American Medical Association, put it:

It is not sufficient that the medical profession should set up a standard of morality for themselves, but the people are to be educated up to it. The profession must be aggressive to those wrongs and errors which it only can properly expose, and successfully oppose. (155)

Unfortunately, with regard to medical issues like abortion, this made the dramas heavily laden with moralizing. In the case of abortion, public health and medical issues suffered at the hands of religious attacks, at least in part because of the very structure of the films themselves.

Abortion played another important role in early cinema: it was set up as the villain by early movements for birth control. Abortion was the evil alternative that justified the need for sexual education and provision of effective birth-control devices to women by doctors at the turn of the century. Abortion could be, and still is, vilified on two fronts: it ends a pregnancy that might otherwise become a baby, and it poses risks to the woman because it is a surgery. As the research of Carl Degler has revealed, with women as the "angels of the house" and the center of morality in U.S. culture at the turn of the last century, and their main role to be good wives and mothers who raise healthy, precious children, both of these aspects of abortion were seen as horrific. In addition, unlike other issues involving sexuality, abortion could not rely on the symbolism used commonly in literature and the arts to represent sexuality, romance, and pregnancy. Explicit sexual scenes and those involving surgery were deemed to be too grotesque or too morally shocking for photographic representation on the screen by the local boards that regulated film distribution. As a result, films pertaining to abortion relied on drama as their primary means of expression, and they used symbolism and veiled hints on screen to get their more controversial points across. Accordingly, abortion dramas were able to avoid some of the aesthetic censorship that films pertaining to eugenics or euthanasia regularly faced (Pernick 121).

Let's look at one of the few still-viewable examples from this time to examine these various elements and how they worked formally on the silent screen. The film *Where are My Children?* (1916), alternatively titled *Ill Born*, was controversial because, as some have argued, it represented a case for the decriminalization of contraception. Contraception is represented as necessary in the film because of the evils that abortion (as its only alternative) presents to wives, women who became victims of male seduction, and the overly fertile poor. The work focuses particularly on the corruption of wives who are at the moral center of American life. As Martin Pernick points out, it also touches on the issue of eugenics, yet it did not encounter the aesthetic censorship common to other eugenic-themed films because it did not directly represent images of actual malformed children or surgery which would be unseemly (127). Instead, it presents viewers with what we would today call a melodrama, but what at the time would be considered a "tear-drenched" drama (Singer 165).

*Where are My Children?* has a two-pronged plot. The primary plot focuses on a district attorney and his wife who have no children. It begins with a court case in which a man is on trial for distributing a book about contraception in violation of what appear to be the Comstock Laws of 1873 against obscenity (Mohr 196-197). The district attorney prosecutes the case and then returns home to speak to his wife about the morality of his battle because he believes in eugenics. His wife, a young socialite, seems in every way to be a good, dutiful young woman fitting the moral codes and standards of the film's era; she is finely clothed and shown caring for her visiting brother and the child of a female friend who has dropped by for a visit. As the story unfolds, however, it is revealed that the wife is selfishly concerned with her own activities and social calendar, so much so that she has been avoiding pregnancy and motherhood by having abortions. This is one of the stereotypes that anti-abortion movements early in the century utilized to make women who wished to delay the start of their families or limit their fertility seem shallow and selfish. It promoted the argument that women should not be tempted to shirk their expected duties as mothers and that doctors should be the ones to decide when an abortion was needed. This was part of the medical profession's push to make doctors moral leaders in their communities, rather than simply technicians and distributors of medicines.

This move against family limitation was not entirely in keeping with the social thought of its time. As sociologists and researchers including Nanette Davis and Carl Degler have pointed out, there was a strong Neo-Malthusian movement in the United States and Europe about this same time. Limitation of fertility was not only a concern of those who did not wish the "burden" of caring for children. It was also a concern of those who believed we would overpopulate the planet and might best concentrate our resources on fewer, better-cared-for children. For example, Davis, a social scientist, noted:

> By the twentieth century, the "law of population" dominated social scientists' thinking. Economists, agronomists, biologists, demographers, sociologists, population planners, and public health groups emphasized the urgent requirements for rational control over individual reproduction. (21)

But this social view did not fit into the melodramatic format when the intended message of the film was to be that contraception was good and abortion was bad. For the tear-drenched drama to work, there needed to be an enemy, and abortion as well as abortion providers were the easiest choices given the overall nature of such films. As Martin Pernick points out:

> Melodrama can only portray such large abstract forces by personalizing them, representing them as individual heroes and villains. The silent screen's reliance on physical pantomime also made it harder to convey that the individuals were supposed to represent impersonal abstractions. Most important[ly], these technical limits of the medium reinforced key ambiguities in the progressive health message. The constraints of silent melodrama amplified the internal contradictions in the progressives' faith that science could be both impersonally objective and a source of moral imperative. (146)

The tear-drenched drama, therefore, acting as propaganda for progressive health movements, needed to create concrete characters and stories to represent the generalities of its ideas. This is what the wife in *Where are My Children?* becomes. She is a representation of the socially mobile, anti-maternal woman who was encouraged and enabled by abortion. Her use of abortion to limit fertility (and, in this case, without her husband's knowledge) undermines her role as the ideal "angel of the house" and eventually leads to her downfall. The film accomplishes its goals by resorting to earlier themes of religious morality in order to focus viewer sentiments against the wife. It becomes clearer how this works when one examines the representation of pregnancy in this film.

From the standpoint of censorship, one of the problems this film encounters involves how to represent the pregnancy of the women in question. The first woman who is presented as having become pregnant is one of the wife's friends; she is married and yet does not want to miss out on her social life because of her impending duties as a new mother. But how could one indicate this on the screen when words were limited and pregnancy and sex were taboo subjects? *Where are My Children?* features a fascinating solution, hearkening back to images of the revelation of the Immaculate Conception from religious paintings.

This approach heightens the religious morality that permeates the film, and weakens the progressive message about the benefits of contraception, because progressive movements saw science as the new religion. It is effective enough by the end of the film to counteract any message about birth control that its makers may have wished to include, transforming the overall meaning of the film into a throwback to pre-turn-of-the-century "family values" as we would call them today.

The image viewers are presented with is that of the wife's friend alone in a garden; an anxious expression passes over her face as the film cuts to an intertitle stating that a soul has been sent down from heaven. We are then greeted with images of the pearly gates opening and a tiny angel descending down the screen. Next, we are shown the woman with a cherub hovering over her shoulder (thanks to the use of a double exposure, which provides an eerie, translucent quality). This representation strongly echoes the images of the Immaculate Conception in famous paintings that would have been known throughout Europe, and by many middle- and upper-middle-class Americans, by the turn of the century. These paintings—by famous artists including El Greco, Bartolome Esteban Murillo, and Samuel van Hoogstraten, to name just a few— represent the Virgin surrounded by cherubs at the time of the revelation of her pregnancy. This image erases the act of sexual intercourse from the equation and makes the issue of impending motherhood entirely a religious and moral issue for the women in question: Will she take on her responsibilities or not?

Upon the friend's revealing to the district attorney's wife that she is pregnant, the following intertitle appears: "If you are determined to evade motherhood, and are willing to take the risk, I recommend you see Dr. Malfit." The district attorney's wife provides the name of a doctor she has used, takes her friend to the abortionist's office, and introduces them. This is the same office she advises her brother to take his pregnant girlfriend to before she learns it is her own servant's daughter. In both instances, when the abortion is performed, we do not actually see a medical situation because, at this time, most local boards reviewing motion pictures forbade films that explicitly included "gruesome and unduly distressing scenes," including "surgical operations," "men dying," or depictions of the "insane" (Pernick 121). When the district attorney finds the servant's daughter dying and goes after the abortionist in order to bring him to justice, he discovers Dr. Malfit's appointment book and the names of his wife and her friend inside. Only then does he find out that he has been denied his rightful children in one of the early arguments for father's rights on screen in the abortion debate. His wife is then shown as now-amenable to having children, praying for pregnancy, but she is denied angels from heaven to descend upon her from the pearly gates. The final scene, accomplished through a series of dissolves, portrays the coupling aging, with a double exposure presenting the shadowy images of the children they should have had surrounding them.

Another noteworthy film in this glimpse at the abortion issue in cinema came twelve years later, and it represents a late offering from the silent period that deals with abortion, contraception, and criminality. *The Road to Ruin* (1928), directed by Norton S. Parker, was produced at the end of this cycle of films about abortion and just prior to the formalization of the Motion Picture Production Code, which would make explicit sexual subject matter even less acceptable on the screen. This film frames its foray into the corruption of a young, innocent girl with a speech by the detective in charge of juvenile delinquents in Los Angeles. It is a case in which, according to the intertitles, a good child goes bad because her parents are not vigilant enough. The film deals with themes of family, romance, and sexuality as it attempts to represent the perils of the new independent woman in the real world, which result from her newfound freedom.

In *The Road to Ruin*, a teenage girl, Sally, convinces her mother to allow her to spend the night at a girlfriend's home; the friend is, symbolically, named Eve. Although her mother trusts her and gives her freedom to stay out all night, Sally starts drinking and smoking with her friend, hanging out with boys, and playing strip poker. Eventually, she spends time alone with one young man in his apartment and, although viewers see nothing to indicate it directly, she later indicates that they have had sex. The strip-poker incident, observed by some adults, motivates a call to the police because the girls are only children. The girls are then brought in and forced to endure examinations by the police doctor, which frightens and horrifies them. But because Sally is a good girl, she is released with just a warning, and her mother agrees that they will keep her transgression a secret.

When Sally realizes she is pregnant (during a scene with an intertitle that reads, "The wages of Sin"), she calls the young man she was with and he promises to help her out if she will do a favor for him: He has a friend who needs another girl to entertain some gentlemen at a speak-easy later that night. This is followed by a scene of the young man taking her to the doctor's office, and a scene of her reclining on her couch at home, holding her stomach to indicate that she is in pain. She calls the young man to try and back out of the promise she made to him, but he insists that she fulfill her part of their agreement if she really loves him. That evening, the young man drops her off at the speak-easy, where she appears young and angelic again, dressed in white; the costuming and lighting highlight her as innocent and pale, a victim of the circumstances she has encountered. This perception is further emphasized when she is traumatized by sexual advances made by her own father, who approaches her in the room. The shock of realizing it is her father who is attempting to kiss her throws Sally into a state of shock and, although she is rushed home and a doctor is summoned, she is beyond help. Her death scene again references an angelic presence because she is dressed all in white and brightly lit, making her glow in an otherwise dark room. She asks her mother for forgiveness and her mother replies that she is the one who is at fault, because she did not share with her "what mothers should teach their daughters." Sally's death redeems her transgressions; a corresponding intertitle reads, "All are redeemed by Jesus Christ."

Although this film shows many more sexual situations than the earlier films (e.g., images of the young girls embraced by their boyfriends and kissing, the game of strip poker which reveals a fair amount of skin, etc.), there are no documentary-footage sequences of operations, no blood and gore to be considered too gruesome for presentation. I believe that this concealing of the operation works in a different way, one that has historically come to plague the pro-choice movement. Much like unseen monsters in horror movies, viewers do not know the unspeakable horrors that await behind the abortionist's door. As such, their imaginations do the work of creating fear.

Such patterns continued into the 1930s, when abortion still showed up as an issue in films, albeit much less frequently. One striking example is *Ann Vickers* (1933). Irene Dunne stars as the social reformer, Ann Vickers, who becomes pregnant by a soldier she falls for while working in a settlement house during World War I. Their encounter is signified by her saying that she should be leaving his room and then, rather than showing her putting on her coat, the camera pans away from the embracing couple to the window. Slowly, the light in the window changes to morning, as if the camera has never been moved. This allows for the indication of sex without the mention of it or the inappropriate removal of clothing on screen. Later, Ann confesses to a socialite friend, whom viewers subsequently learn is a female abortion doctor (although this is never stated directly), that she is in trouble. Her friend suggests a nice rest at her "country place" in Cuba. It is interesting to note that Dr. Malvina Wormser (played by Edna May Oliver) is never referred to as the doctor performing Ann's surgery until after the abortion is complete. Even then, she is indicated as the abortionist only by the nurse saying, "The doctor is on the phone—she will be right in," which is followed by Malvina entering and sitting down to chat with Ann about how she is feeling. Ann talks about her guilt and what she would have named her girl: "Pride Vickers—that is what I named her. Pride of work, pride of character." Malvina tells her it is not good to dwell on such things and Ann resolves to throw herself into her work, "jobs for women." This can be seen as a not-so-subtle critique of women replacing family values with career goals. It is clear that Ann is not just interested in her own social life. She turns down the opportunity to marry a rising litigator who later becomes a judge. If she were simply a socialite like the district attorney's wife in *Where are My Children?*, that might have been appealing to her. Instead, it is her ambition for social change, as well as her feminist agenda, that brings her to choose abortion and eventually see this as the destruction of her happiness. It is implied by the rest of the narrative that Ann chooses to live either alone or in relationships that can never be traditionally happy because of her guilt and regret over her abortion. Also, it is noteworthy that her career success and personal achievement never make up for what she gave up by having that abortion. Ultimately, she is redeemed only as a tragic figure who is doomed to suffer as the mistress of a former judge who loses everything because of his involvement in corruption. Viewers see that, rather than improving her own position and the position of all women more generally, she ends up trapped in a tiny apartment with a child and an unemployed husband with few prospects.

What I want to suggest with this latter example is a shying further and further away from any real contact or understanding on the part of the viewer as to what abortion really is or what these women are going through. Abortion shifts from part of a movement to educate the public about health matters to simply a tragic plot twist that dooms the heroine to tragedy. I would also suggest that this is partly the result of industry self-censorship, based on aesthetic sensibilities, that was motivated by the establishment of the Motion Picture Production Code in the early 1930s.

By the 1950s, U.S. cinema was even further removed from representations of abortion as a reality. From the late 1800s onward, abortion had been the subject of crime stories in newspapers such as *National Police Gazette*, which offered lurid accounts of the trials of abortionists and the confessions of their "victims/witnesses" (i.e., the women who sought out abortions). However, public opinion of the women who sought abortions was still doubly pronged: Some women were viewed as "good women" who became victims of circumstance or evil men, whereas others were regarded as evil women who used abortion to avoid responsibility for their actions. The 1951 film *Detective Story* represents both of these types of women. Like the earlier films, it talks of children who are "born dead" instead of using the term abortion, but it is nevertheless clear what the subject is. In this film, Detective McCloud (played by a very young Kirk Douglas) is a self-righteous cop with a vendetta against abortion doctors. He is seen early in the film as a hardworking man fighting against evil, which makes viewers like him as a hero character. We see him with his sweet, seemingly innocent wife, Mary (played by Eleanor Parker), who has just come from the doctor, disappointed that she is not pregnant. She seems everything a proper wife of the late 1940s and early 1950s should be: she is devoted, obedient, and praying to start a family. Even the other characters comment on what a good woman she is, and how she has saved the life of

McCloud by keeping him from falling too deeply into his obsession with smiting evil. As the story progresses, we find out that McCloud's father was either an abortionist himself or forced McCloud's mother to have abortions against her will. When viewers meet the first woman in the film who is a patient of the doctor, she is the negative stereotype of a woman who desires abortions. She has obviously been paid off by the doctor to claim that she does not know him and is happy about her choice. Once again, this is a jab at the typically social-climbing, ambitious women who serve as evil figures in abortion narratives. But as the film draws to a close, viewers learn that Mary, McCloud's wife, was also a patient. Unlike in the earlier films, sympathy here is generated for the wife from the beginning. Her ex-boyfriend is brought in and explains that it was his fault, because he did not tell her he was married. The lieutenant confronts Mary with this revelation and she says that it is true, but because she never told McCloud, it cannot possibly be the source of his vendetta. To be certain, the lieutenant brings in McCloud and confronts them all together. Unfortunately, the detective is unable to overcome his anti-abortion sentiment, and his wife leaves him just hours before he is killed on the street.

Based on these four examples of how abortion has been represented (or not represented, as the case may be) historically in U.S. cinema, I would argue that, as social sentiments have shifted through the decades, women who have abortions and the men involved in their lives have received more sympathetic representations. Although many films still represent abortion as a source of deep personal trauma or as clear-cut battles between good and evil, others have softened with the times. For example, the teen experimenting with sexual pleasure and in need of an abortion can become a figure of sympathy in films such as *Fast Times at Ridgemont High* (1982). Abortion doctors can become reluctant, if still tragic, heroes in films such as The *Cider House Rules* (1999). The exaggerated battle between pro-choice and pro-life groups can even be used as a source of black comedy in films such as *Citizen Ruth* (1996).

## Works Cited

Benjamin, Walter. *Illuminations*. Trans. Harry Zohn. Ed. Hanna Arendt. New York: Schocken Books, 1985.

Christian, E. P. "The Pathological Consequences Incident to Induced Abortion." *Detroit Review of Medicine and Pharmacy* 2.4 (1867): 155.

Davis, Nanette. *From Crime to Choice: The Transformation of Abortion in America*. Westport CT: Greenwood Press, 1985.

Degler, Carl N. *At Odds: Women and the Family in America from the Revolution to the Present*. New York: Oxford University Press, 1980.

Mohr, James C. *Abortion in America: The Origins and Evolution of National Policy, 1800-1900*. New York: Oxford University Press, 1978.

Pernick, Martin S. *The Black Stork: Eugenics and Death of "Defective" Babies in American Medicine and Motion Pictures since 1915*. New York: Oxford University Press, 1996.

Singer, Ben. "Female Power in the Serial-Queen Melodrama: The Etiology of an Anomaly." *Silent Film*. Ed. Richard Abel. New Brunswick, NJ: Rutgers University Press, 1996. 163-193.

CHAPTER NINE

DANGEROUS BODIES: THE REGULATION AND
CONTESTATION OF WOMEN'S SEXUALITY
AT THE MOVIES IN VIRGINIA

MELISSA OOTEN

In 1922, the General Assembly of Virginia created a motion-picture
censorship board to regulate out of popular culture images its cultural arbiters
ruled detrimental to state officials' attempts to modernize and "clean up" the
image of Virginia. On-screen depictions of women's sexuality repeatedly fell
prey to the board's "protectionist" ideology, by which censors argued that their
work "protected" society's most vulnerable citizens. In reality, such an ideology
served as an extension of state power to keep subjective, realistic portrayals of
these already marginalized citizens out of popular culture in order to justify their
continued status as "second-class" citizens within the state.

## Regulation of Sexuality in 1920s Virginia

The regulation of sexuality came to the forefront of Virginia's legislative
agenda repeatedly during the 1920s. According to historian Philippa Holloway,
Virginia's leaders of that decade "identified a broad spectrum of sexual
behaviors and sex-related activities that they considered dangerous to public
welfare" and thus initiated specific policies to control and curb the effects of
deviant sexuality (27). Between 1922 and 1924, the General Assembly of
Virginia passed three laws that expanded public intrusion into private sexual
matters. First, the Assembly passed the Motion Picture Censorship Act, which
allowed censors to view each movie requesting entrance into the state before it
could be shown on any theater screen. Second, the state passed the Racial
Integrity Act of 1924, which narrowed who could be "white" in the state of
Virginia. Finally, in that same year, legislators passed the Virginia Sterilization
Statute, which allowed the sterilization of any resident of the state's four mental
institutions or the Lynchburg State Colony. Holloway points out the significance
of such regulation in her assessment that "feeble-minded individuals were not

new to Virginia in the 1920s, but the suggestion that they could damage the Commonwealth was" (27, 32).

Not only did the government begin to expand its intrusion into citizens' sexual behaviors, but it also solidified white elites' belief that "certain kinds of sexual behavior presented dangers to the state and that government should undertake serious efforts to prevent these threats" (Holloway 30). For the first time, Virginia's elites began to view segments of the Commonwealth's citizenry as enough of a threat to their "progressive" vision to allocate state funds to censor the movies, regulate whiteness, and sterilize some of its poorest and least politically empowered citizens.

Sexual deviance has long been associated with social disorder, and the control of the sexual by Virginia's elites in the 1920s must be understood in the context of their broader mission to cultivate an orderly, efficient, economically prosperous, "modern" state in the 1920s. The General Assembly instituted statewide prohibition in 1914, and it was during this campaign that state elites began to support government efforts at moral reform (Holloway 8, 9, 14). The expansion of the government into the realm of sexuality was done in the name of economic progress. Touting "business progressivism," Virginia's elites promoted a "clean" state as a prosperous one, hoping to paint the state as "morally clean" in order to lure more business and economic prospects into the state. It became a driving interest of state officials to ensure that Virginia was not full of "degenerates" and that these socially and politically marginal citizens did not drain the state's coffers as welfare recipients. Virginia's elites "embraced a vision of progress that involved controlling disorderly individuals in the interests of efficiency and social order, and they passed sex-related legislation to promote this vision" (Holloway 67).

State officials in Virginia concerned themselves with cultivating an economically efficient state, not one based on social welfare programs, and they enlisted scientific "experts" across the state in their cause. For example, medical professionals throughout the state promoted eugenics-based sterilization as being in the best economic interest of the state. Once sterilized, these individuals could be "safely" released from state institutions (Holloway 33). These institutions, then, were not "for" the mentally ill. They instead functioned to "protect" Virginia society as a whole—and the state's treasury—by containing certain individuals until their "threat" was eliminated (that is, until they were rendered sterile and state authorities could be ensured that these individuals could not produce a "degenerate" child that could become a future economic burden on the state).

At the crux of this study is the fact that, throughout the twentieth century, state officials in Virginia expanded the state's sexually coercive regulations in order to cultivate an image of the state (as exemplified by both its public officials and its citizens) as moderate and progressive, especially in economic terms. Understanding state officials' regulation of citizens' sexual behavior, especially of its poor residents and/or citizens of color, cannot be detached from its program to lure lucrative economic and industrial development into the state (Holloway 213). To this end, censors began to regulate a medium of popular culture—films, in this case—in order to protect their own elite status as cultural arbiters, and they attempted to confine certain images of "the other"—in terms of races, classes, and "deviant" sexualities "other" than their own white, middle-class heterosexuality—to shore up their entrenched power and authority. In essence, these censors engaged in a cultural war in which they and the societal contingent they represented actively worked to prevent authority that was established politically and economically—placing themselves and their constituents at the top of the hierarchy—from being undermined or contradicted by images viewed in popular culture by mass, diverse audiences. Thus, the battle the censors fought was one to maintain their own cultural authority as white, politically empowered elites.

The issue of sexual knowledge—who controls it and who has access to it—operates at the core of these debates over sexuality among both censors and citizens. In order to entrench themselves as the chief controllers of sexual knowledge, censors employed the rubric of "protection" to regulate popular culture and to protect their own elite status as cultural arbiters and protectors. These emergent and contested sexual discourses that came to surround the censors' "protective" actions involved inextricably linked subtexts of gender, race, and class. While censors spoke about forbidding certain images of white women and African Americans to "protect" them, they actually censored these images as a mechanism to control how these individuals were depicted on film as an extension of the control state officials already issued over their African-American, working-class, and female citizens (D'Emilio and Freedman 106; Pernick 109).

## The Censorship of Sexuality at the Movies Through Sex-Hygiene Films

Sexual topics on film presented a particular set of problems for Virginia's movie censors. The medium of film itself furthered the propulsion of sexuality into the public eye, pushing the effort for governmental regulation. Film and its connection with potentially provocative displays of female sexuality—initially portrayals of prostitutes, glimpses of bare legs and thighs, sexually evocative dialogue, and later full nudity—combined to invite a particularly potent attack by movies' detractors (Ullman 109; Staiger 180). The censorship board's debates revolved around who controlled, and who would have access to, sexual knowledge. While not officially involved in sexual education, the censors judged whether the medium of film constituted an "appropriate" venue for educating (and controlling) the public with regard to issues of sexuality and whether individual movie efforts were aimed at sexual education or exploiting the gaps in censorship laws to allow for showing sexual situations on film in order to turn a quick profit. Individual censors had to decide whether each individual film educated the public or cultivated prurient interests in its viewers. Since most of these films fell into the loosely defined genre of "sex-hygiene films," it would be through these films that censors pointed their regulation of displays of on-screen sexuality.

The term "sex hygiene" refers to the promotion of practicing hygienic, "healthy" sexual relations for both individual good and the good of the community. Sex-hygiene campaigns began as part of much broader Progressive-era reform efforts to scientifically "clean up" society as a whole under the rubric of social hygiene. As reformers sought to control venereal disease as a health problem, sex-hygiene films, which addressed a range of health issues such as pregnancy and venereal disease, were born. Sex-hygiene films as a genre began in the 1910s as a direct result of—and often in association with—campaigns against venereal disease (Pernick 120). The history of sex-hygiene films involves productions created by both "legitimate" medical and public-health institutions as well as those produced by "exploitation" filmmakers who masked their products as educative sex-hygiene works in order to secure the censors' approval of their films. While medical and public-health officials billed their fare as strictly educational, "exploitation" filmmakers were much more intent on earning a profit from audiences seeking a bit of nudity and on-screen discussions of sex.

Sex-hygiene offerings that filmmakers brought before Virginia's censors for approval function as a lens through which to study censors' and citizens' responses to depictions and discussions of sexuality in popular culture. The board's heavy-handed regulation of such films also illustrates how the board used the rubric of protectionist ideology to undermine subjective on-screen representations of sexuality for certain groups of people, including people of color, working-class individuals, and, especially, women.

Nearly all of the sex-hygiene films seeking entrance into Virginia concerned the question of who was to be blamed for sexual deviance. A brief look at the titles of these films—*Wasted Lives* (1925), *Wages of Sin* (1929), *Girls of the Underworld* (1940), *Because of Eve* (1948)—suggests that women overwhelmingly bore the blame for venereal disease, promiscuity, and pregnancy outside of marriage, while other titles such as *Is Your Daughter Safe?* (1927) and *Unguarded Girls* (1929) connoted women's vulnerability and their need for male patriarchal authority and protection. For example, the mainstream

Chadwick Pictures produced the film *Is Your Daughter Safe?*, a "white slave traffic" film. As such, it portrayed urban men in the prostitution trade luring innocent girls into work at "houses of ill repute." Since these films often linked sex education to questions of morality, blame—specifically, who was to blame for sexual deviance—was always a consideration, and it fell heavily upon women.

Overwhelmingly, these films presented women as one of two extremes: either good or bad, the classic virgin or whore binary. Filmmakers and Virginia's censors alike sought to codify and promote the idea of strictly dichotomous behavior in women. Thus, both cultural entertainment and state actors mutually reinforced the construct that women were either sexually pure or sexually corrupt and "deviant." It did not seem to matter particularly to the censors whether women were corrupted by their own actions or from the lack of protection by a male or socially imposed authority. These films, however, sometimes offered "redemption" for corrupt or deviant women who showed regret for their actions and righted their wrongs over the course of the film. The Motion Picture Production Code, a form of industrial self-censorship that began to be rigidly enforced in 1934, would assure "redemption" by requiring any immoral behavior to be properly punished on screen in a Hollywood production.

## The Ideology of Protection

As white, middle- to upper-class, politically connected elites working in a state-funded government agency, Virginia's censors sought to enshrine their own power by using the rubric of "protection" to regulate on-screen sexuality. In terms of protecting women, their actions followed two strains of logic. They argued that by censoring women's sexual actions on the screen, they were protecting both women's physical and moral well-being. First, they suggested that films portraying women as sexually promiscuous and desirous of sex presented women in a negative light and contained the potential to subject women to physical violence. Presumably, male audience members would interpret women being portrayed as sexually available on the screen to mean that all women were sexually available and, thus, these men would become sexual predators. Second, censors argued that they protected women's morality by not allowing images that would "sully" women's collective reputation to be viewed on the screen, including scenes of live births. Such tactics worked to further the censors' efforts to present only "moral" material at the movies and to craft an image of a state in which promiscuous white women, and certainly prostitutes, did not exist—not even on the movie screen.

Virginia's censors reviewed dozens of sex-hygiene films and completely rejected several of them from exhibition within the state. The subject matter of the films included abortion, childbirth, female endangerment (both physical and the endangerment of one's reputation and perceived morals), reproduction, sexual relations, and venereal disease. Many of these films dealt with some or all of these issues, along with other prominent issues of the day such as eugenics, sterilization, and medical malpractice.

As stated earlier, control of sexual knowledge functioned as the central controversy surrounding sex-hygiene films in two ways. First, while filmmakers of sex hygiene films—both "legitimate" and "exploitation" producers— promoted their films as educational, historian Allan Brandt reminds us that "the necessity for sexual control underpinned all educational efforts" (31). Sexual-education programs sought to "properly" educate the public by emphasizing restraint and promoting what educators deemed to be the "correct" ordering of sexual relations between men and women. In short, sexual-education programs "destroyed the conspiracy of silence—a seemingly radical act—to uphold the conservative sexual mores of their time" (Brandt 31). Second, the censors' regulation of these films represented their attempts to control Virginians' access to certain kinds of sexual knowledge. The question of what sorts of sexual knowledge the films attempted to "educate" the public about and how the films treated such "education" concerned the censors from the board's inception.

## Race and Class Frameworks

Furthermore, sex-hygiene films operated within raced and classed frameworks that consistently located sexual deviance and defined sexual deviants outside of the white middle class. Film theorist Annette Kuhn has shown that the content of many early venereal-disease films portrayed sexually active, working-class white women as the source of venereal disease (Kuhn 63). These working-class women, either as prostitutes or simply as "sexually accessible" women, inflicted their "working-class" diseases upon middle- to upper-class white men. Filmmakers not only located disease in the bodies of working-class women, but they also portrayed working-class, sexually active women as dangerous disease-carriers who threatened the middle-class family while suggesting that middle-class men who had sex with these women were simply victims of working-class women's deviant sexuality.

Such depictions, however, did not concern Virginia's censors, for their work implicitly promoted the idea of the morally pure and "clean" white, middle-class populace. Censors were concerned that some sex-hygiene films purporting to be educational might actually only be using the vehicle of the educative sex-hygiene film as a method to depict nudity and explicit sexual discussions, and they found their security in preventing scenes and dialogue they considered to be sexually explicit. In 1927, the board reviewed the film *Is Your Daughter*

*Safe?* In response to this film and others like it, the state health commissioner, himself an opponent of increased sexual education, wrote to inform the board that such pictures often alleged to be educational but were instead shrewd money-making schemes "capitalizing [on] salaciousness" (VBMP n.pag.). The board ultimately refused to allow *Is Your Daughter Safe?* to play in the state, concluding that "while purporting to be a health film, and to point a strong moral, [the film] embodies so many features that are obscene and indecent that it is offensive, and in our opinion could do no possible good and might do harm" (VBMP n. pag.). Thus, the film's potential for offensiveness overrode any educational value it might contain.

Sex-hygiene films in general addressed a range of topics relating to sexuality and reproduction (Schaefer 5). During the early to mid-1920s, the production and distribution of sex-hygiene films, especially those produced by "legitimate" ventures, declined due to public concerns over the appropriateness of the topic and the rise of censorship boards. The films came back into vogue in the late 1920s, especially "exploitation" ones, with a string of films—*Is Your Daughter Safe?, Unguarded Girls, The Road to Ruin*—issuing warnings about the "new" dangers urban life posed to young women's morality. For the most part, these films positioned an idea of rural purity against urban corruption, promoted the idea that unchecked desire (especially for women) could be deadly, and usually placed "fallen" women (single women engaging in sexual relations outside of marriage) into disease-ridden houses of prostitution while offering no similar repercussions for single men engaging in sex (Schaefer 173, 177). In addition, while such films portrayed "fallen" women as decidedly working-class, single men who patronized houses of prostitution were nearly always middle-class men "slumming" in behavior and in neighborhoods "beneath" what their privileged racial and class status entitled them. According to these films, had working-class women acting as temptresses not lured middle-class men to them, then such diseases would be an affair solely of the working class.

## Keeping the Middle Class "Pure"

Censors often weighed the class element of certain films in relation to whom they, as censors, would be policing. For example, one of the censors' reasons for censoring the 1929 sex-hygiene film *Unwelcome Children* was that "it might incite some classes to crime" (VBMP n. pag.). The board ultimately condemned the film because it "treated of things forbidden in the medical practice and represented the youth of today in such a way that the showing…might do incalculable harm" (VBMP n. pag.). The board described the film as "a photoplay with a clearly defined, well-acted plot," but they were concerned that it addressed "such delicate questions as eugenics, birth control and abortion, contraceptives and the like. It is the unanimous opinion of the members of this division that these questions, whatever their merit, are not fit material for exploitation on the motion picture screen" (VBMP n. pag.). The board was also concerned with "a most repulsive scene, the rape of a young woman social worker by an imbecile whom she has befriended" (VBMP n. pag.). The scene was made worse, according to the censors, because "on this hideous crime the plot hinges; to eliminate it would destroy the continuity of the story and make it senseless" (VBMP n. pag.). Yet they refused to leave the rape scene in the film, which in itself is significant. According to scholar Sabine Sielke, representations of rape found in literature and popular culture often function as rhetorical devices to address other social, political, or economic concerns. Sielke argues that "narratives of sexual violence ponder…the power dynamics of a particular culture" (2). The censors likely found the rape aesthetically repulsive; however, I would argue that their reason for censoring it, and the entire film, was politically motivated. They did not want to acknowledge the existence of sexual violence in their culture and in their state, and they worked to keep it out of the public mind as much as possible, thus contributing to the continued culture of silence surrounding the sexual assault of women and the lack of state services available to victims of such crimes. Furthermore, this rape scene would have been especially troublesome to the censors if the assaulted woman had become pregnant with a child fathered by an individual the censors defined to be an "imbecile." Such a circumstance would have proven to be a potent situation indeed in a state that refused abortion services to women yet simultaneously sought to systematically use sterilization to prevent mentally ill or poor children from ever being born.

## Selling "Exploitation" Sex-Hygiene Films

Board members believed they had good reasons to look at sex-hygiene films suspiciously. By 1919, independent producers and distributors working outside of Hollywood produced cheap films addressing "forbidden" subjects and using "salacious" modes of depiction—sex, venereal disease, vice, prostitution, drug use, and nudity—and independently distributed them nationwide. Film scholar Eric Schaefer calls these films, which began being produced in the 1920s and continued through 1959, "classic exploitation films." This term refers to early "exploitation" films, ones that used over-the-top promotional techniques to gain an audience because they contained no identifiable celebrities and no recognizable, traditional genres (Schaefer 4). Such film distributors relied upon creating a carnivalesque atmosphere to promote such offerings, as the topics of these movies were often "forbidden" by Hollywood's self-censorship controls. "Classic" exploitation films were characterized as a whole by their "forbidden" topics, low budgets, independent distribution methods, and their exhibition in theaters not owned by Hollywood studios (Schaefer 5, 6).

Nearly all sex-hygiene films, both "legitimate" and "exploitation" ones, utilized scenes in hospitals and clinics to show characters on the screen (and, by proxy, theater audiences) the effects of venereal disease or the course of pregnancy. Reliance on such scenes attempted to embody the medical authority associated with these institutions to help endorse the films as educational while complicating the question of whether they also functioned as entertainment. To further the idea that these films functioned strictly as educational endeavors, they typically contained one or more "square-ups." In a "square-up," a film displayed a rolling title that talked about morality and the importance of viewers watching such "educational" films as a way to further both individual and public morals. In reality, these square-ups also validated the audiences' viewing of potentially "illicit" material by emphasizing the social and moral value of doing so. Film distributors billed these motion pictures as an appropriate means to extend sexual education into public, commercial venues in an effort to reach individuals outside of the sexual-education programs being established in school systems.

Distributors of "exploitation" sex-hygiene films, however, developed techniques specific to their films in order to counter efforts to censor their products. "Hot" and "cold" versions of these films—including "hot" and "cold" advertising campaigns—existed, and producers marketed them according to the existence or absence of a censorship board or a conservative audience base (Schaefer 73). "Hot" and "cold" versions were alternate varieties of the same film that differed in the amount of censorable material they contained, especially nudity. Distributors used "hot" versions in states and locales without heavy censorship laws; they often included graphic scenes of childbirth and the effects of venereal disease on the body through the use of partial or complete nudity. Marketers exhibited "cold" prints, or self-censored versions of the film, in markets known for their strict censorship boards. Then, at individual "cold" showings, the roadshowman could illegally exhibit a "hot" reel of film at the movie's end if he so desired (Schaefer 73, 74, 79).

A continual problem confronted by the censors involved their duty to control not only a film's sexual content but also the sexual content of its advertisements. Presuming that many more people would be exposed to film advertisements than would actually see the film, censors wanted to be certain that advertisements did not emphasize the explicit sexual content of the films to lure in more audience members. With regard to the film *Unguarded Girls,* for example, the censors insisted that the film's distributors "must not advertise *in any way* the scene which shows Mary Foster lying on a couch in a state of semi-nudity" (VBMP n. pag.). When the censors approved the movie, they made sure its distribution company knew that their "action in this matter does not mean that the picture met our unqualified approval" but rather that they could not pinpoint a specific law that the picture violated and were, therefore, forced to approve it (VBMP n. pag.). The censors offered detailed instructions about what must not be shown in the film's advertisements, which can be summarized by their mandate that advertisements "must abstain from any suggestion that it will satisfy those looking for salacious entertainment" (VBMP n. pag.). The board spent two full days deliberating the fate of *Unguarded Girls* before they ultimately accepted it. However, when they found a different version of the film being shown than the one they approved (perhaps an unscreened "hot" version whereas the board had approved a "cold" one), they ordered a round of additional cuts. They required the film's makers to cut a "close-up scene as girl crosses her legs making an indecent exposure of her person," "both scenes in the house of ill fame in which couple are shown in passionate embrace," and "the entire series of scenes in house of ill fame in which couple are shown on couch" (VBMP n. pag.). When advertisements began appearing for the film, several individuals wrote to the board and included clipped advertisements they found to be offensive with their letters. In response to a scathing letter written by Reverend W. B. Jett of Petersburg, which condemned the board's approval of the film, the board attempted to "convince [the reverend] that we are trying hard to keep the motion pictures within decent bounds" (VBMP n. pag.).

In order to "sell" the respectability of their films to censors, distributors of sex-hygiene films created separate showings for men and women, recommending that fathers attend with their sons and mothers with their daughters as an educational outing. Sex segregation was key to "protecting" the audience (as well as film distributors, whose films often would not have been allowed screenings in co-ed settings) because same-sex viewings cast the screenings in an air of "respectability." Segregating audiences by sex was a common approach of sex educators by the 1930s. State officials, including censors, believed that sex segregation of audiences made the showing of such films "respectable" because the fear of intermingling individuals of different sexes in the audience was removed, a concern that individuals had voiced about the movies from their inception. Also, sex segregation supposedly allowed distributors to show reels of childbirth scenes and the effects of venereal disease on women's bodies only to female audiences, while showing reels chronicling the effects of venereal disease on men's bodies only to male audiences. In other words, distributors used segregated audiences as a means to convince censors that viewers of one sex would not have the opportunity to view partially nude bodies of the opposite sex even though, once inside a theater, movie exhibitioners could theoretically show whatever reels they chose. Producers of these films also used "adults only" widely in their advertising, both as an attempt to appease censors (by arguing that no children would see the film) and as a signal to alert potential audience members that these films contained titillating material. Such strategies could be skillfully blended together by movie distributors to generate customer interest by suggesting that these films contained material that was too illicit for men and women to view in the same room and entirely unsuitable for children (Kuhn 68). Thus, distributors used conventional defenses of their films to actually attract a larger audience.

## Conclusion

World War II marked a watershed in the history of sex-hygiene filmmaking. "Exploitation" sex-hygiene films waned as mainstream Hollywood productions began to include sexual topics and material the industry had previously forbidden. At the same time, sex-education campaigns had firmly entered many of the nation's schools, making "legitimate" sex-hygiene films increasingly seem unnecessary. These changes—the saturation of sexual issues and nudity in Hollywood films, solid sexual-education efforts in public schools, and a Supreme Court committed to extending the First Amendment's free speech protections to the movies—increasingly hampered censors' efforts at heavy censorship in the postwar era. And with sex-education campaigns in the hands of public-health officials and professional educators, the censors' role in controlling the dissemination of sexual knowledge waned. Hollywood's producers and the industry's censors also lost some of their ability to attack exploitation films because of the increasingly open production of films showcasing "deviant" behavior by "mainstream" Hollywood studios. Such films submitted to the Production Code Administration would still be denied a seal, but the stakes simply seemed smaller in the more permissive atmosphere of postwar American culture (Schaefer 163).

In the end, most proponents of sex-hygiene films believed that corrupt minds would seek out the obscene in such films—characterized by those powerful enough to do the defining as sexually suggestive or bawdy language, actions of heterosexual contact that might simulate or suggest sex (such as dancing), and women defined as "scantily clad"—but that the obscenity of some should not prohibit the film from being distributed. In other words, if the film functioned as educative to some, then it should be shown. The Circuit Court of Richmond struck down the censors' banning of films by stating:

> If [the viewer's] mind tends toward obscenity or indecency, he may see [the obscene], but if his mind is not so bent he will see something that is educational and wonderful. (Sova 165)

The court thus declared that the potential for voyeurism should not be used to condemn a film in light of the positive effects it might have on conscientious viewers.

Taken as a whole, Virginian censors' regulation of sex-hygiene films spoke directly to the idea of "protection." As legally empowered actors of the state, Virginia's censors sought to "protect" certain standards of morality. Their decisions served as barriers against "pollution"—in this case, pollution from the "taint" of women's sexual expression and, in race films, against the pollution of interracial mixing or African-American advancement in a society hierarchically positioning white elites at the top. Simultaneously, censors reasoned that they suppressed certain films or scenes from films in order to protect the vulnerable in society, namely African Americans, women, and youths. In other words, they "protected" everyone but the most powerful—white elites—through the regulatory practice of film censorship. However, in 1965, the U.S. Supreme Court ruled that a priori film censorship was illegal; as a result, censorship boards such as Virginia's could no longer require distributors to submit their films for censorial approval before they were allowed exhibition in the state. With such submission, and the accompanying fees, now voluntary, arguments of citizen "protection" and control of sexual knowledge were no longer enough to keep Virginia's film censorship board afloat. State agents censored their last films in 1965. Censorship then shifted to local and municipal authorities.

## Works Cited

Brandt, Allan. *No Magic Bullet: A Social History of Venereal Disease in the United States Since 1880.* New York: Oxford University Press, 1987.

D'Emilio, John, and Estelle Freedman. *Intimate Matters: A History of Sexuality in America.* Chicago: University of Chicago Press, 1998.

Holloway, Philippa. "Tending to Deviance: Sexuality and Public Policy in Urban Virginia, Richmond and Norfolk, 1920-1950." Ph.D. Diss. Ohio State University, 1999.

Kuhn, Annette. Cinema, Censorship, and Sexuality: 1909-1925. New York: Routledge, 1990.

Pernick, Martin. *The Black Stork: Eugenics and the Death of "Defective" Babies in American Medicine and Motion Pictures since 1915.* New York: Oxford University Press, 1996.

Schaefer, Eric. *Bold, Daring, Shocking, True: A History of Exploitation Films, 1919-1959.* Durham: Duke University Press, 1999.

Sielke, Sabine. *Reading Rape: The Rhetoric of Sexual Violence in American Literature and Culture, 1790-1990.* Princeton, NJ: Princeton University Press, 2002.

Sova, Dawn. *Forbidden Films: Censorship Histories of 125 Motion Pictures.* New York: Facts on File, 2001.

Staiger, Janet. *Bad Women: Regulating Sexuality in Early American Cinema.* Minneapolis: University of Minnesota Press, 1995.

Ullman, Sharon. *Sex Seen: The Emergence of Modern Sexuality in America.* Berkeley: University of California Press, 1997.

Virginia Board of Motion Picture Censorship (VBMP) Archives. Library of Virginia. State Records Division. Richmond, Virginia.

# CHAPTER TEN

# RECONNECTING THE BODY "IN" TO THE BODY "OF" PASOLINI WITH *PORCILE*

# MATTIAS FREY

Pier Paolo Pasolini's *Porcile* (1969) remains his most maligned and least successful film (Greene 139). It interweaves two seemingly disparate tales through alternating montage, a la Godard's contemporaneous *One Plus One* (1968). One story takes place presumably in medieval times on the barren slopes of Mt. Etna. A young, unnamed man (played by Pierre Clementi) ekes out a primitive existence, eating a butterfly and a snake he finds in the otherwise empty landscape. He happens upon a man, whom he kills and then eats. After a time, others join him to prey on passersby. The town authorities eventually catch up with the band and sentence the men to death. The entire story has taken place without dialogue, but before dying the protagonist shouts: "I've killed my father. I've eaten human flesh. I tremble with joy."

The second story is set in 1967. Its main figure is Julian (played by Jean-Pierre Leaud), who lives in an opulent West German villa with his mother and his father, the industrialist Herr Klotz (played by Alberto Lionello). The narrative tension derives from a secret Julian won't divulge, one that prevents him from attending a student demonstration in Berlin with his fiancée, Ida (played by Anne Wiazemsky), as well as joining his father's business, and one that also causes him to lapse into a catatonic state: Julian likes to have sex with pigs. Klotz's rival and ex-Nazi criminal Herr Herdhitze (played by Ugo Tognazzi) ascertains this information and proceeds to blackmail Klotz. Klotz, in turn, threatens to uncover Herdhitze's past. In the end, the two decide to form a strategic alliance. Just before the party for their new joint venture, peasants arrive with the news that Julian has been eaten by the pigs. When it is revealed that the pigs have devoured every last trace of the boy, Herdhitze ensures that the episode is hushed up.

*Porcile* has long been bemoaned as an obvious work, a tedious, ideological lesson on Marxism from the time preceding May 1968. A great number of auteurist studies of Pasolini consider it to be his "least interesting work" because of the film's "allegory" and "verbality" (Snyder 121). Moreover, the film has never been convincingly situated in Pasolini's body of work. Instead, it has traditionally been marked as an exception, a fluke, or as a part of his corpus to be forgotten or dismembered. The film demands a re-reading that moves away from Marxist dialectics and politics and toward a consideration of sexuality as marker of difference, and architecture and landscape as the sites of these inscriptions. Such an approach does not attempt to de-politicize Pasolini, but rather to lead the discourse away from an obsession with which particular shade of Marxism his films might activate. As a result, this chapter seeks to investigate how the bodies in *Porcile* (e.g., physicality, sexuality, and their relation to and inscription upon their surroundings) relate to the body of the film (e.g., textuality, intertextuality, and self-referentiality).

*Porcile* bursts with physicality. The camera lingers on close-ups of body parts. The medieval scenes are structured by violence. In fact, in the absence of dialogue, the Pierre Clementi character's nonverbal encounters necessarily foreground the body as narrative site. The film puts forth a plethora of body shapes and body parts: crippled Nazis, faces transformed and hidden by plastic surgery, an errant soldier's decapitated head, Herr Hirt's collection of Bolshevik Jews' skulls, the central motif of cannibalism, and Ida's insistence on pissing on the Berlin wall, to name just a few.

This is certainly not out of keeping with Pasolini's body of work. Indeed, the camera's fascination with Terence Stamp's crotch in *Teorema* (1968) and a constellation of crotches in *Il Decameron* (1970), or the composition of the writhing Ettore in *Mamma Roma* (1962) taken directly from Mantegna's portrait of Christ, spring quickly to mind; the complete list of examples is too extensive to include here. Indeed, Pasolini himself saw his project as the investigation of "bodies...and of their culminating symbol, their sex" (Pasolini, "Trilogy," 49; cf. Bruno 37 for the physicality of Pasolini's theoretical work).

But "bodies" do not signify in a vacuum in Pasolini's films. Vital to note is the body's interaction with its environment: architecture and landscape. This very topic was an important subject of discussion in postwar Italian cinema. Luchino Visconti, for example, talks in his essay on "Anthropomorphic Cinema" of the way that the landscape should be the star of the film, intimating a dynamic relationship of the human subject and its surroundings. Michelangelo Antonioni, for his part, conceptualized and shot a film in which the river Po is the main character. This is an important exercise, so Antonioni, because of the "special intimacy" and emotional connection between the Italian and his environment. Perhaps Giuseppe De Santis, Visconti's collaborator on *Ossessione* (1942) and the director of *Riso amaro* (1949), formulates the sentiment most programmatically in his essay "Towards an Italian Landscape." De Santis calls for a correspondent cinema of affect in which "the landscape [is] neither rarefied nor picturesque, but which correspond[s] to the humanity of the characters either as an emotive element or as a clue to their feelings" (127).

To be sure, these essays were written during World War II by a generation of filmmakers looking ahead to ensure the legitimacy of a post-fascist Italian cinema. Thus, we need to regard these thoughts as points of departure, rather than ready-made paradigms, in understanding Pasolini. Even in Pasolini's earliest films, he channeled, quoted, and subverted the neo-realistic project rather than committing himself to it. To contemplate the body and its relation to architecture and landscape in the films of Pasolini means to be mindful of De Santis' idea of the environment and subject as affective reflections of one another, but also to realize that Pasolini transgresses this one-to-one model.

Karsten Witte's essays on Pasolini are useful in further clarifying Pasolini's concept of bodies and spaces, *corpi e luoghi*. He describes the power of Pasolini's cinema in what he coins its *Körperort*—literally "body-place." Witte defines Pasolini's *Körperort* as the localization of deformation in the shape of grotesque bodies, an inseparable economy of place and body in which the more Pasolini emphasizes physicality, the weaker the historical topography in which his bodies move, becomes (54). For Pasolini, the body is a setting, *the* setting. In contrast, his actual settings are border zones, wastelands, and city steppes. Thus, according to Witte, bodies and places signal in Pasolini's films a crossing of boundaries, whether into topographic liminal states or into utopian zones, in which the bodies are not attached to any place.

With these theoretical approaches in mind, let us now turn to the body of the film's text itself and a general assessment of *Porcile*'s approach to bodies in space. Many commentators have ascribed to Pasolini a brand of vulgar pastorality. According to these critics, Pasolini (for example, in his Trilogy of Life) posits the pre-industrial peasant society as a pure and utopian situation that was ruined by centralizing structures and language (cf. Indiana 18). *Porcile*, however, seems to refute this model, even on first glance. The film's alternating montage presents two configurations of setting: the pre-industrial landscape and the overdetermined architecture of post-Auschwitz West Germany. Crucially, Pasolini hardly draws a binary opposition between the two thematically.

The German sequences are, above all, remarkable for the way in which the body is trapped in circumscribed spaces. Pasolini foreshadows Fassbinder's emotional architecture in *Ali: Fear Eats the Soul* (1974). Like Ali in Fassbinder's film, Julian is a troubled young man caught between two fronts, in this case his radical girlfriend and his reactionary father. In the mise-en-scene, Julian is framed by doorways and windows; his body is correspondingly masked and weighed down by fur coats and baroque hats. Moreover, the entire German sequence is marked by a stifling Renaissance perspective and an eerie organization of space into tableaux. The acting and dialogue only exaggerate this. The actors forsake psychological realism and lifelessly intone their lines. The dialogue itself is lines of poetry, quotations, misinterpretations of the other characters, or complete non sequiturs.

But the main locus of this phenomenon in *Porcile* is concentrated in its central structure, the Klotz villa. This edifice echoes the family's house in *Teorema*, both in its architecture and in the static, imposing way that it occupies the screen via Pasolini's camera. The villa in *Porcile* functions as the tangible representation of "civilized" institutional power. We might see this as the reification of an idea from Pasolini's theoretical work. Pasolini formulated a symbolic connection between architecture and institutional power in his *Corriere della Sera* cover article "Ma a che serve capire I figli?" In this essay, he uses the architectural metaphor of *il Palazzo* to stand in for Foucauldian notions of dominant discursive practices (cf. Bruno 38). He who stands "fuori dal Palazzo" remains marginalized in and/or from society. Indeed, this is born out across Pasolini's body of work; it is the crucial corporeal link between *Teorema*'s sexual *ronde* and *Salò*'s (1975) sadistic stage. In these films, the idea of institutional hegemony and sexual perversion is reified into, and takes place in, an architectural structure: *il Palazzo* (cf. Viano 219-220). *Porcile*'s architecture and its inscriptive and circumscriptive force extend graphically Mary Ann Doane's remark that the "body is always a function of discourse" (26) to the male body.

If the German scenes present a mannerist architecture of bodily repression, then the film's Pierre Clementi metahistorical scenes depict, at first inspection, the exact opposite: landscape pure. Landscape is a language, as Anne Whiston Spirn programmatically formulates, and these scenes are geographically and linguistically empty—until the very last frame of the story. Here Pasolini twists De Santis. The landscape does not necessarily represent an affective reflection of its characters, but it does match linguistically and semiologically. The setting is the bare hills around Mt. Etna. Pierre Clementi's body roams the very same slopes through which the father wanders at the very end of Pasolini's previous film, *Teorema*. The two bodies connect across Pasolini's corpus. David Forgacs has written about how, in Italian cinema of the fascist era, the trope of exterior space functioned as the setting through which the masculine hero can move and dominate and in which he feels liberated (164). In that cinematic tradition, the man's journey is interrupted, deflected, and arrested by an encounter with a fatal woman and fits closely with the pattern of masculine narratives of ego formation. This is indeed an old narrative template, and we find this model in Pasolini's earlier *Oedipus Rex* (1967). But Pasolini turns this tradition on its head in *Porcile*'s landscape portrait. There, the sexual encounter is homosexual and cannibalistic: the Pierre Clementi character kills and eats the male he encounters in the barren landscape. When a woman does arrive, he can only idly look on and watch as another man brutalizes her. Moreover, the Clementi character's aimless wandering contrasts with the purposeful strut of the female streetwalker in *Mamma Roma*, captured in extended tracking shots. The relationship of man to landscape in *Porcile* is not one of mastery and liberation, as in Forgacs' description of wartime Italian films. Indeed, the Pierre Clementi character is not only implicated in dismemberment in his decapitation and devouring of the soldier, but is also subject himself to the terms of disembodiment on the level of the film's mise-en-scène: he does not command the center of the frame and is often cut off, skewed, or shot from long or illusory distances. Pierre Clementi's character—like Julian vis-à-vis *il Palazzo* in the German sequences—is a body trapped by the landscape and, furthermore, inscribed by Pasolini's body of work and legible filmographic intertextuality.

The basic physicality of *Porcile* is perhaps above all made pregnant by the guiding metaphor of cannibalism. Cannibalism surely stands in for a circuit of devouring and being devoured. The scene in which the Pierre Clementi character kills and eats the soldier, transmitted to the spectator by a decidedly homoerotic camera gaze, corresponds to the final scene of the story, when the Clementi character is burned at the stake, dogs waiting to consume his remains. Julian, for his part, is also physically eaten by the pigs, after having committed bestiality with them. In *Porcile*, Pasolini equates perverse sexuality with "devouring."

In most accounts of the film, commentators take Pasolini's political statements on the film quite literally—that the film is to be understood as a critique of capitalism's "consuming" tendencies (cf. Indiana 79). But there is a way in which the bodies in the text can be connected to the body of text itself. Giuliana Bruno has noted how in Pasolini's theoretical writings on the cinema he dismembers the classic Vertovian metaphor of cinema as the "kino-eye" and, following from an Italian name for the movie camera (*macchina da presa*, literally, a machine to capture or to devour) re-embodies it as the "*occhio-bocca*"—the "eye-mouth," the "voracious devourer" (Pasolini, "Res sunt nomina," 255). In 1967, the year he made *Porcile*, Pasolini suggested that the cinematic apparatus has an oral function as a machine of reproduction and perception (Bruno 34). Thus, we might interpret the cannibalism and the general obsessive attention to eating and digestive elimination in the film as meta-cinematic commentary (Snyder 124).

Indeed, there is an enormous amount of cinematographic self-reflexivity evident in *Porcile*, moments at which the body of the text consciously calls attention to itself and its position in film history, and moments at which Pasolini refers to his own body and body of work. Let us look to *Porcile* for these moments of meta-cinematic cannibalism, instances when the *macchina da presa* turns on itself. Several of these references have already been mentioned:

*Oedipus Rex, Teorema*, as well as Pasolini's conscious re-visioning of *Roma citta' aperta* (1945) and the neo-realistic project, achieved in no small part by his usage of Anna Magnani in that film (see Indiana 34 and Viano 87-93). In *Porcile*, Pasolini again plays with star semiotics and film historical contiguity by featuring Anne Wiazemski and Jean-Pierre Leaud. These actors, who had just appeared in Jean-Luc Godard's *La Chinoise* (1967), were also committed to the French student revolutionaries' cause and their casting here no doubt deliberates on what Pasolini deemed to be the bourgeois faux-revolutionaries of the student movement.

Above all, however, the figure of Ninetto Davoli is of utmost importance. Davoli was a young Italian boy whom Pasolini found during his cruising of Roman slums, and with whom Pasolini fell in love. From *Il Vangelo secondo Matteo* (1964) on, Davoli appeared in nearly every film Pasolini made, occasionally in a starring role, such as in *Uccellacci e uccellini* (1966), but more often, as in *Oedipus Rex, Teorema*, and *Porcile*, as a chorus figure or messenger. In *Porcile*, Davoli appears in both stories, the only figure to do so. In the West German story, he plays an Italian peasant who watches Julian go off to the pigpen and then brings the news that Julian has been eaten by the pigs. In the Pierre Clementi story, Davoli's appearance is even more curious. He appears suddenly as the Clementi character is about to be executed, watching on as witness—but in anachronistic late-1960s clothes: a leather jacket and bell bottoms.

Nino Davoli's presence in *Porcile* ties together a number of concerns. First, it sutures the two stories together and problematizes the historicity of the cannibal story. Davoli functions as a meta-cinematic surrogate spectator. This is redoubled by the last image of Pierre Clementi as an over-the-shoulder shot from the point of view of Davoli, thereby raising him to the role of privileged observer. Second, Davoli contextualizes *Porcile* within Pasolini's corpus by way of filmographic continuity. Upon seeing Davoli, the spectator knows he or she is watching a Pasolini film. Third, Davoli's presence inscribes Pasolini's body, his homosexual desire, onto the film and makes the film legible as part of an autobiographical discourse. And fourth, all of these meta-cinematic devices call attention to the constructed nature of the film as a body of text. In *Porcile,* bodies in the text, the body of the text, and Pasolini's body of work all point to themselves and to each other as the *macchina da presa* devours itself.

# Works Cited

Antonioni, Michelangelo. "Concerning a Film on the River Po." *Springtime in Italy*. Ed. and trans. David Overbey. Hamden, CT: Archon, 1978. 79-82.

Bruno, Giuliana. "Heresies: The Body of Pasolini's Semiotics." *Cinema Journal* 30.3 (1991): 29-42.
De Santis, Giuseppe. "Towards an Italian Landscape." *Springtime in Italy*. Ed. and trans. David Overbey. Hamden, CT: Archon, 1978. 125-129.
Doane, Mary Ann. "Woman's Stake: Filming the Female Body." *October* 17 (1981): 22-36.
Forgacs, David. "Sex in the Cinema: Regulation and Transgression in Italian Films, 1930-1943." *Re-viewing Fascism*. Eds. Jacqueline Reich and Piero Garofalo. Bloomington: Indiana University Press, 2002.
Greene, Naomi. *Pier Paolo Pasolini. Cinema as Heresy*. Princeton, NJ: Princeton University Press, 1990.
Indiana, Gary. *Salo, or The 120 Days of Sodom*. London: BFI, 2000.
Pasolini, Pier Paolo. "Ma a che serve capire I figli?" *Corriere della Sera* 1 Aug. 1975: 1-2.
—. "Res sunt nomina." *Heretical Empiricism*. Ed. Louise K. Barnett. Trans. Ben Lawton and Louise K. Barnett. Bloomington: Indiana University Press, 1988. 255-260.
—. "Trilogy of Life Rejected." *Lutheran Letters*. Trans. Stuart Hood. Manchester: Carcanet New Press, 1987. 49-52.
Snyder, Stephen. *Pier Paolo Pasolini*. Boston: Twayne, 1980.
Spirn, Anne Whiston. *The Language of Landscape*. New Haven, CT: Yale University Press, 1998.
Viano, Maurizio. *A Certain Realism: Making Use of Pasolini's Film Theory and Practice*. Berkeley: University of California Press, 1993.
Visconti, Luchino. "Anthropomorphic Cinema." *Springtime in Italy*. Ed. and trans. David Overbey. Hamden, CT: Archon, 1978. 83-85.
Witte, Karsten. *Die Körper des Ketzers: Pier Paolo Pasolini*. Berlin: Vorwerk 8, 1998.

CHAPTER ELEVEN

"TELL ME I'M A MAN!": HOMOEROTICISM AND
MASOCHISM IN *JACKASS THE MOVIE*

MARY E. PAGANO

Imagine a group of late twenty-something white males who perform shockingly dangerous, completely moronic, and undoubtedly violent stunts: taking a sledgehammer to the groin; provoked standoffs with agitated alligators and sharks; public displays of defecation, urination, and vomiting. Moreover, not only do these guys seem to enjoy such antics, but they also record and air them on film and television, with great success, for the amusement of others. First of all, we can presume that there is a decent-sized audience segment of the U.S. population that enjoys these displays, thus begging the question, Why? Upon initial examination of such antics, we might simply dismiss these men as jackasses—and we would be right, for that is precisely their point. Yet to leave it at that and to dismiss these texts as too lowbrow, too vulgar for serious contemplation, is to overlook the more compelling aspects that speak to the current conditions of white male masculinity and the male body in late-capitalist America.

Using as its prime example the MTV film *Jackass the Movie* (2002), this chapter demonstrates how the seemingly irrational and irreverent exploits of this group of young men play with cultural conceptions of masculinity, a play that is most often graphically and violently enacted on the white male body. More specifically, it employs a queer-theory-guided analysis in order to focus on the ways that *Jackass the Movie* contends with the problematic figure of the on-screen male, which has historically been (and still remains) a quite troubling figure for theories of cinematic structure and spectatorship.

As Steve Neale has rightfully noted:

Male homosexuality is constantly present as an undercurrent, as a potentially troubling aspect of many films and genres, but one that is dealt with obliquely, symptomatically, and that has to be repressed. (19)

Drawing from Neale, it is my argument that *Jackass the Movie*, when compared to competing mainstream representations of masculinity, makes more explicit this implicit male homosexuality, but it does so only to a certain point—there are definite lines that even the jackasses won't cross, certain taboos that they will not break (at least not in front of the camera). Regardless, therefore, of the strands of this text that can be interpreted as subversively deviant, in the end the jackasses—for all of their shocking and defiant behavior—uphold a model of mainstream masculine representation that draws a distinct line between legitimate homosocial bonding and illegitimate homosexuality, with homoeroticism remaining in the middle, in a constant state of flux.

The notion of the homosocial on which this analysis relies is drawn from Eve Kosofsky Sedgwick's work *Between Men: English Literature and Male Homosocial Desire*. On the most basic level, Sedgwick describes homosociality as "social bonds between persons of the same sex" (1). Significantly, Sedgwick points to the inherent contradiction within the term homosocial: while the root of the word is derived from "homosexual," "homosocial" gets its meaning by distinguishing itself from the more deviant realm of the homosexual. For men, homosocial means "men-promoting-the-interests-of-men" (3). Accordingly, male-bonding rituals—and male-dominant or male-exclusive organizations such as fraternities, sports teams, and the military—all fall under the acceptable rubric of homosociality. Yet, as Justin Wyatt points out in an essay on the movie *Swingers* (1996), such texts in which the presence of straight male friendships cannot be contained within, or explained by, institutional factors (such as those mentioned above) are threatening, in that the potential to breach the boundary between homosocial and homosexual seems especially present (55). This threat is due, in large part, to the relationship between spectator and screen, theorized most canonically by Laura Mulvey and expanded upon, as noted above, by Steve Neale; moreover, such a threat speaks to the perpetual and unavoidable problem of displaying the male. Drawing from this model of spectatorship, media scholar Clay Steinman explains:

> This fear of the feminine would seem to have several effects on relations between the "male" gaze and male images. To look at another man's exhibitionism is to risk admitting pleasure in the sight, to risk imagining glances exchanged, to risk being thought out of line. At the same time, the exhibitionist image threatens to become an object of identification, and as such may trigger fears that it might represent a feminine aspect of the viewer himself. (202)

Continuing along this line of queer theory, Judith Halberstam explores the racial variations that dot the New York City drag-king scene in her ethnographic piece, "Mackdaddy, Superfly, Rapper: Gender, Race, and Masculinity in the

Drag King Scene." Commenting upon the drag king's performance of white masculinity, or lack thereof, Halberstam posits:

> We might explain the nontheatricality of dominant white masculinity by noting that masculinity in white men often depends on a relatively stable notion of the realness and the naturalness of both the male body and its signifying effects. (111)

Furthermore, Halberstam argues that, when performed on stage, white masculinity is often shown through a parodic lens, in which ridiculous imitations of masculinity dull the potentially transgressive nature of such gendered performances. Importantly, however, Halberstam also points to some of the more mainstream cultural instances in which the performativity of masculinity is brought to the forefront, such as the television show *Seinfeld*, or the *Wayne's World* films of the 1990s (112). She argues that, in such media texts, men use comedic tropes to deconstruct and "deligitimize" the supposed naturalness of white masculinity (Halberstam 112). In this vein, Halberstam argues that drag kings must first make visible and theatrical the cultural markers of white masculinity, in order to then problematize and interrogate it.

In many ways, Halberstam's model of the drag kings' performance of white masculinity is quite similar to what the jackasses do in their film. Many skits involve the jackasses donning fat suits or transforming their bodies to appear as elderly men; in *Jackass the Movie*, one of the ways in which the change in scenes is indicated is through a Laurel-and-Hardy-inspired vignette in which Preston Lacy, the fat jackass, chases Wee Man, the aptly named little-person jackass, throughout the streets of Hollywood. Both men wear only undergarments.

Yet just as these representations may help to "delegitimize" mainstream masculinity, it is important to note that the unmodified bodies of the majority of the *Jackass* stars represent current accepted notions of masculinity. Thus, most of these men, most of the time, represent the "extreme sports" version of men: tattooed and pierced, scarred and bruised, and daringly athletic (many of them are proficient skateboarders and/or BMX bicycle riders). Many of their stunts, while admittedly idiotic and inane, involve a good deal of athletic skill and talent to pull off, although their numerous scratches and bruises (constantly displayed in extreme close-ups for the audience) speak to the dangerous nature, as well as to the relatively frequent failure, of such stunts. I would argue, however, that the jackasses' numerous unsuccessful attempts do not call their masculinity into question; on the contrary, they reveal to the audience their incredibly high tolerance for pain—their ability, in a sense, to *take it like a man*.

Accordingly, despite obvious displays of such pain, the jackasses almost always complete their stunts. One of the more visceral examples of this tolerance can be found in a skit from *Jackass the Movie* entitled "Papercuts." Shot entirely on video with a handheld camera (and thus evoking the aesthetics of documentary), the scene opens with a medium shot of Johnny Knoxville, the leader of the jackasses, announcing his intention to have papercuts deliberately inflicted on the webbings of his fingers and toes. After two such cuts are made on his toes, fellow jackass Ryan Dunn advises Knoxville to let him do one on his hands, so that he "will forget about the pain in [his] foot." Knoxville agrees and, shortly thereafter, the focus of the scene shifts to Lance, a cameraman, who is nauseated either by something he ate or what he is currently filming (it is not made entirely clear), vomits, and falls to the ground. The jackasses involved in the skit actually antagonize Lance until he vomits and then laugh hysterically when he hits the floor. Thus, despite the fact that he does admit pain, when compared to Lance, Knoxville comes out on top as the more "manly" man: while Knoxville physically endures the pain, Lance cannot even bear to witness it. Significantly, Lance is marked as effeminate not only because of his inability to handle viewing the infliction of the papercuts, but also because he has a high, squeaky voice that is quite comical.

In *Male Impersonators: Men Performing Masculinity*, queer theorist Mark Simpson addresses masculinity and bodybuilding, arguing that "every time men try to grasp something consolingly, sturdily, essentially masculine, it all too easily transforms into its opposite" (30). Thus, there are a number of scenes in *Jackass* in which a seemingly conventional masculine activity—sharing pain and displaying its rewards—slips into the murky territory of the homoerotic. For instance, a graphic scene from early in the film, "The Muscle Stimulator," involves a group of four jackasses—Knoxville, Chris Pontius, Dave England, and Ehren McGhehey—who attach electrodes to various parts of their bodies and shock one another. The scene opens with Knoxville shocking his cheeks, and then jump cuts to England holding the electrodes in his hand and receiving shocks, as well. A medium shot of McGhehey and Knoxville follows in which McGhehey, on the left, is shirtless with the electrodes attached to his chest, while Knoxville, fully clothed on the right, watches. Importantly, Knoxville is also in charge of administering the shocks. As McGhehey shrieks in pain and the other men look on, Knoxville reassures him, "Come on, daddy's got you, daddy's got you."

The next sequence of "The Muscle Stimulator" begins with Knoxville exclaiming that one of the jackasses should attach the electrodes to "the gooch—the spot between your balls and your butthole." A quick cut reveals a medium shot of England sitting on the couch between McGhehey and Knoxville, in which the naked England is spread-eagled, displaying the electrode and cupping his hands over his genitals. After two shocks and, of course, the obligatory reaction shot of the other jackasses laughing hysterically,

England rips off the electrode and pulls up his pants. Interestingly, Knoxville smells the electrode after it has been placed near England's anus, and he then forces McGhehey to do the same. This, however, is shown to be a ruse, for once the electrode is near McGhehey, Knoxville shoves it onto his face and shocks him once again. The last shock of the scene—literally and figuratively—begins when Chris Pontius declares, "Alright, let's zap my nuts." Pontius takes his testicles out of his shorts and attaches an electrode onto each one. As Knoxville initiates the shocks, Pontius dances around and screams, while the other three men watch and laugh. Impressively, Pontius endures about six shocks before he removes the electrodes. The camera pans left to a medium close-up of Knoxville, holding his head in his hands and laughing, before fading to black.

Clearly, at least a tinge of homoeroticism is evident in this vignette, yet I described it in full detail not only for its obviousness, but also to point to that which it omits. In other words, for all of its homoerotic overtones, this skit is careful not to venture into the homosexual; the men never touch one another's bare flesh, and while the men definitely call attention to both the anus and the male genitalia, ultimately there is no penetration. Because of this, audience members—the majority of whom, I would speculate, are white males between the ages of twelve and thirty—can read this skit simply as a group of good friends hanging out, most likely drinking, and just acting stupid: stereotypical frat-boy stuff. Yet such an interpretation should be tempered by Halberstam's analysis of the areas in which comic pressure is applied to normative masculinity. While I do not consider *Jackass* to wholly expose white masculinity as fragile or "delegitimized," I would certainly argue that it interrogates notions of acceptable masculinity. I acknowledge that there is a large amount of "play" going on within these skits, but I also maintain that, in the end, *Jackass'* representation of masculinity is not entirely subversive or transgressive.

One of the reasons why I hold to this interpretation is because the jackasses' sense of humor is largely juvenile. They derive a good deal of their stunts from toilet humor—literally. One memorable clip involves a jackass who publicly defecates into a floor-model toilet in a hardware store, although a large part of the joke comes from the fact that, in the first take, he soils himself before arriving at the store. Another stunt depicts jackass Steve-O launching bottle-rockets from his anus, and yet another anal-oriented skit involves a jock strap, a bungee cord, and an extreme wedgie. This connection between the anus (and its byproducts) and humor is a well-known comedic trope, although it is more often employed in tamer forms, such as Jim Carrey-style fart jokes.

In one of the final scenes of *Jackass the Movie*, "Butt X-ray," jackass Ryan Dunn is documented while inserting a toy car into his anus. The ensuing skit involves him going to the hospital to get an x-ray, and the joke develops around the unsuspecting doctor's reaction to the radiographic image of the toy car in Dunn's ass. Much focus is placed on Dunn's preparation for the stunt. The segment opens with a medium shot of Dunn sitting on a hotel-room bed, displaying for the camera the tools needed for this skit: a tube labeled "Anal Lube," a blue toy car, and a condom into which the car will be placed before it is inserted into his anus. Yet despite all of the focus on the preparations for and the aftermath of the stunt, the actual physical insertion of the car into Dunn's anus is never shown. Moreover, the men in the room with him express their disgust and discomfort with the skit, and certainly no one offers to help Dunn with the task at hand. The only man who touches him—a fellow jackass, not a medic—does so to effectively "medicalize" the event (by donning a latex glove and using a stethoscope to listen to Dunn's heartbeat), to put it in the realm of scientific inquiry as a likely attempt to lessen its homosexual implications. This interpretation also partially accounts for the text's insistent focus on the body's waste products (blood, feces, urine, and vomit), as well as the bodily marks and wounds mentioned earlier. Accordingly, the "Butt X-ray" skit does not end there; more medical evidence is needed in the form of a doctor's visit and an x-ray, not only to confirm that Dunn truly performed the stunt, but that he did so for a purpose other than sexual pleasure. As Mark Simpson points out, "It is the sublimated eroticism of the anus that makes men social" (80). To acknowledge pleasure as anally derived would be to ostracize oneself from the realm of homosocial bonding, landing instead in the unacceptable world of homosexuality. Comedy and curiosity are acceptable outlets for anal inquiry; sexual arousal is not.

It is impossible to fully account for the jackasses' behavior without taking note of the prevalence of masochism, or the taking of pleasure in physical pain. *Jackass* can be interpreted psychoanalytically in terms of an anxiety over homosexuality and homosexual desire, and this is precisely where theories of masochism come into play. Particularly compelling is Freud's connection between masochism and a repressed homosexual drive. Therefore, I invoke masochism here in accordance with Kaja Silverman's interpretation of two of Freud's works, "The Economic Problem of Masochism" and "A Child is Being Beaten." Silverman details the implications of Freud's assertion that the super-ego is always a substitute for a longing for the father, demonstrating how this proves to be especially problematic for men, since to act upon this longing would require an acknowledgement of one's incestuous, homosexual desire. Accordingly, Silverman argues that, for Freud, "feminine masochism is a specifically *male* pathology, so named because it positions its sufferer as a woman" (189, author's emphasis). She continues:

Feminine masochism, in other words, always implies desire for the father and identification with the mother, a state of affairs which is normal for the female subject, but "deviant" for her male counterpart. (190)

For the male subject, then, such desire for the father is inevitably a same-sex desire, thus venturing into the dangerous realm of the homosexual.

The adaptive male masochist must therefore repress this homosexual desire, while at the same time constantly and graphically relive the Freudian beating fantasy. In this sense, aspects of masochism are tied to exhibitionism; the trauma of this repressed longing for the father is brutally enacted upon the male body, and then displayed for public consumption (Silverman 190). Recall Johnny Knoxville's paternalistic reassurance of Ehren McGhehey: "Daddy's got you." Importantly, however, Silverman interprets Gilles Deleuze's re-reading of masochism as one that "celebrates…a pact between mother and son to write the father out of his dominant position within both culture and masochism, and to install the mother in his place" (211). Feminine masochism in the male, therefore, is linked to a usurping of authority; it can be read as an act of deviance or defiance in that the male refuses to identify with patriarchal authority, instead retaining a primal and infantilized attachment to the mother. The jackasses revel in their chosen state of perpetual adolescence and, in doing so, perhaps assist in the dethroning of the adult white male within contemporary late-capitalist culture.

Moreover, the style of humor that the jackasses typically employ is also in dialogue with this psychoanalytic model of deviance and masochism. In *Beyond Laughter*, Martin Grotjahn, M.D., offers concise summaries and applications of Freud's work on humor. Grotjahn profiles the "practical joker," the category under which such jackass-style humor falls:

He is the eternal adolescent who indulges in a dangerous pastime. The practical joke represents a primitive form of the funny which often is so cruel and so thinly disguised in its hostility that the sensitive, esthetically minded person can hardly enjoy it.… It lacks symbolization, elaboration, or disguise; by using not words but aim-inhibited action, it stands less than halfway between an intended aggression and its witty, verbal expression. The practical joke is so close to uninhibited and unexpressed cruelty that one needs a robust conscience and a lax censorship as protection against a reaction of guilt. (40)

Interestingly, Grotjahn's description is rather similar to comments made by mainstream film critics and reviewers of *Jackass the Movie*. Yet, if we take into consideration that a good deal of the jackasses' practical jokes are played on themselves, it becomes clearer as to how this type of humor is related to both theories and practices of masochism. In one sense, such humor is an extension of the argument that the male masochist resides in a perpetual state of adolescence because he is unable to achieve proper Oedipal identification, and thus can never legitimately achieve male adulthood. Moreover, as practical jokers, the jackasses often enact this aggression and hostility onto their own bodies; although it may provide a source of amusement for spectators, ultimately, the jackasses are made the butts of their own jokes. Or, in reality, the jackasses' butts become the sights and sources of their own jokes. This is especially interesting in that Freud links the development of laughter and the enjoyment of the comedic—produced by one's mastery of the bowels—to the anal phase of childhood development (Grotjahn 74, 80). Furthermore, as Silverman argues, masochistic practice as a whole involves a regression to the anal stage of human sexuality (210).

On a more applicable and less theoretical level, then, it becomes clear how masochism ties in with the jackasses. On the one hand, this abuse of the body is intended to prove what real men they are, as a high tolerance for pain has continually been associated with a high measure of masculinity—of guts, or balls. Yet if one thinks about what this gratuitous display of masochism may be covering up—namely, homosexual desire—then the construction of the jackasses as "real men" begins to break down. The compensatory nature of their stunts is nearly self-evident; the need to abuse and mutilate the male body to this degree in order to prove oneself a man ultimately reveals the degree to which one is insecure about his own masculinity. By introducing Silverman's psychoanalytic conception of masochism to the jackasses' construction of masculinity, Halberstam's interpretation of the drag kings' performances of white masculinity is made even more useful. Ultimately, this psychoanalytic understanding of masochism renders fragile the mainstream, heteronormative representation of masculinity, but does it serve to fully "delegitimize" it?

In this vein, while I believe that one valid reading of *Jackass the Movie* is that of deviance and subversion—that their ridiculous antics and abuse of the male body subvert dominant cultural conceptions of white masculinity and patriarchal authority—for all their irreverence, in the end, the jackasses still hold tight to the keystone of acceptable masculinity: heterosexuality. Regardless of the homosexual drive underlying their masochistic displays, the jackasses never truly cross the line, oscillating instead between "crazy friends having a good time" and "crazy friends having a good time, but with a little *somethin'-somethin'* going on there, *if you know what I mean.*" In the end, the jackasses uphold their actions as indicators of their masculinity, even if some of their stunts are so precarious as to need reassurance from other men. Accordingly, while lying on the bed in the missionary position, inserting a lubricated condom containing a toy car into his anus, Ryan Dunn begs of crew member Manny Puig, "Oh, Manny, tell me I'm a man!"

The implications of this analysis point to the variety of contemporary media conceptions of acceptable masculinity. To say that there is currently a "crisis of masculinity" is perhaps clichéd, predictable, and overdramatic, but to claim that masculinity, in the present moment, is in a state of transition and flux is accurate and apparent. All one needs to do is turn on the television to be bombarded with a number of competing versions of acceptable (and unacceptable) masculinity: the All-American NFL quarterback, the X-Games pro-skater, the loyal husband and doting father, the "big, fat, obnoxious fiancé," and the metrosexual, to name just a few. It is only through an investigation of such easily overlooked texts as *Jackass the Movie* that heterosexuality and white masculinity can truly be deconstructed and delegitimized, and that the complex concepts of "acceptable" and "normal" can begin to be broken down.

## Works Cited

Deleuze, Gilles. *Masochism: Coldness and Cruelty*. New York: Zone Books, 1991.

Freud, Sigmund. *Three Essays on the Theory of Sexuality*. Trans. James Strachey. New York: Basic Books, 2000.

—. *Jokes and their Relation to the Unconscious*. Trans. James Strachey. New York: Penguin Books, 1976.

Grotjahn, Martin, M.D. *Beyond Laughter*. New York: McGraw-Hill, 1957.

Halberstam, Judith. "Mackdaddy, Superfly, Rapper: Gender, Race, and Masculinity in the Drag King Scene." *Social Text* 52/53 (1997): 104-131.

Neale, Steve. "Masculinity as Spectacle: Reflections on Men and Mainstream Cinema." *Screening the Male: Exploring Masculinities in Hollywood Cinema*. Ed. Steven Cohan and Ina Rae Hark. New York: Routledge, 1993. 9-20.

Sedgwick, Eve Kosofsky. *Between Men: English Literature and Male Homosocial Desire*. New York: Columbia University Press, 1985.

Silverman, Kaja. *Male Subjectivity at the Margins*. New York: Routledge, 1992.

Simpson, Mark. *Male Impersonators: Men Performing Masculinity*. New York: Routledge, 1994.

Steinman, Clay. "Gaze Out of Bounds: Men Watching Men on Television." *Men, Masculinity, and the Media*. Ed. Steve Craig. Newbury Park, CA: Sage, 1992. 199-215.

Wyatt, Justin. "Identity, Queerness, and Homosocial Bonding: The Case of *Swingers*." *Masculinity: Bodies, Movies, Culture*. Ed. Peter Lehman. New York: Routledge, 2001. 51-65.

# Part IV
# Cinematic Strategies, Identification, and Spectatorship

# CHAPTER TWELVE

# WOMEN AND THE LAW: SPECTATORSHIP AND RESISTANCE IN *FEMALE PERVERSIONS* AND *A QUESTION OF SILENCE*

## CYNTHIA LUCIA

In her discussion of Hollywood films with female protagonists acting as legal investigators, ranging from FBI agents and police officers to crime victims themselves, Yvonne Tasker explains that "women, it seems, are involved in transgression even and to the extent that they are represented as lawmakers or enforcers," a condition influenced, she argues, by "a working out of issues around women's sexuality which, like women's ambitions and their friendships, is a realm seemingly in need of almost constant policing" (92-93).

Attempting to mask or elide the conditions of such policing, mainstream American films involving women and law often place powerful women, such as female lawyers or investigators, in positions of (ostensible) control. Such positioning, however, offers simultaneously the embodiment of an intellectually and sexually empowered woman *and* the stereotypical pathologies attendant to such female empowerment in our culture, usually centered on personal unhappiness, so often the yardstick against which professional accomplishment is measured. Women in these films ultimately pay for their power—typically with their agency delimited by the phallocentric imperatives of the law and conventional narrative—as "more capable" male agents eclipse the female protagonists. But what does this state of affairs mean for women in the audience who seek pleasure from images of female empowerment? Although such strictures exist, particularly in the films of the 1980s and 1990s, degrees of textual incoherence ever so slightly expose the construction beneath stereotypical pathologies and the policing mechanism at play, providing some grounding (as uneven as it may be) for female viewers, who perhaps oscillate

---

The discussion of *Female Perversions* appearing in this chapter is a modified version of the discussion appearing in *Framing Female Lawyers: Women on Trial in Film,* ©2005, written by Cynthia Lucia, and published here by permission of University of Texas Press.

between cautious ambivalence and genuine pleasure in the momentary empowerment offered the characters.

*Female Perversions* (a 1997 independent U.S. film) and *A Question of Silence* (a 1982 Dutch film), both directed by women outside the Hollywood mainstream, are works that overtly challenge conventional positionings of women in relation to the patriarchal law they serve, particularly as influenced by "the look" of spectatorship as it is defined and delimited within the courtroom, the cinema, and the marketplace. Both films complicate their arguments by presenting viewers not only with powerful women—an ambitious prosecutor in *Female Perversions* and a highly regarded court psychiatrist in *A Question of Silence*—but also with women incarcerated for crimes ranging from shoplifting to murder. In multiple ways, the films reflexively expose conventional narrative tropes to reveal women in the grip of a masculinist culture that promotes female objectification and commodification and inhibits expression of female desire, whether personal, professional, or sexual.

## *Female Perversions*

*Female Perversions* explores issues of female sexuality, eroticism, and the positioning of women within the patriarchal structures of law and of culture (Lucia 206-223). An independent American production directed by Susan Streitfeld, the film presents a character who is very much shaped by patriarchal culture and who, as a result, struggles for control and self-possession. Eve Stephens (played by Tilda Swinton) is a highly successful public prosecutor and candidate for a judgeship in the California Court of Appeals, to be appointed by the governor. Aptly named, Eve is obsessed with obtaining knowledge and control, yet as one of her lovers, Renee, a psychologist (played by Karen Sillas), tells her, ostensibly in jest: "You are a deeply impulsive and a terribly neurotic, extremely co-dependent woman who more than likely loves too much, or too little." A childhood memory haunts Eve: her mother openly expresses sexual desire for her father, an acclaimed scholar. When she lowers herself onto his lap as he sits reading and taking notes, he violently pushes her to the floor. After repeatedly playing out fragments of this memory, Eve ultimately confronts what she has been suppressing all along—the fact that, as a young child secretly watching this incident, although she may have felt sympathy (or pity) for her mother, she ran to her father as her mother lay on the floor. Portions of this flashback interrupt the narrative throughout, but we never see Eve within the flashback, and this final moment of alignment with her father is never shown. We learn about it as Eve describes the memory to her sister Maddy (played by Amy Madigan). The flashback, in withholding images of Eve as a child, is aimed less at eliciting sympathy or creating a direct causal link to Eve's present life and more at revealing the generalized power of "the father" to regulate female desire and consequently to constrain female agency.

As the inscribed "spectator" of this scene, Eve feels divided, but ultimately is drawn to the "true" agent whose masculine power and will prevails. "How much more self-enhancing it is to identify with the father," observes psychoanalyst Louise Kaplan in her book *Female Perversions: The Temptations of Emma Bovary*, upon which the film is based, going on to explain that "if the girl discovers that this same powerful and beloved mother is a denigrated household slave or worthless female or is regarded by the father as a nagging witch, she starts to repudiate the feminine aspects of her own self" (183). Eve's flashbacks further bring to mind Tasker's observations about Hollywood women in the legal professions who tend to identify with their fathers, providing "very little space for the heroine as articulating an identity for herself, one that is beyond the terms of the masculine, mother or Other" (102). While *Female Perversions* seems to adopt this Hollywood cliché, it does so from a consciously feminist position.

Eve's sister Maddy most literally seems to have assumed her father's place—he is a highly acclaimed philosophy professor, recently retired; she is about to defend her dissertation in anthropology. In her work as a lawyer, it would seem, Eve wishes to take her father's place in a more Lacanian sense, as evident when she speaks with Renee about her preference for law, saying, "That's the problem with psychology—nothing's concrete. I prefer the law. Black and white. Obey the rules or suffer the consequences. Guilty or not guilty." On why she is interested in becoming a judge, Eve explains that "ever since I was a little girl...I wanted to be a judge because I wanted to be dressed in a long black robe. With nothing on underneath." Clearly, for Eve, the law is pleasurable in its absence of (feminine) ambiguity and in its promise of (sexual) empowerment. Perhaps Eve wishes to use the judge's robe as phallic dress to replace the strategic accoutrements of femininity that signify an absence of cultural power. Such feminine accoutrements, when employed by the powerful woman, as Joan Riviere suggests, become her means of reassuring the male establishment that she poses no serious threat—that she means to steal nothing from that establishment. In reversal of Riviere, then, Eve's reference to the robe might also imply her unapologetic assertion of desire for masculine knowledge and power. In this same scene, Eve goes on to make love aggressively and somewhat forcefully with Renee, assuming dominance without apology. Although Eve asserts her unequivocal ambition and desire in this scene with a woman, she has trouble expressing such unmodified dominance in scenes with powerful men, in which she often dons a reassuring feminine masquerade, albeit sometimes inflected with a dominatrix code.

In order to appreciate fully Eve's wavering between the two states of masculine assertion and womanly masquerade, it is useful to look more closely at Riviere, whom Kaplan also examines in her book. In her 1929 paper "Womanliness as Masquerade," Riviere describes one of her patients, a highly intellectual, professional woman who, after her lectures, felt compelled to seek the approbation of men attending, usually older father-figures. Beyond the need for such approval, the lecturer would then go on to flirt with male members of her audience, "impersonating a seduction," as Kaplan points out, and thus reassuring the men "that no actual sexual performance would be expected" (270), while at the same time reassuring herself of her attractiveness to the men whom she perceived as having genuine power. According to Riviere, her patient "performed" flirtatious, womanly behavior to cloak her phallic power in an attempt to maintain that power, lest it be discovered and "stolen back" by the male establishment from which she imagined having stolen it in the first place.

Eve's great despair is in being relegated to the status of "woman," as represented by the memory of her mother's weakness. Chris Straayer's notion about the desire of women to be men, in terms of the cultural power men wield, seems especially relevant to Eve. She both embraces the disguise imposed by men in an almost obsessive dependency on the beauty and fashion industries men have erected to disguise women "as their opposite" (146) and resists it in her rejection of the feminine as represented by her mother. Embracing the imposed disguise, Eve is held hostage by an excessive concern with image—one powerful aspect of our culture that keeps women from attaining genuine power. For Eve, this involves buying the newest shade of lipstick and the sexiest lingerie, as well as reading women's magazines to discover the latest fashions and learn how to conduct and contain her emotional life. In a telling scene, Eve sits late into the evening at her office desk, answering a magazine quiz titled "What's Your Fight Style?" On the page facing the quiz is an image of a woman posing in a fashionable black suit, with arms playfully open, yet with her figure confined by black horizontal bars, and copy that reads, "Forgive Me for Being Powerful," a literalized representation of Riviere's concept of womanly masquerade. Eve seems caught within the cultural contradictions typified by these two pages of the magazine. She embodies the aggressive, successful professional who at the same time is imprisoned, lacking in self-assurance, and plagued by self-doubt.

As Eve scribbles her prospective new title, "Judge Eve Stephens," on a legal pad, she imagines hearing a man's mocking laughter. This man—the subject of her earlier courtroom prosecution—grabs her from behind, forcefully rubbing his hands over her body and holding her head in a vise-like grip, as he crosses out the title "judge" and whispers:

No, no, no. Flabby ass and thighs. Stinking, rank, rubbery cunt and drooping tiny
tits. Vulgar, lascivious, insatiable beast. Stupid and devious. Nothing about you is
genuine, and everyone knows you're a fraud.

Eve imagines pushing him away, at the very moment she realizes no one is
there. She rips the paper with her scribblings and crumbles it, repeating, "I have
nothing. I have nothing at all." The words of this imagined male figure are
directed at Eve's body and sexuality, through which she imagines her value is
measured ("Nothing about you is genuine"). This moment makes explicit the
very common cultural syndrome of the self-loathing "superwoman," who has so
internalized her state as object of the male gaze, even in the process of
attempting to escape it, that she is unable to see herself clearly. This internalized
male perspective, through which she confirms her insecurities and failings,
becomes her primary measure of self-worth, and it reinforces a deep-rooted
sense of herself as an interloper whose privileges could be "stolen back" at any
moment.

The film seems to argue that the cosmetics and fashion industries, as well as
the media (most notably women's magazines), create and perpetuate this
syndrome of women as objects to be looked at *by other women* and, in so doing,
not only invite female readers to see themselves as objects but also *shape female
readers in the mold of masculine viewers*—though disempowered masculine
viewers—when assessing these "other" female objects. Having thus internalized
the masculine gaze, the female reader/viewer will see those "others" both as
models to emulate and competitors to envy, objects to be evaluated; she will see
herself as object, as well, enlisting her "masculine" pair of eyes to scrutinize and
stand in judgment of her own appearance, ambitions, and desires. And, of
course, she will always find herself (and others of her sex) lacking, having thus
internalized the phallocentric "standard" and its attendant attitudes.

This emulate/envy binary, offered women in relationship to other women, is
best illustrated when Eve meets the beautiful lawyer her office will hire to
replace her, should she be chosen for the judgeship. When Langley (played by
Paula Porizkova) runs into Eve as Eve applies lipstick while waiting for the
elevator, she notices that she and Eve are wearing the same shade. Asserting that
this could not possibly be the case having just purchased hers, the latest fall
shade, Eve is surprised to find that Langley does, in fact, own that same lipstick
and, moreover, that she is "tired" of it. After Langley ditches her tube in a
nearby ashtray, Eve is left with very little alternative but to do the same. As
Langley first enters the frame, she observes Eve as Eve assesses herself in her
compact mirror, creating multiple lines of "looks" and objects: Eve as object of
her own look, Eve as object of Langley's look, and both as objects of an
"internalized" male gaze. The women are framed with the elevator door

dividing them into "separate" spaces, almost as facing pages in a magazine.

Before emulating Langley in throwing away her tube—an act rooted in envy—Eve "attacks" herself by smearing the lipstick on her white blouse, clearly an expression of self-loathing. As if to confirm and reassert her "value" through "genuine" masculine eyes and desire, Eve presents herself in her boyfriend's office, inviting him to shave her pubic hair; it becomes clear that Langley's female gaze, with its internalized male standard, has so shaken and destabilized Eve's own internalized (masculine) "measure" of her desirability and of her power.

The film further illustrates female internalization of a phallocentric standard when Eve arrives at a small town police station, where her sister is being held for shoplifting. Angry that she cannot arrange for her sister's immediate release, Eve shouts her complaints into a telephone at the station. This time, Eve imagines that she is violently grabbed and reprimanded by the *female* clerk who works at the station: "Hysterical, loud-mouthed bitch. Ball-buster. Battle-ax. Strident. Unfeminine. Grotesque. Out of control. You, a judge? Never!" Using the language that men traditionally have employed to demean women, this clerk (as internalized by Eve) has so internalized the attitudes behind that language that she (Eve) can find nothing redeeming in Eve (herself). Eve imagines her punishment for aggressive, assertive, "unfeminine" behavior as exclusion from the world of powerful men ("You, a judge? Never!"), and also from the world of other women who are her competitors in aspiring to masculine positions of empowerment. Following this hallucination, Eve can only whisper, "I'm sorry. I'm sorry."

The singular courtroom sequence, appearing very early in *Female Perversions*, further represents the pervasive male gaze, persistent in its power to contain female agency. As she argues before a judge for strict sentencing of the defendant, Mr. Rock, who "channel[ed] toxic waste into a landfill," Eve proclaims that Mr. Rock "understands only one thing—dominance." As "a small, mean, dangerous criminal masquerading as a sophisticated person of means," Mr. Rock "deserves no mercy"; "force is required." "The only appropriate course of action," according to Eve, "the only thing to which he will respond is the seizing of his assets." Beyond its mild sexual double entendre, Eve's language might just as easily be read as her own imagined judgment of herself as an "independent" woman with "stolen" phallic power—she will be punished and dominated, her assets seized for her masquerade in presuming to occupy this place where, truly, she does not belong. Shot composition, editing, and sound achieve an interesting duality of perspective in this scene. In the eyes and minds of the judge and various other men in the courtroom, the effectiveness of Eve's argument has less to do with legal skill than with her physical (erotic) presence. As Eve speaks, the bailiff, most notably, removes his hearing aid, ensuring his fantasies full play around Eve's lips, elbows, and hips, undisturbed by her words. This scene foregrounds the bailiff's subjectivity, as sounds of tinkling glass and female voices whisper in fractured melodies on the soundtrack and accompany images of Eve's fragmented body and face, framed in extreme close-up, decontextualizing Eve and serving her up in parts. Erasing Eve from the frame, as lawyer and as person, the film thus hyperbolizes and satirizes a strategy at the core of female representation in classical narrative film. Seamlessly inscribing male subjectivity, conventional male-centered narratives often wed us to that perspective; in this scene, *Female Perversions* so foregrounds that perspective as to divorce us unequivocally from it. In so doing, the film represents a self-reflexive narrative version of historicized spectatorship, perhaps in an attempt to empower and confer agency upon its female spectators.

The film announces its premise before the narrative begins, with a printed epigraph from Kaplan's book:

> For a woman to explore and express the fullness of her sexuality, her emotional and intellectual capacities, would entail who knows what risks and who knows what truly revolutionary alteration of the social conditions that demean and constrain her. Or she may go on trying to fit herself into the order of the world and thereby consign herself forever to the bondage of some stereotype of normal femininity—a perversion, if you will.

In her book, Kaplan examines sexual perversion in men and women, as well as the history of psychological and psychoanalytic discourse on perversions, revealing changing definitions and cultural attitudes toward the subject. Through case studies of actual patients and an interesting case study, of sorts, focusing on Flaubert's Emma Bovary, Kaplan argues that female perversions result from and are manifested within the very behaviors our culture deems as feminine or as "required" for women to adopt, including some of the very behaviors to which Eve is addicted—revolving around obsession with body, image, and control—all of which involve a distortion of female desire and sexual expression. As Kaplan points out, "perversions, insofar as they derive much of their emotional force from social gender stereotypes, are as much pathologies of gender role identity as they are pathologies of sexuality," going on to assert that "socially normalized gender stereotypes are the crucibles of perversion" (14).

Just as independent women feel they must walk a tightrope between self-assertion and self-effacement in order to avoid being perceived as threatening to the male establishment, so, too, must women walk a sexual tightrope between giving themselves over to pleasure and containing pleasure or desire in an effort to properly "perform" the gender/sexual role to which they have been assigned.

In a series of silent, stylized tableaux, the film literalizes the tightrope metaphor, as Eve is shown tentatively attempting to traverse it or confined in bondage by it. Masked figures, both male and female, pull the rope tighter, prompting the question of whether Eve is experiencing pain or pleasure as she acts or is acted upon.

Kaplan argues that all perversion is reactionary in that it enables subsistence, through accommodation, within a culture that defines gender and sex roles with such rigidity that perverse strategies become necessary, to greater or lesser degrees. The tightrope sequences connect with this notion in two possible ways. First, if read as nondiegetic inserts, the sequences can be understood as allegorical representations suggesting that the conditions motivating perversion merge with the enactment of perversion. Played out in a highly stylized S/M setting, in which character movement is almost balletic and make-up and costume create caryatid-like figures placed dramatically against a black background, the tightrope sequences bring to mind Elizabeth Cowie's notion of fantasy as the *setting for desire* rather than as the *object of desire* (133). Considering Kaplan's premise as it might dovetail with Cowie's contention, then, these sequences could be understood to imply that fantasized perversion as reactionary accommodation never can arise from true desire, elicit free expressions of desire, or become objects of desire but rather can function only as the *setting for displacement of desire*.

A second way of thinking about the tightrope sequences potentially reinforces this first reading, if we understand the sequences as representing Eve's subjective sexual fantasies/anxieties. The film opens with a tightrope sequence, directly followed by an image of Eve and her boyfriend, John (played by Clancy Brown), in bed together. We see the tightrope sequence again, after Eve provocatively enters John's office with shaving cream and razor, and tightrope sequences are twice intercut during Eve's sexual encounter with Renee. At a climactic point later in the film, as Eve dreams, the tightrope sequence is interwoven with images of Eve's recurrent childhood memory of her father's rejecting her mother's sexual advances, thus collapsing woman and child, mother and Eve. In the context of the "real" sequences within which they appear, the tightrope sequences remain ambiguous in terms of whether Eve experiences pain or pleasure yet, more often than not, she appears anxious, frightened, and uncertain, struggling for control. In another sense, then, these images can be seen to represent both the condition and the manifestation of Eve's perversion in that they provide both a setting for desire and a setting for the displacement of desire, particularly in the context of Kaplan's argument that stereotypes of femininity work to "disguise" the female desire for masculine (sexual) empowerment (18).

While the film, at times, partakes in mischievous humor (as in the courtroom sequence), it seems nevertheless to adopt Kaplan's theory that true sexual pleasure cannot be attained in a culture built upon active male dominance and passive female submission. Although men and women may exchange roles of dominance and submission in both straight and gay sexual relationships, the general model remains intact. Here, Kaplan is very much at odds with Pat Califia, who, as Cowie explains, sees the "play" and potential subversion in dominance and submission (Cowie 125). While characters in the film take on varying roles in the dominance/submission model, that basic model ultimately appears to hold them in a form of bondage, underscoring missteps, doubts, and recriminations in living through and living out these roles, even with the erotic charge they may deliver.

Interspersed throughout the film, quotations from Kaplan's book appear within the frame in unlikely places; for example, they are embroidered on a pillow ("Perversions are Never What They Seem to Be"), painted on a bus-stop bench ("In a perversion there is no freedom, only rigid conformity to a gender stereotype"), and scrolled across the bottom of a TV screen ("Perversion keeps despair, anxiety, and depression at bay"). The incongruously banal settings suggest the pervasive presence of perversion in our everyday lives, which the film represents in various ways.

Through parallel editing, we see Eve shop for lipstick and lingerie as her sister Maddy shoplifts a scarf and a garter belt. Both actions are graduated expressions of the perverse strategy, as Kaplan defines it. Compulsive shopping and kleptomania are "accusation[s] against the social environment" (287) that has forged "the domestic imprisonment of women, who are trained from childhood to find the satisfaction of all their desires in material goods" (305). This "imprisonment" arises from "commodity fetishism of modern industrial societies" (305) that entices women to accept the (false) empowerment offered through the purchase of merchandise displayed as "visual temptation" (304). While the boutique—as featured in both *Female Perversions* and *A Question of Silence*—and the department store may appear to be spaces designed by and for women, they ultimately become "fantasy spaces" that establish the mise-en-scene or setting for the displacement of female desire, as Anne Friedberg implies in her discussion of the flâneuse, the female flâneur "whose gendered gaze became a key element of consumer address" (61). Just as applicable to the contemporary department store are Friedberg's observations concerning the nineteenth-century department store, where the woman found that "new desires were created for her by advertising and consumer culture; desires elaborated in a system of selling and consumption that depended on the relation between looking and buying and on the indirect desire to possess and incorporate through the eye" (63). Both spaces invite a visual consumption—a form of spectatorship, if you will—serving capitalist consumerism. Eve's shopping and Maddy's shoplifting are perverse strategies acted out in a repressive setting in order, ultimately, to feed the fantasy of empowerment and therefore to displace desire.

Both Eve and Maddy are aggressive and determined in their enactment of their chosen perverse strategies. Eve emerges from a dressing room wearing only a sheer body suit a size too small, displaying herself as other customers shop; Maddy exits a store with the stolen garter belt, which she promptly throws in a trash can on the street corner. The film further illustrates how fully women participate in perpetuating the perverse strategy in relationship to other women. The female clerk at a cosmetics store tells Eve that she could "use something" when Eve asks if a certain moisturizer "really works"; another female clerk encourages Maddy to buy one of the "miracle bras" on display, stating, "I haven't met a girl yet who doesn't enjoy cleavage. They create cleavage like a crevice after an earthquake. Men just fall into it." While the humor of this moment is undeniable, the self-consciously stark, almost painterly set design and shot composition bring to mind the convergence of the boutique and the Foucauldian prison. Friedberg refers to the department store as "the panopticon of the sexual market" (62), following Walter Benjamin, who spoke of the employment of female salesclerks in department stores as the merging of buyer and seller and as "'seller and commodity in one'" (qtd. in Friedberg 62). Benjamin's observation makes all the more apparent the emulate/envy binary offered women as "spectators" of other women, now in the context of capitalist/consumerist imperatives.

Such moments in *Female Perversions* force a spectatorial distance imbued with acknowledgement, rather than judgment, of the female protagonists within this particular culture, thus constructing a rather complex female viewing position. The film attempts to create a conscious and self-conscious (female) spectator through overt inscriptions of spectatorship within the narrative itself, creating multiple subject positions, often associated with the more traditional woman's film, as Judith Mayne points out of those films (64-72), while self-reflexively foregrounding and commenting upon those positions. *Female Perversions* achieves this through its representation of the various cultural texts addressed to women, including some film hybrids, women's magazines, and advertising; in its foregrounding of the contradiction between woman as defined by patriarchal ideology and women as historical subjects, as well as through its representation of women who both have the power of the look yet recognize themselves as the objects of the male look; and in its representing female characters who identify with contradiction itself.

This commentary on female subjectivity and (generalized) female spectatorship is most evident in a series of sequences set outside the small town of Fillmore, where Maddy lives and is arrested for shoplifting. In this rural

desert setting, Maddy rents a room from Emma (played by Laila Robins), a
dress designer with an adolescent daughter, Edwina (played by Dale Shuger),
who goes by "Ed." Having retreated from the onset of puberty through her
boyish manner, short hair, and loose-fitting T-shirt and shorts, Ed furtively
washes the blood from her shorts when she gets her first period and
ceremoniously buries her bloody napkins in a kind of makeshift cemetery,
explaining to Eve, "I'm burying the baby.... Every month a baby tries to take
hold, then it gets washed away." Within scenes set in Emma's home, Ed's
perspective becomes pivotal as she watches and responds to the various models
of femininity offered her. She is drawn to Maddy, intrigued by Eve, impatient
with her mother, and amused by her Aunt Annunciata (played by Frances
Fisher).

In this location, the film represents various female "types," their perverse
strategies, and the subject positions they potentially adopt and create, playing
these feminine differences through and against each other. While Maddy, as a
compulsive shoplifter, displaces "aggression, lust, envy, vengeance, anxiety,
depression, and agitated madness from personal relationships to material goods"
(Kaplan 287), Eve enacts the womanly masquerade rather self-consciously, her
actions centered on "posing," on presenting herself and persistently testing out
power relations. Annunciata, in her career as a stripper, appears to display a
certain power in her exhibitionism but it is tempered by large doses of cynicism.
Of this perverse strategy, Kaplan points out that "the countless women who
dress up in...semi-exposing female garments to pose in...sexually suggestive
postures do so to reassure themselves that they will not be abandoned or
annihilated" (257).

Emma, an avid reader of romance fiction, manufactures romanticized images
of desire that place her at the mercy of men for a sense of self-definition and
validation. As Kaplan describes it, the reader of romance fiction "attends as the
virgin patiently peels away each of the many shells of phallic hardness until at
last she arrives at the soft custard of domestic desire at the center of the man's
being—the caring, protective, loving *husband*" (325-326). Emma will not allow
Eve to use her telephone, for instance, fearful that her boyfriend Rick may try to
call, and she agonizes over what she will wear on a weekend date, when she
plans "to get him to tie the knot." Having read Maddy's dissertation about a
matriarchal Mexican community, she tells Eve, "It's wild—the women have all
the power," to which she quickly adds, "The awful thing is that they're all so fat
and unattractive. That happens in a matriarchy. So fat."

And Ed, as the reluctant adolescent girl whose fear of adult femininity is
manifested in delicate self-cutting, enacts a less serious form of self-mutilation
which, as Kaplan points out, is an expression of unease with a changing body
through both "active and defiant gestures...most directly a means...of

forestalling final gender identity and denying that the illusions and hopes and dreams that made life endurable are lost forever—in this life at least" (364).

As the hypothetical, impressionable, young female spectator, Ed admires Maddy's intelligent, straightforward manner and her independence from make-up and men. She takes up a defensive position when her mother bemoans the fact that Maddy ("poor thing") has not had a boyfriend in over a year. Ed hangs out in Maddy's room, reading her dissertation and working at her computer. Having surreptitiously followed Maddy into town, she watches from a distance as Maddy is arrested. Intrigued by Eve's self-assertion, Ed positions a mirror in order to watch as Eve sits at the kitchen table and talks with her mother. When Ed's aunt, Annunciata, arrives on the scene, bringing a gift of lace lingerie for Ed in celebration of her becoming a woman (i.e., getting "the curse"), Ed is amused. She feels strangely comfortable with this warm, hyper-feminized woman, so different from what she seems to be choosing for herself. As Ed photographs Annunciata, who models her skimpy, striptease costumes, she explains to Eve that Annunciata is "body doubling," which, as Ed puts it, means that "ugly bodies become perfect by magic." Annunciata instructs Ed on womanly behavior, saying, "It's not something that comes naturally. You have to work at it...by studying other women." Here, the film explicitly articulates the condition of female spectatorship in a masculinist culture.

In one beautifully choreographed scene, the women interact and enact multiple positions of female spectatorship, resulting in an interplay of attitudes and approaches to self-definition. Shot composition is richly layered, playing various planes of the image against each other, while always strongly foregrounding the reactions of Eve and Ed as they respond to the versions and perversions of femininity articulated. While Ed and Eve are most strongly inscribed as spectators, each woman becomes a spectator of the others. Emma arrives home unexpectedly, crushed that her date with Rick ended in a break-up rather than a marriage proposal. As she tearfully tells her story, close-ups of Ed reveal her annoyance and disappointment that her mother seems so weak and dependent. Through Ed's reactions, we sense that it is not the first time this sort of scene has played itself out. When Annunciata proclaims that Emma should be grateful now that she will have more time, Emma appears dumbfounded, asking, "For what?" Barely containing her hostility, Eve replies, "Your business." Expressing stereotypical dependence and self-deprecation, Emma sobs, "That will never mean anything. I miss him. I know he doesn't give as much as I do...but he's scared. I love him so much."

For the film viewer, Emma becomes linked with Eve's mother as we see her in the repeated flashbacks. Not only are Emma's expressions of desire entirely regulated by men, but her costuming also recalls that of Eve's mother. Her lacy, white dress—overly girlish and virginal, perhaps expressing her romance-novel aspirations—recalls the lacy blue-gray robe worn by Eve's mother in the flashbacks. The fabric of the dress and the robe, as well as the lace curtains in Emma's home, create a cloying atmosphere of self-imposed weakness and femininity, as Eve seems to perceive it. In a culture that so devalues the feminine, Eve has come to fear this version of femininity. As a woman shaped by an oppressive culture, Eve is not ready to acknowledge her mother's circumstance as one shaped by those same conditions.

In a clever reversal, the *women* serve as internal audience to Annunciata's performance as she demonstrates her latest striptease routine, narrating as she moves slowly and seductively, "You got to be everybody's dream. Everything to everybody." At this moment, Annunciata's torso, covered in black fishnet, fills the right half of the frame, as she stands in front of Eve, whose discomfort is powerfully registered. For a split second, Eve's childhood flashback is intercut, and Annunciata's dance melts smoothly into the movement of Eve's mother as she lowers herself onto the father's lap.

When Annunciata says, "You got to erase yourself. You got to become, like, generic," reaction shots of Ed reveal her playing with a pair of scissors, cutting at the skin on her fingers and hands, metaphorically "erasing" herself, perhaps. A second time we see Ed, she snips at the lace bridal veil on one of her mother's mannequins. As internal audience, Ed is the reluctant spectator, *uncomfortable* with the positions offered by her mother and her aunt. In fact, neither woman provides a coherent subject position at all; each has molded herself, with radically different results, to the desires of men. Just as Annunciata suggests, both she and Emma *are* generic, each reflexively representing a stereotypical female character present in any number of genre films from the western to the melodrama and the musical: the dependent, domestic woman whose only concern is supporting her man, and the good-hearted, tough-edged, world-weary prostitute, whose transgressions are punished either by death or emotional isolation. Ed is confronted with a culture that offers few truly positive alternatives for a girl growing into womanhood.

As Annunciata dances with Emma, who moves trance-like, moaning "Rick, I'm yours," a tight close-up of Eve registers her suffocating sense of entrapment and, at this moment, a more extended portion of the childhood flashback is played out. Eve's mother seductively reaches for the father's pen, tracing a circle around her breast nipple and leaning toward him, as he pushes her to the floor. She looks up humiliated, her lip bleeding. The link between her mother and Emma, whose behavior prompts this memory, is overpowering for Eve. As internalized audience or spectator within this scene, Eve adopts two positions simultaneously: (1) a masculine subject position, dismissive, as male critics were of weepies or women's films; and (2) a feminine subject position, deeply affected and disturbed by what she sees. She recognizes her own dependence and vulnerability played out in exaggerated terms. Eve is thus positioned as a spectator in much the same way that Elaine Showalter argues women writers are positioned in a masculinist culture, having been exposed primarily to the literary traditions and culture of men. Linda Williams suggests, following Showalter, that this positioning—as women who develop their own "culture" within the overarching male-dominated culture—results in a "double-voiced discourse" for women (433), an observation that parallels the internalized masculine position many female spectators adopt with regard to other women as well as themselves.

Like *Female Perversions*, *A Question of Silence* presents women in the context of cultural conditions which purport to grant them agency and power only to disguise their restraints, leading women both to embody and act out the meaning of those restraints in the form of commonplace and not-so-commonplace behaviors. But both films also represent points of resistance. In Eve's case, resistance comes in the form of recognition.

When the governor interviews her for the judgeship she so desires, questioning her status as a single, childless woman ("Don't you feel isolated? Do you miss not having a family?… I suppose living alone just gives you more time to read, doesn't it?"), Eve can only stumble through a reply, later recriminating herself for not having pretended to be engaged. Later that evening, Eve and Maddy watch a home movie from their childhood, one that Maddy has played several times throughout *Female Perversions*. Shot on the very afternoon of the incident depicted in Eve's childhood flashback, the movie prompts Eve to remember what she has been repressing all along: that she ran to her father, rather than comforting her rejected mother. That night as Eve dreams, images from the home movie converge with images from the flashback and images of the tightrope Eve feels consigned to walk. In the dream, Ed appears and cuts the tightrope with a razor—the very razor she presumably uses when delicately cutting her skin—as Eve plunges into a cross-shaped swimming pool at her parents' home, a pool we recognize from the home movie. At that moment Eve awakens, crying and frightened, as Maddy soothes and consoles her. Shortly thereafter, Eve walks outside in the blue-gray light of dawn and secretly follows Ed through the desert landscape to the makeshift cemetery she has created. As Ed runs, frightened, Eve pursues her and calms her, just as Maddy had earlier comforted Eve. Perhaps, metaphorically, Eve is now ready to console her own mother.

These final images present us with a comfort in female unity but, to its credit, the film avoids suggesting that the differences separating these women, or the difficulties of women in the context of a phallocentric culture, can be easily resolved. If anything, these final scenes provide for recognition of the "double-voiced discourse," thus potentially presenting points of resistance to the pervasive emulate/envy dichotomy offered women in relationship to other women within a culture of commodification.

## A Question of Silence

*A Question of Silence*, perhaps, picks up from where *Female Perversions* leaves off, although this film appeared well over a decade before *Female Perversions*. Intriguing in its complexity, Marleen Gorris' film exposes the conditions of constraint under which women exist in a patriarchal culture, concentrating its greatest attention on points of resistance. Three women who have never before met are shopping in a boutique. When the owner spots one of the women, Christine (played by Edda Barends), slipping a dress into her bag, he removes it with the smug satisfaction of having caught her in the act. The other two women, Annie (played by Nelly Fruda) and Andrea (played by Henriette Fol), watch as Christine defiantly places the dress in her bag once again. The three women slowly and deliberately surround and attack the owner—kicking, hitting him with a shopping cart and mannequin stand, ripping him open with the jagged edge of a glass display shelf and broken plastic hangers—in stylized, choreographed movements, as though well-rehearsed and destined for performance. Four additional women who are shopping in the boutique silently witness the crime. After being arrested, all three women confess and stand trial to determine their mental competence. A female psychiatrist, Janine Van den Bos (played by Cox Habbema), is called in to evaluate the women and present her findings in court, although it becomes clear that the Dutch magistrates already have concluded insanity as the only rational explanation for this seemingly unmotivated crime. When Janine fails to confirm the magistrates' conclusion, the film powerfully places the patriarchy, as well as the Dutch legal system, on trial, an action reversing the typical trajectory as Tasker defines it.

Given its structural complexity, any synopsis of the film's plot cannot begin to capture the textured and nuanced interplay of power and resistance central to the film. Interwoven with flashbacks to the women's lives before and immediately after the crime are scenes involving Janine's life and her series of interviews with the women. Disruptions in space and time further result when portions of Janine's interviews, as heard on tape in her study, slide into the actual space and time of the interviews conducted in the Dutch prison.

In its radical disjuncture of spatial and temporal continuity, the film further acknowledges that an understanding of its female characters and their actions can neither be obtained from, nor reduced to, the simple linearity of cause-and-effect relationships, as impelled by concretely discernable motives and as driven toward closure in which truth is revealed and resolution offered. The film calls into question this narrative paradigm of conventional cinematic structure and, with it, the positioning of spectators within that paradigm. In so doing, it further challenges a similar narrative paradigm employed by the legal system in which motive must be established, chains of cause and effect reconstructed over a linear plotting of time, truth discovered, and resolution offered, usually in the form of a verdict and the punishment or absolution to follow. Through its form, thematics, and content, *A Question of Silence* exposes and indicts the Dutch magistrates, for their inability to understand women's lives, as well as the legal institution as a whole, for its reductive, linear, absolutist structuring of "plausible" explanations. Moreover, the film's structure reveals that, in all of its power, the male-dominated legal profession is foolishly blind to itself and its effects upon the lives of the women who exist under its authority and oppression.

As a psychiatrist, Janine, much like Eve in *Female Perversions*, initially stands in for the male-dominated power establishment she serves; however, unlike Eve, she appears to live a happy and balanced personal as well as professional life. Married to a lawyer, Janine lives a comfortable middle-class life, having achieved a state of rapprochement with the patriarchal power structure. This is not so for the three incarcerated women, whose social status has taught them a great deal more about the lives of women than the female psychiatrist assigned to evaluate them can understand. The film traces Janine's growing awareness of the patriarchal constraints under which the three women, and she, must operate, leading her to question the patriarchal institutions of law, psychiatry, and marriage.

Linking *A Question of Silence* with *Female Perversions* is Kaplan's notion that perverse strategies express unconscious rebellion or resistance to society's rigid gender-role definitions. In *A Question of Silence*, however, resistance takes on conscious and deliberate forms. The viewer catches telling glimpses of each woman, intercut with the opening credits, on the day after the murder. Christine appears fearful and distracted as she cautiously parts the curtains drawn on her living-room window. This image of a woman at the window is the first of many others, recalling this trope within the woman's film, where the window acts as an "interface between inside and outside, the feminine space of the family and reproduction and the masculine space of production," as Mary Ann Doane points out (288). For Christine, at this moment, the window functions as Doane describes it, for beyond the window lies the law. However, the window becomes a more complicated "interface" in this film, since the women often stand at windows within the patriarchal prison. With all of its Foucauldian implications, the prison is a space within which all privacy is denied. Yet the prison in this film deceptively replicates private space, with the women living in single rooms resembling fairly commodious college dorm rooms, thus creating the illusion of private space within the confines of a public institution. The image of women at prison windows thus exposes the imprisoning qualities of the home, constructed as much by patriarchy and its system of laws designed to contain female expression and transgression.

*A Question of Silence* implies that there is no unequivocal feminine space. When arrested, the women go quietly and without protest, suggesting that it makes very little difference; they simply exchange one form of incarceration for another, a notion that is made explicit as Andrea, gazing out the prison window, tells Janine, "I'll never have to type again!... The government will take care of me.... They'll let me go quietly crazy in here." Substitute the words "my husband" for "the government" and we are led directly to Christine's domestic circumstances, in which her husband provides little more for her than the house in which she experiences a maddening isolation. Once arrested, Christine stops speaking; she sits, head lowered, sometimes rocking ever so slightly as in a state of mild catatonia.

Imbedded within a scene in which Janine interviews Christine's husband is a scene representing a typical morning in Christine's household. She serves her husband and children as they go off to work or school, neither speaking nor being asked to speak. From her husband's point of view, "We had a good marriage. A very good marriage," yet he betrays his perception of Christine as a satellite on the periphery of his own orbit. "How could she do this to me?" he complains. "She should have known I'm useless with kids." In prison, Christine refuses to see her husband and she speaks only once, saying simply to Janine, "Please remind my husband to speak to Simon's teacher." Her only other form of communication is to draw pictures of stick-figure families framed within boxes that resemble houses, images that resonate with the same contradictions as do images of the women standing at the windows of their prison. Christine's silence is a clear and conscious act of resistance, passive yet aggressively aimed at the culture that systematically has silenced her and rendered her invisible.

Annie, on the day after the murder, is involved in teasing banter with a group of men who sit at the coffee shop where she works. Her laughter and self-deprecating humor reflect her own accommodation with the oppressive conditions of her job and her life. She is a divorced, middle-aged woman, rejected not only by her husband but by her daughter as well, a circumstance echoing Eve's rejection of her mother in *Female Perversions*. During her meetings with Janine, Annie talks incessantly. Yet her talking functions very much as Christine's silence; with all of her conversation and laughter she reveals very little of herself, yet her isolation and loneliness seep through. When Janine asks whether Annie is happy in her job, she replies, "'Happy' is a big word. I can't complain, but 'happy'?" Wondering if Annie ever tried to find another job, Janine confronts a cultural and economic reality she seems never to have considered. "You're pretty naive, aren't you?" asks Annie. "Who'd want an old woman like me?'

This is not the only time Janine is called naive. Aware that she has simply exchanged one form of imprisonment for another, Andrea challenges Janine: "You're not naive enough to believe you can help me. [Your report] will influence nothing." Intelligent, articulate, and insightful, Andrea is amused but also angered by Janine's sheltered naiveté concerning the realities of women's lives. When Janine asks Andrea whether the murder victim could have been a woman, Andrea replies, unequivocally, "No." When Janine asks if she has always worked "with men," Andrea immediately corrects her: "*For* men."

On the day after the murder, Andrea is shown taking dictation in her boss' office. Here it becomes apparent that she knows a great deal more about the business than he does, something he takes for granted, viewing her knowledge merely as a tool for his capricious use. Imbedded within Janine's interview with Andrea's boss—who claims Andrea was "the best worker I ever had; my right hand"—is a sequence in which Andrea serves coffee at a meeting of the all-male board of directors. As she returns to her place at the table to resume taking notes, she speaks knowledgeably and eloquently about an issue under discussion. Because she is a "secretary" (interchangeable with "woman," as her boss points out when Janine asks whether he ever considered appointing her to the board), neither the boss nor the other board members acknowledge Andrea's remarks. As Andrea, in muted anger, stirs her coffee, the boss places his hand on hers to silence the persistent ringing of the spoon against her cup. The camera tracks slowly in to an extreme close-up of her eyes as she stares fixedly ahead. Recalling Christine's determined silence, Andrea's eyes reflect the enforced shutting down of her intellectual and emotional life. It is the stare of an invisible woman. Andrea articulates so much of what Janine does not understand. Christine's silence, she points out, arises from her recognition that "nobody is listening."

In keeping with Kaplan's commentary on shoplifting and kleptomania, we can read Christine's initial act of shoplifting as an unconscious act of resistance, a perverse strategy, staving off a sense of depravation, powerlessness, and anxiety. The mutilation/murder itself seems to fall somewhere between an unconscious and conscious act of resistance. Carried out calmly and with deliberation, yet with a stylized quality suggesting almost somnambulistic movements on the part of the women, the murder can be understood as a turning point from unconscious to conscious acts of resistance. And, of course, in response to that pivotal moment, literal imprisonment must follow.

The fact that the murder occurs in a boutique has been the subject of some critical commentary. Williams, again referencing Showalter, explains that "women's culture is not so much a subculture as a dual perspective of living and participating in a dominant male culture with boundaries that overlap, but do not entirely contain, the non-dominant, 'muted' culture of women" (434). Williams further points out that this "muted culture" is a "no-man's-land," "entirely off limits to men," and that "there are few such places outside the home, but a woman's dress shop is certainly one of them" (434). She argues that the boutique in *A Question of Silence* is one such no-man's-land and that "the crime could not have taken place in a more male-defined space; nor could it have taken place in that space if the shop owner had been a woman" (434). Yet, I would argue that the boutique, like the home, is a space defined by a phallocentric culture that addresses women as consumers by manufacturing and preying upon feminine insecurity, as we have also seen in *Female Perversions*. It is precisely because the dress shop is a *male-defined space in drag*, so to speak—*falsely posing* as a no-man's-land—that the murder must take place there. That factor, perhaps, also explains the brutality of which the coroner reports: "The genitals are barely recognizable as such." In its false form of address to women, in its deceptively posing as a no-man's-land (a deception made more apparent, in this case, by the male owner), the boutique becomes the site of violent retaliation. Like the home, the boutique represents yet another form of women's cultural confinement, made apparent through the design of the space, with its horizontal racks, mirrors, and tight spaces constraining the movement of the women.

If images of women standing at the window of the patriarchal prison serve to uncover the home as a male-defined space in disguise, then the events unfolding in the patriarchal space of the courtroom work to uncover the boutique as a male-defined space in disguise. The incident at the boutique, of course, becomes a direct subject of interrogation in the courtroom, just as the home, more often than not, becomes the primary subject of interrogation in the prison as Janine interviews the women. Within the courtroom, the same seven women are gathered: the three accused and the four witnesses. The four women who witnessed the murder never come forward to the authorities, nor do the accused women speak of their presence in the boutique. Whereas the home and prison are places of confinement and passive resistance—unconscious resistance in the home and conscious resistance in the prison—the boutique and the courtroom pose, ironically, as spaces of empowerment, where women are "granted" the power to purchase and the power "to speak," respectively, and both spaces in all their deception become stages for acts of resistance. While a man is murdered and mutilated violently in the boutique, patriarchal law is "mutilated" in this courtroom, if only for the moment, by Janine's refusal to offer evidence supporting insanity and by her exiting the proceedings in mid-testimony. The patriarchal law is further mutilated by the three accused women and four witnesses, who burst into laughter at the absurdity of the process and are hence removed, creating an even more absurd situation. The pomposity of the prosecutor when he questions Janine's professionalism unmasks the sham of the law's objectivity insofar as women are concerned. When he questions Janine's conclusions, stating that they are "incompatible" with his own views and thus questioning their "objectivity," he brings to mind legal theorist Catharine MacKinnon's argument that the very notion of "objectivity" in law is a concept that supports patriarchal dominance. As MacKinnon points out:

> The state will appear most relentless in imposing the male point of view when it comes closest to achieving its highest formal criterion of distanced aperspectivity. When it is most ruthlessly neutral, it will be most male; when it is most sex blind it will be most blind to the sex standard being applied. When it most closely conforms to precedent, to "facts," to legislative intent, it will most closely enforce socially male norms and most thoroughly preclude questioning their content as having a point of view at all. (435)

In her essay on the film, Mary Gentile observes that "the women are caught in a patriarchal trap: the doctor's 'defense' assures them of the harshest sentence. Gorris has turned the courtroom 'rationality' upside down" (402).

The first glimmer of resistance among the accused and the four witnesses comes from Christine, who quietly giggles when the magistrate points out that surely she must understand "the court will take her social and psychological background into account." Christine's giggle later turns into raucous and rebellious laughter when the prosecutor refers to "shopping for dresses" as a "harmless pastime" and when he goes on to say that he can see "no difference between this case and, let's say, if they had killed a female shop owner, or, yes, the other way around—if three men had killed a female owner of a shop." Annie is the first to laugh and, soon after, is joined by one of the four witness/spectators until the point that all three of the accused, the four witnesses, and Janine burst into laughter at this absurd articulation of a patriarchy so blind to itself. Of course, it was not so long before that Janine herself suggested a similar possibility.

The idea of spectatorship is very much inscribed within *A Question of Silence* and is developed through the ways in which the prison and the home, the boutique and the courtroom, are played through and against each other. The trope of the woman at the window inscribes spectatorship while uniting the spaces of the home and the prison. In the prison, spectatorship takes the form of surveillance, as we are constantly reminded with images of surveillance monitors, long corridors, multicolored panels of buttons that lock and unlock doors, and even a rather anachronistic-looking device that copies out in longhand a message sent from another part of the prison. In a certain sense,

Janine is part of the surveillance machinery as she probes into the lives of the women, taping their conversations and traversing the spaces of the prison and the home. Janine enters Christine's home, and she plays and re-plays the prison tapes in her own home. The filmmaker's camera itself becomes an instrument of surveillance as it reflexively tracks forward, circling Christine and Annie in their homes, connecting the home and prison as male-constructed spaces.

In the boutique, spectatorship takes on the qualities of the "mobilized gaze," as Friedberg defines it, linking it closely with the boutique in *Female Perversions*, where Maddy does her shoplifting. As Annie, Andrea, and the four witnesses shop, their gaze becomes fixed on Christine, who resists her role as the "empowered" spender consigned to perpetuate the system that enslaves her. The four "spectators" are also witnesses whose refusal to speak in court links the boutique and the courtroom as patriarchal spaces within which conscious rebellion ensues and prescribed forms of gendered spectatorship/witness are shattered, at least temporarily. The three accused women unveil the "harmless pastime" of buying dresses for what it really is, as their gaze becomes fixed upon the shop owner whose very presence and challenge to Christine unmasks the masculinist underpinnings of this ostensible no-man's-land. Speaking neither in the boutique nor in the courtroom, the witnesses, as David Black has pointed out, are "uninferable, and undiscoverable to the law" (177). So, too, is the sanity of the three accused women. Having assigned and constructed the "mobilized" female gaze in the first place, relegating it to "harmless pastime," the patriarchal establishment would, in recognizing the sanity of the women, be forced to recognize its own lack of objectivity, aperspectivity, and sanity.

In recognition of the very real cultural power of patriarchal law, the film chooses not to posit anything transformative in this momentary breakdown of the Dutch judicial system, though it may be a transformative moment for the women and for Janine herself. As Linda Williams aptly points out, the film does not end on a "note of solidarity" but rather "on a moment of suspension between the known world of patriarchal light and the unknown world of matriarchal shadow" (438). Outside the courthouse, as her husband impatiently honks the car horn, Janine's gaze is locked in freeze-frame with that of the silent witnesses, a look in which "the spatial, experiential, and metaphysical realms of female difference are recognized...though they still have not been spoken" (Williams 438).

A similar "moment of suspension" exists in *Female Perversions* in the final freeze-frame of Eve as she gently caresses Ed's face. Williams' remarks might likewise be applied to *Female Perversions* when she observes that "the power of *A Question of Silence* as feminist art thus lies in its resistance of all the male paradigms by which female deviance has been understood...[and] in its refusal to narrate the positive, utopian identity of women" (439).

# Conclusion

Attempting to consciously take hold of Hollywood's tendency to police the lives of women, then, *Female Perversions* and *A Question of Silence* expose and shift the terms of argument away from the necessity of policing female sexuality and behavior, and toward the necessity of policing patriarchal institutions in their historical oppression of women. The legal institution in *A Question of Silence* and consumerist culture in both films, as supported by a patriarchal network, become subjects of close scrutiny. And as part of this examination, the films interrogate the commodification of women sometimes perpetuated in the guise of liberation: the female is "empowered" to purchase, only to create herself as a commodity desirable enough to be "purchased." Yet from this dichotomy emerge tenuous points of resistance, sometimes in the form of perverse strategies as defined by Kaplan, which ultimately are not liberating at all but do signify (rebellion against) patriarchal constraints, or sometimes in the form of potentially self-destructive behavior. We see the deformation of Eve in *Female Perversions*, in which she is forced to walk a tightrope as a female lawyer who is intelligent and ambitious but feels compelled to masquerade her desires and ambitions, fearful that she will be expelled from the patriarchal paradise that promises knowledge and power—a tightrope Janine is also consigned to walk in *A Question of Silence*, though initially she may not be aware of it. In exposing the uneasy quality of Eve's masquerade, *Female Perversions* further exposes the cultural conditions that encourage the deforming masquerade in the first place. The perverse strategies enacted by the women in both films, moreover, serve as an argument for policing *not the women* but the cultural institutions that confine and oppress them.

Through inscriptions of spectatorship, both films further shift the terms of Tasker's argument, representing multiple viewing positions and inviting film spectators to take up multiple positions, thus allegorizing—and at moments perhaps valorizing, though not unproblematically so—the fluidity of such (identification) strategies. The films illustrate the complications of spectatorship, suggesting that it often involves identification with contradiction itself, as Mayne suggests, allowing for the recognition and appreciation of complications involved in feminist address within a phallocentric cultural context. Female spectatorship is a not a simple matter within this context, and both films inscribe complex models of female spectatorship while creating equally complex viewing positions that challenge or rub against the grain of the conventional tendencies Tasker describes.

And herein resides the pleasure these films provide. By opening spectatorship to a multiplicity of positions and by examining the complicated interplay of power and resistance, dominance and submission, on the levels of content, theme, and structure, these films, for the most part, avoid creating overly reductive containment/subversion strategies, enabling the viewer likewise to avoid such overly reductive dichotomies in relationship to female characters. *Female Perversions* and *A Question of Silence* end on freeze-frames that capture moments of genuine, unspoken connection between women, traversing generational and social class divisions. Layered with the very real problematics of women existing in a phallocentric culture, the films perhaps suggest that such moments of unity and the new forms of empowerment they promise can, at this point at least, exist only as moments: frozen and isolated.

## Works Cited

Black, David A. *Film In Law: Resonance and Representation.* Chicago: University of Illinois Press, 1999.

Cowie, Elizabeth. *Representing the Woman: Cinema and Psychoanalysis.* Minneapolis: University of Minnesota Press, 1997.

Doane, Mary Ann. "The Woman's Film: Possession and Address." *Home Is Where the Heart Is: Studies in Melodrama and the Woman's Film.* Ed. Christine Gledhill. London: BFI Books, 1987. 283-298.

Friedberg, Anne. "Cinema and the Postmodern Condition." *Viewing Positions: Ways of Seeing Film.* Ed. Linda Williams. New Brunswick, NJ: Rutgers University Press, 1994. 59-83.

Gentile, Mary C. "Feminist or Tendentious? Marleen Gorris's *A Question of Silence.*" *Issues in Feminist Film Criticism.* Ed. Patricia Erens. Indianapolis: Indiana University Press, 1990. 395-404.

Kaplan, Louise J. *Female Perversions: The Temptations of Emma Bovary.* London: Jason Aronson, 1991.

Lucia, Cynthia. *Framing Female Lawyers: Women on Trial in Film.* Austin: University of Texas Press, 2005. [Please note that the discussion of *Female Perversions* appearing in this chapter is a modified version of the discussion appearing in *Framing Female Lawyers: Women on Trial in Film,* ©2005, written by Cynthia Lucia, and published here by permission of University of Texas Press.]

MacKinnon, Catharine A. "Feminism, Marxism, Method, and the State: Toward a Feminist Jurisprudence." *Feminist Legal Theory: Foundations.* Ed. D. Kelly Weisberg. Philadelphia: Temple University Press, 1983. 437-453.

Mayne, Judith. *Cinema and Spectatorship.* New York: Routledge, 1993.

Straayer, Chris. *Deviant Eyes, Deviant Bodies: Sexual Re-orientation in Film and Video.* New York: Columbia University Press, 1996.

Tasker, Yvonne. 1998. *Working Girls: Gender and Sexuality in Popular Cinema.* New York: Routledge, 1993.

Williams, Linda. "A Jury of Their Peers: Marleen Gorris's *A Question of Silence.*" *Multiple Voices in Feminist Film Criticism.* Ed. Diane Carson, Linda Dittman, and Janice R. Welsch. Minneapolis: University of Minnesota Press, 1994. 432-440.

# Chapter Thirteen

# Marianism in the Movie *Elizabeth*: Femininity, the Law of the Father, and the Maternal Semiotic

## Jaime Bihlmeyer

As a system of signs not dependent on Lacan's Symbolic Order, motion pictures lend themselves to the enunciation of Julia Kristeva's maternal semiotic (Kristeva, *Revolution*, 41; Silverman 106). In contrast to the latter, spoken language and its secondary form, the written word, work to suppress the extra-logical power and instability of pre-lingual precedence. Further, the written word as a cultural tool for political dominance functions to diminish the institutional role of women in society. The film *Elizabeth* (1998), also known as *Elizabeth: The Virgin Queen*, adroitly (re)presents the intersection in a mainstream movie of the Symbolic Order and the maternal semiotic while creating an intertextual dialectic between its imagery, the historical record, and spectatorship (Kristeva, *Revolution*, 59-156). The film accomplishes this not only by featuring the culminating historical and political moment when the pre-h(y)st(e)rical goddess image reached its zenith of resurgence in European culture but also by exposing the maternal semiotic in the cinematic apparatus.

## FEMININITY versus The Law of the Father

The oppositional bias inherent in language—that is, the primary artifact of the Symbolic Order—taints FEMININITY because the latter stems from the pre-lingual and so (re)presents biological precedence and extra-logical influences. Body-centered primacy is always already construed to be in binary opposition to the Symbolic Order. The maternal semiotic, which consists of the subconscious pulsations and repressed pre-memory experienced in the pre-lingual developmental stage, by nature enfolds FEMININITY and remains disavowed by the Law of the Father. Within the image-making constructed by the mainstream film artist, FEMININITY corresponds to the enunciation of the maternal semiotic through subtle emphasis placed on the split seams and fissures of the narrative, a construct of the Symbolic Order. These gaps in the narrative amount to the extra-logical play of images and dialogue as well as the overt referencing of the maternal and the sensory. Mainstream filmmakers, especially those harboring aesthetic impulses, intuitionally highlight these fissures in narrative film structure, which are analogous to the disavowed crevices in the Symbolic Order through which the subconscious seeps onto consciousness.

Director Shekhar Kapur taps into the artist's semiotic urge in *Elizabeth* from the very first frames of his film. The opening montage, consisting of symbols on a bloody background superimposed with images of Henry VII, Queen Mary, and Elizabeth, is striking in its multi-layered graphic work topped with simple titles recounting the immediate historical events leading to the opening moments of the bio-narrative. The background is visceral in its resemblance to amorphous organic ooze, in and out of which period renderings of the principals appear in rack focus, from blurred blobs into crisp detail and back out of focus again, as they disappear along the z-axis. At one point the titles state "THE COUNTRY WAS DIVIDED" and a large cross, semi-translucent like a cell's membrane in the bloody background, splits in two, as if a microbe were cloning itself to make a double image. The motif of the double reoccurs shortly afterwards as the name "Elizabeth" dissolves into the center of the screen and we suddenly recognize that the rectangular shapes in the background also form the name Elizabeth in a much less symbolically transparent manner than the previous foreground letters' signifying display. This multi-layered strategy in the opening montage obliquely references the amorphous tenacity of the Symbolic Order vis-à-vis the semiotic, as well as the illusionism of the written word as signifier. Within the context of Kapur's film, the organic struggle between the Symbolic and the maternal semiotic in this opening title sequence kick-starts the Kristevan intertextual dialectic that rapidly spills over into the recounting of the historical record in terms of the cult of the Virgin Queen(s): overtly, the chronicle as well as the self-construct of Elizabeth I and her ascension to the role of queen mother of England; covertly, the myth and the iconography of Mary, Mother of Jesus as Queen of Heaven.

Near the beginning of his film (in fact, during the final opening credits), Kapur directly references the maternal semiotic by displaying the abject (Kristeva, *Powers*, 8) in the grisly form of a dismembered head suspended above a cavernous moat that the young Elizabeth witnesses while being escorted by boat and under arrest to the Tower of London. Since Elizabeth's stepsister, Mary, is the Queen of England and sole monarch—the one who does not lack— the tower (re)presents the phallus of the Phallic Mother (Ian 12-13), the primordial (m)Other, the abhorrent tower that always already harbors all the connotations reminiscent of the dripping, abject maternal residue, the pre-Symbolic trauma and quasi-subjectivity. This dire circumstance of captivity is what conjures the intervention of the Virgin Mary as Phallic Mother par excellence. One night, Elizabeth is ushered from the tower just as she muses out loud that tonight she thinks she will die. Her short journey takes her by carriage through the night of mayhem in the street, as depicted by a montage of women brutalized by soldiers. Suddenly, the screen is filled with the painting of the Madonna with Baby Jesus at her breast, her nipple erect. The Madonna's eyes are closed in jouissance (Barthes 9; Parker 159). Next, the panel of the painting that contains the Baby Jesus at the Madonna's nipple shifts open and the upper body of Elizabeth leans in. We then realize this is a hidden doorway in a mural. Elizabeth steps in, closes the door, and stands there, nearly covering the Baby Jesus, side by side with the extra-proportional Madonna towering over her in jouissance. This heavy-handed yet exquisitely photographed composition lays bear the director's conceit and opens the space for all the textual intersections between Elizabeth I and the Virgin Mary, including the disavowed leaks of the maternal semiotic.

## The Virgin Mary and the Maternal Semiotic

Milk and tears became the privileged signs of the *Mater Dolorosa* who invaded the West beginning with the eleventh century, reaching the peak of its influx in the fourteenth. But it never ceased to fill the Marian visions of those, men or women (often children), who were racked by the anguish of a maternal frustration. Even though orality—threshold of infantile regression—is displayed in the area of the breast, while the spasm at the slipping away of eroticism is translated into tears, this should not conceal what milk and tears have in common: they are the metaphors of nonspeech, of a "semiotics" that linguistic communication does not account for. The Mother, and her attributes evoking sorrowful humanity, thus become representatives of a "return of the repressed" in monotheism. They reestablish what is nonverbal and show up as the receptacle of a signifying disposition that is closer to so-called primary processes. (Kristeva, *Tales*, 249-50)

The Virgin Mary's mystique lies in her Otherness. She is other than man, other than the Law of the Father, and other than other women: she is "alone of all her sex," to use the words of Marina Warner, and Queen of Heaven. She is the milk of the pre-lingual developmental stage and she cries the tears of death. As Kristeva implies in the quote above, representations of the Virgin mark the return of the repressed Otherness to the cult of monotheism. Christianity was and is the cult of monotheism that dominates the European cultural arena. The Virgin Mary has accumulated a wide following among the faithful, if not among the Fathers of the Church(es) that subscribe to Christianity. This implies that the Virgin's otherness, that is, her link to the body-centered and repressed semiotic, strikes a chord in the populace. This is not surprising when considering the long (pre-)history of goddess worship among the common folk and the difficulties the leaders of the monotheistic cults have had in their avid attempts to eliminate her influence. What is surprising is the mystical and convoluted adaptation of the earth goddess eventually canonized within the opportunistic doctrine of the Virgin Mother that obliquely references the friction and the collusion between the Law of the Father and the semiotic. Further, the Roman Catholic Church exploited regressive imagery in the depiction of the Virgin in order to retain the medieval peasantry within the monotheistic fold. A similar skewed and regressive iconography found its way into the cult of Elizabeth I and will be examined later in this chapter.

The pre-h(y)st(e)rical goddess image reflects the fecundity and excess of the body and draws much association from the concept and the phenomenon of the Earth as (m)Other (Getty 3). The Palaeolithic Venus of Willendorf is a prime example of the excess and the opulence, as well as abjection and jouissance attached to the maternal semiotic. She is robust and fecund like a nubile consort. She is compact, round, and folded like a turd (see the movie *The Thirteenth Warrior*, based on Michael Crichton's book, particularly the small stone icons that a Viking holds up on his sword so as not to touch it). She is encoded and revered. Ultimately, she is milk, blood, and sensation. Gradually, through the eras of spoken history culminating in the written word, she becomes, on the one hand, the disavowed repressed singularity, while on the other hand, the milk, tears, and fetish for the disenfranchised. This is the telltale transformation through the filter of language, particularly the written word, which affects the skewed goddess incorporated within the linguistic and iconographic depictions of the Virgin Mary. The distortion of the earth goddess within the Virgin Mary liturgy constitutes not only the co-opting agency of the Law of the Father, but also the myriad folds of the maternal semiotic as it performs its symbiosis within and outside the Symbolic Order. The Virgin goddess became Mater Dolorosa, Madonna della Misericordia, Maria Regina, and ultimately "alone of her kind." As goddess she retained the maternal, but as the Virgin she was distanced from the Earth. Unofficially sanctioned by the Church of Rome as Queen of Heaven and Mother of the Church since the Dark Ages (officially sanctioned as such in 1954 and 1964, respectively), the Church nevertheless censured the Virgin Mary in paradoxical ways. She was detached from carnal knowledge, but not from birthing. She was freed from the stigma of Eve by means of the Immaculate Conception and granted Dormition/Assumption because she was the mother of Jesus Christ. The Church then acknowledged her as mystically part of the Trinity previously thought of as composed only of the three incumbents—the Father, the Son, and the Holy Spirit—for whom she became wife, daughter, and sister in an incestuous caldron of repressed extra-logical fusion. Her subversive significance in this arrangement, however, is that she carries with her to the Trinity the maternal component from the human pre-lingual condition: the (m)Other. And so she impinges on phallogocentrism unless she can be co-opted.

Kristeva describes the psycho-social dynamics of the Virgin iconography:

> A skilful balance of concessions and constraints involving feminine paranoia, the representation of virgin motherhood appears to crown the efforts of a society to reconcile the social remnants of matrilinearism and the unconscious needs of primary narcissism on the one hand, and on the other the requirements of a new society based on exchange and before long on increased production, which require the contribution of the superego and rely on the symbolic paternal agency. (*Tales*, 258-259)

In a sense, the Law of the Father, in the form of the doctrines of the Catholic Church, has salvaged the abject jouissance of the body-centered goddess, filtered her through paternal agency of language, and then placed her on a new pedestal of liturgical imagery and dogma. However, the maternal semiotic is extra-lingual and so seeps and leaks its subversive influence onto the psyche despite culture's disavowal. Without the co-opting of the goddess into the Virgin Queen, society might lack the display of the primordial (m)Other.

## Elizabeth I and the Maternal Semiotic

Elizabeth I was two-and-a-half years old when her nineteen-year-old mother was beheaded and she was branded a bastard. She was barely a speaking subject when the (m)Other was severed from her Oedipal equation by her father (patron) because Elizabeth was born lacking the organic/Symbolic appendage. Her proximity to the pre-lingual during this abandonment certainly suggests a potential in the child for the return of the repressed not only in her monotheistic upbringing but in her psychological state as subject in process. As Martha Reineke explains in terms of the Kristevan perspective:

> What does Kristeva mean by fascinated rejection? With this paradoxical term, Kristeva refers to intertextual practices of negativity—jouissance and rejection—undertaken by the subject. These practices attest to the work of the unconscious. A maternally marked metaphor, fascinated rejection marks the emergence in the world of a nascent subject in process and on trial.... Historically, fascinated rejection has alluded to the stance of one who would become the master of its house by repressing all that is heterogeneous, wholly sacrificing to subjective and societal order all vestiges of the unbounded economy of the semiotic. (39)

Young Elizabeth was certainly in process and on trial from the start and, given her resilient fortitude, she packaged her interrupted and stunted "fascinated rejection" into a survival mechanism that implemented the vestiges of the maternal semiotic, the negativity that affirms, the unconscious that is not quite repressed and resonates with primal jouissance. If she must suffer abandonment, then independent and heterogenous she shall remain—especially in the face of Symbolic disavowal and abject horror.

Elizabeth I *masters* the Law of the Father despite being a subject in process in whom disavowal of the pre-lingual connection has not been fully inculcated. She is free to implement the extra-logical force of the repressed as well as the structure of the Symbolic Order. Her connection to the semiotic melds with all of the always a priori pre-lingual implications, that is, the caldron of perverse bodily excesses that have attached themselves as well to the iconography of the Virgin Mary and the Trinity.

> The Virgin assumes the paranoid lust for power by changing a woman into a Queen in heaven and a Mother of the earthly institutions (of the Church). But she succeeds in stifling that megalomania by putting it on its knees before the child-god. (Kristeva, *Tales*, 257)

Popular interpretations of Queen Elizabeth I's monarchy that allege the monarch's exploitation of the cult of the Virgin Mary support Kristeva's take on the paranoid power lust assumed by and developed iconographically for the Virgin image, which, in turn, results in the pseudo-disavowal of megalomania in the name of the ultimate male offspring/phallus: the Son of God. In hindsight, the Virgin Queen of England interpreted and implemented the cult of the Virgin within the schism of Christianity to perfection in terms of sustaining her role as female monarch. Elizabeth I professed virginity in all its paradoxical Symbolic construct while fostering its skewed body-centered heterogeneity in poetic and pictorial self-representation. By doing so, she discovered that the Law of the Father was not able to effectively place her in binary opposition. In this regard, and considering the censorship of religious imagery in the Protestant worship, her figurative displacement and replacement of the cult of the Virgin Mary in her own likeness and vice versa established her sovereignty. This phenomenal psychological and iconographic sleight of hand comes into play emphatically in the film *Elizabeth*.

## The Virgin Queen(s) and the Written Word

Before focusing entirely on the film in relation to the Virgin Queen(s), our inquiry turns to the examination of the struggle between the written word and the emergence of the iconography of the Virgin. This discussion will underscore the FEMININITY in iconography and motion pictures that arouses artists and spectators as if drawn to an altered state of the human condition where the repressed returns.

## Mary, Mother of Jesus

The goddess image was depreciated aggressively in the patristic canon and therefore ostracized despite the emergence of the cult of the Virgin. Even before St. Augustine's influential onslaught against the Virgin, the deliberate marginalization of the goddess was apparent in literate societies (Shlain C30).

The Immaculate Conception that is the Christ's virgin birth is only mentioned once in the gospels. The first English translation of the New Testament (and one of Elizabeth's biblical sources) translates Matthew 1:18 this way:

> The byrth of Christe was on this wyse, When hys mother mary was maryed unto Joseph, before they cam to dwell togedder, she was founde with chylde by the holy goost. Then her husbande Joseph beinge a parfect man, and loth to defame her, was mynded to put her awaye secretly. Whill he thus thought, behold the angell of the lord apered unto him in slepe sainge:
>
> Joseph the sonne of David, feare not to take unto the, Mary thy wyfe. For that which is conceaved in her is of the holy goost. She shall brynge forthe a sonne, and thou shalt call his name Jesus. For he shall save his people from theire synnes.
>
> All thys was done to fulfill that which was spoken of the lorde be the prpht saynge: Beholde a mayde shall be with chylde, and shall brynge forthe a sonne, and they shall call his name Emanuel, which is a moche to saye be interpretacioun, as God with us. Joseph as sone as he awoke out of slepe, did as the angell of the lorde bade hym, and toke hys wyfe unto hym, and knewe her not tyll she had brought forth her fyrst sonne, and called hys name Jesus. (Tyndale 22)

The Book of Luke also references Mary as a virgin when visited by the angel Gabriel and yet remains significantly less forthcoming about Immaculate Conception:

> And in the. vj. moneth the angell Gabryel was sent from god unto a cite off galile, named nazareth, to a virgin spoused to a man, whose name was Joseph, of the housse of Davide, and the vergins name was Mary. And the angell went in unto her, and sayde: Hayle full of grace, the lorde is with the: blessed arte thou amonge wemen. When she sawe hym, she was abasshed att his saynge: and cast in her mynde what maner of salutatcion that shulde be. And the angell sayde unto

her: feare not Mary, thou hast founde grace with god. Loo: though shalt conceave in thy wombe, and shalt beare a childe, and shalt call his name Jesus. He shalbe greate, and shalbe called the sonne off the hyest. And the lorde god shall geve unto hym the seate off his father David, And he shall raygne over the housse off Jacob forever, and of his kyngdom shalbe none ende.

Then sayd Mary unto the angell: Howe shall this be, seinge that I know no man? And the angell answered, and sayd unto her: The holy goost shall come apon the, and the power off the hyest shall overshaddowe the. Therfore also that holy thynge which shalbe borne, shalbe called the sonne of god. (Tyndale 89)

Several telltale signs of intertextual dialectic occur within each gospel verse above, as well as between both texts. In Matthew, Mary is only betrothed to Joseph when her pregnancy is discovered and the angel appears to him in a dream. In Luke's version, Mary and Joseph are already married when the angel Gabriel appears to Mary, who is fully awake during the event. Further, Matthew, at the end of the verse, implies that Joseph had sexual relations with Mary but not until after Jesus was born—which makes sense since Jesus is credited with having a brother named James in other scriptures. Luke, on the other hand, suggests that the "holy goost" will affect her some way, and that God's power will "overshadow" her. But Luke stops just short of saying that the conception is consummated by the Holy Ghost. Finally, in Luke we find a true Annunciation reflecting the popular legend of the cult of the Virgin Mary, whereas in Matthew, Joseph is the one who receives the angelic vision in a dream, while Mary remains objectified and peripheral to the event.

Not only do the two writers differ in terms of the status of Mary in proceedings leading to the birth of the Messiah, but Matthew's version, by specifying the appearance of the angel in Joseph's dream, seems to be consistent with the conventional concepts of accessing the repressed subconscious. Joseph's contact with the workings of the Trinity takes place in the surrealist state of a dream, whereas in Luke, the extra-logical experience is afforded directly to Mary while she is conscious. Supported by the irrefutable link to the Immaculate Conception found in Matthew's gospel, Luke's version becomes canon once the cult of the Virgin Mary starts to pervade the European liturgical ritual, specifically in rites concerned with spiritual intervention between heaven and earth.

## Elizabeth I

The schitzophrenic nature of the gospels' recounting of the same events, but from different perspectives, coalesces in the arena of both ritual and institutional identity in a manner that opens space for strategy in manipulating the same. Elizabeth, as a precocious youngster, would have recognized the overt implications of the two differing gospels in relation to women in general and the Virgin Mary specifically. Given popular readings of Elizabeth's political career in particular as regards the cult of the Virgin, and the political ramifications of the schism between the Catholic orthodoxy and the Reformation, especially in terms of her father's opportunistic revisionism, it is feasible that she was influenced greatly to take advantage of the contemporary cultural and political currents.

At the very least, Elizabeth would have sensed, if only intuitionally at first, the institutional and political potential of the sparse canonized references to the Virgin and their influence on the Reformation and on her future as monarch of England. In addition to having a thumb on the religious pulse of her era, and in full recognition of her precarious role in the political environment, she also connected extra-consciously to the potential of the maternal semiotic disavowed in culture. She could intuit that the longevity of the cult of the Virgin Mary lies in the suggestive silences of the iconography, which succeeded despite the disavowal from the Symbolic and which closely paralleled her own exceptional situation in the following overtones: the myth and multivalence of virginity, the assumption to queen (specifically in relation to earthly institutions), and the uncanny link to the extra-logical maternal singularity attributed to the Virgin welcomed paradoxically in the collective intuition of the people and in their liturgy.

Elizabeth's political machinations appropriated extremely well the schisms and the fissures in the Symbolic Order. Her published writings and strategically implemented self-representation, both verbal and iconographic, were emblematic of the cult that arose around her rule and the myth that was promoted after her death. Despite the structure of the secondary political machinery of her government that demanded compromises (Levin 14), Elizabeth held her own and created an image of integrity and singularity that reached her citizenry at multiple levels of awareness. Through her intuitionally profound grasp of the maternal semiotic, as it leaked through the fissures in religious dogma and linguistic construct of the Law of the Father, Elizabeth's propagated mythology functioned to stabilize the eruption of the abject that the Reformation, as an instance of the exaggeration of linguistic dependence and consequence in culture, aroused.

Elizabeth was known for her ability to put together words, which is verified in her poetic works and, above all, in her well-documented speeches. One of Elizabeth's lesser-known yet more poignant literary presentations that demonstrates her precocious perspicacity in the apprehension of the relationships between the Symbolic Order and the maternal semiotic, as well as the significance of her precarious position in the Tudor megalomanic dynasty, takes the form of an editorialized translation of Queen of Navarre Margaret

Angoulome's *Le Miroir de l'ame pecheresse.* Elizabeth was eleven years old when she accomplished this literary marvel. The original text reflects a meditation encompassing several themes that recur in the politics, religion, and psychology of the times, and Elizabeth's translation, which verges on adaptation, serves as a microcosm of the cultural transformations that would culminate in her monarchy. Mark Shell succinctly argues for the importance of this translation in the understanding of the women principals of the period and specifically for Elizabeth as a young female in the Tudor line:

> What is most interesting about the "Glass" may go some way toward explaining its relative obscurity. Elizabeth's work expresses, as we shall see, an ideology both important and discomforting in its personal and historical aspects. Its treatment of bastardy and incest, for example, has potentially disconcerting ramifications for ideas of liberty and politics generally and illuminates the historical rise of the English nation and biographical role of Elizabeth herself. For the most profound themes of the "Glass" involve the reworking and expansion in nationalist and secular terms of such medieval theological notions concerning kinship as universal siblinghood, whereby all men and women are equally akin, and dormition, wherein the Virgin Mary plays at once the role of mother and daughter as well as wife. Above all, the "Glass," whose French original had a subtitle about the human conflict between flesh and spirit (*Discord etant en l'homme par contrariete de l'esprit et de la chair*), concerns the transmutation of the desire for or fear of physical incest into the desire for or fear of spiritual incest. It thus reflects the beginnings of a new ideal and real political organization, which, partly out of Elizabeth's own concerns with incest and bastardy and partly out of political exigencies of the time, England's great monarch introduced as a kind of "national siblinghood" to which she was simultaneously the mother and wife. (6-7)

Elizabeth's early journey through adult mediation on religious and psychosexual themes that traverse multi-linguistic protocol and spiritualistic maternal iconography speaks for her sense of self-possessed FEMININE identity. At the age of eleven, Elizabeth connects extra-linguistically to aspects of FEMININITY, the limitations of female influence in society and monarchy that signal as much the symbiosis of the maternal semiotic and the Law of the Father as the semiotic virulence of the structural fissures pervasive in the latter. The featured symbol in Shell's essay as well as Elizabeth's literary work is the mirror or "glass," which becomes, several centuries later, the symbol for the crucial developmental stage that amounts to a self-reflective threshold signaling the entry into subjectivity that is the process of splitting from the pre-lingual morass of maternal objectivity (Elliot 62). Elizabeth references this threshold, which, for her, corresponds to a jubilant primordial transformation, by choosing Margaret's melancholy text to translate. This translation signifies a turning point in Elizabeth's precarious and exhilarating young life that reinforces her primary identification with the pre-lingual maternal singularity as (re)presented by the construct of the Virgin Mary.

Kapur's film presents the *image/imago* of Elizabeth's self-possessed extra-subjectivity that is embodied in Cate Blanchett's performance and punctuated by multivalent images of Tudor royal lineage and Marian iconography at turning points in the Virgin Queen's bio-narrative.

## The Maternal Semiotic and the Virgin(s) in the Film *Elizabeth*

After Kapur's Elizabeth enters Queen "Bloody" Mary's regal sanctuary, resplendent with Catholic iconography of the Virgin Mary, she is fearful of death at the whim of her elder step-sister, who has summoned her unexpectedly from imprisonment in the horror of the Tower of London. After tormenting her with the threat of death, Queen Mary suddenly pleads with Elizabeth to promise not to "take away from the people the consolations of the Blessed Virgin, their Holy Mother," to which Elizabeth fights back a sigh of relief, followed by an infinitesimal smile of victory, and promises only to follow her conscience as Queen. This verbal exchange and the opulent display of the Virgin Mary imagery condense the historical record and provide a foreshadowing accompanied by a real sense of the self-possessed strength of the future monarch. Elizabeth has clearly won the war, although she must remain under house arrest until Queen Mary's rapidly approaching demise.

When Queen Mary dies, Elizabeth assumes the throne and the film co-opts the event of the announcement to Elizabeth in order to revisit the Virgin Mary iconography in an extra-logical and cinematic way. The event is bracketed by a fade to white that signals a spiritual intertext and attaches the subsequent scene to the biblical Annunciation according to Luke. The stylistic trope also signals, in poetic grandeur, a quasi-departure from the linear structure of the mainstream film by drawing attention to the cinematic transitions that comprise a bookends effect. This breach in illusionist structure has a payoff in the proclamation "The Queen is Dead, Long Live the Queen!," in a composition dominated by a large tree in the foreground that veritably dwarfs the crucial event that is both paradoxically pastoral and regal. However, the unorthodox use of this bracketing in the film, with the interjection of the brief white screen, suggests as much spirituality as virginity and so remains consistent with the themes explored in the film. The composition of the main shot in the bracketed sequence reinforces the separateness of Elizabeth, alone in the middle of the frame, with attending maids like a chorus of angels at a distance and the kneeling messenger also at a distance, bowing toward the new monarch. Elizabeth, in turn, proclaims her approval in a triumphant manner tapered with a caveat: "God has done this and we find it pleasing!" In referencing the Virgin Mary obliquely in this scene with the allusion of the Annunciation, Kapur acknowledges the multifaceted importance of the Virgin as metaphor. Kristeva concurs with the significance of the Virgin:

> Extending to the extra-linguistic regions of the unnamable, the Virgin Mother occupied the tremendous territory on this and that side of the parenthesis of language. She adds to the Christian trinity and to the Word that delineates their coherence the heterogeneity they salvage. (*Tales*, 250)

Kapur's interpretation of Elizabeth's jubilant assumption to Queen, with its overtones of biblical events (such as with the overtones of the Annunciation), signals the heterogeneity of the Virgin that England will salvage from Elizabeth in this period of unmitigated cathexis of the written word.

Heterogeneity, in its multifaceted and contrasting (even extra-logical) implications, surrounds the cult of the Virgin and the cult of Elizabeth. One example of this diverse scope of Elizabeth's existence is featured in her official virginal state juxtaposed with her documented relationship to Sir Robert Dudley, who is featured in legend and in the movie as Elizabeth's lover. In the one scene that shows them in the royal bed making love, the transparent drapes that surround the bed have eyes and ears painted on them in a reference to the Rainbow Portrait of Elizabeth, in which she wears a dress decorated with ears and eyes to represent the vigilance of her courtesans who inform her of the goings-on in the court. However, transferred to the Virgin Queen's bed, the reference is conflated with the surrealist enunciation of the maternal semiotic as much as the implication of courtesan voyeurs privy to Elizabeth's romantic interludes. In terms of the maternal semiotic, the eyes and ears, as disembodied organs and body parts, in conjunction with the sexual activity and a brief appearance of an aroused nipple, seem to reflect an argument that Kristeva presents referring to the Virgin Mary:

> The Virgin obstructs the desire for murder or devouring by means of a strong oral cathexis (the breast), valorization of pain (the sob), and incitement to replace the sexed body with the ear of understanding. (*Tales*, 257)

The drapes in the boudoir of Kapur's Virgin Queen contain the eye that sobs, the ear of understanding, and the corporal signifier of the oral cathexis. These objects are body-centered and precede the Symbolic because they reference the maternal semiotic and the return of the repressed. The film's pictorial emphasis on these signs of extra-logical and surrealist incongruity bolsters the film's theme of heterogeneity that colludes with, and flies in the face of, the Symbolic Order.

Soon, Elizabeth's reign suffers a derailment because her armies are defeated in Scotland. In her moment of anguish over this obvious sign connoting incompetence as leader, she falls to her knees, dejected, and vents her tears. Then she looks up to see a huge painting of her deceased father, King Henry VIII. Kapur skews the inspirational cliché subtly to lend emphasis to the strong influence of the maternal semiotic in Elizabeth's life. In front of the picture, and duplicated in the background, are positioned two cloth-covered statues of a form reminiscent of the Virgin with Child. The covering of the statues is a historical reference because images of the Virgin and the saints for Protestants were censored as objects of idolatry during the Reformation. The connection and implications between the elements in the composition are *uncanny*. The resi*dual*ity and semiotic display of the Virginal form, tethered as if an abject object prepared for disposal and yet preceding the Symbolic reference that is the colossal portrait of Henry VIII, itself an iconic (re)presentation of the Law of the Father, is mirrored, as if to reiterate the semiotic reference, in the background with a similar censored and camouflaged statue of the Virginal form. These elements of the composition conjure the pre-lingual developmental stage at the moment that the pre-subjective entity recognizes the outside presence of the third party, who is separate from the (m)Other, separate from the pre-lingual subject in process: and that is the father, the displaced phallus-to-be. The residue of the maternal object manifests itself in the abject signs: the rope like a severed umbilical cord inundates from the top of the frame; the decrepit cloth-covered shapes that contain soft lines and yet frighten because they contain cold stone and death; the dirt and filth of abandonment in the air as the subject in process slices herself from the jubilant Oedipal drama/trauma. Elizabeth, resolute, exits the scene, at once inspired by Henry's phallic posturing and yet bolstered in her connection to FEMININITY, the enunciation of the maternal semiotic.

Not long afterwards, however, the abject resurfaces as Elizabeth yields to violence against the Catholics who are conspiring for her downfall and a return of the Church's dominance in England. Walsingham, Elizabeth's joint secretary of state, starts a pogrom and we witness the death of a Catholic bishop while the cast shadow of a Virgin with Child is projected on the bloody wall, as if watching over the entire assassination as the slumped body bleeds out. The subsequent montage of state-sanctioned murders features the abject: the bishop flagellates his back to a bloody pulp; one of the treasonous victims sits on a communal wood-plank toilet attending to bodily functions; and another victim, Norfolk, is arrested while consorting with his mistress, who betrayed him to Walsingham, and then beheaded. Soon, and in a display of the abject and jouissance, the four dismembered heads of the prime traitors to Elizabeth are displayed on stakes in gruesome detail, setting up the culminating burst of semiotic Marianism in the movie.

In the aftermath of the pogrom, Elizabeth languishes in her chapel, tormented about her role as phallic Queen. Walsingham counsels her that "all men need something greater than themselves to look up to and to worship." Every shot in which Queen Elizabeth finds herself in this soul-searching scene contains Elizabeth's personal, and illicit, statue of the Virgin Mary with the Baby Jesus, except for one shot that is at the turning point when Elizabeth seems to heed the cryptic advice of her council, Walsingham. In that shot, the camera framing is the closest to Elizabeth and at her eye level, which is significant because all of the other shots of her are from a high angle looking down on her, as if from the point of view of a divine presence. The last shot of the sequence varies from this high-angle strategy, consisting of a close-up on the statue of the Virgin Mary's face from a low camera height and upward angle, replicating the relative position of Elizabeth looking up at the statue's face; however, the camera then cranes upward while tilting down, keeping the Virgin's stone face in the center of the frame. This is a curious strategy to end the sequence because it draws so much attention to itself. If we analyze the beginning of the shot as from Elizabeth's perspective, then the subsequent camera movement in the shot seems to give her an ability that exceeds the human—at the very least, it indicates that she is able to levitate. But since we cut away to another scene, the message seems to be more metaphorical, suggesting that Queen Elizabeth is about to self-elevate her stature at least to the level of, if not higher, than the Virgin Mary in the eyes of her citizenry, which she effectively accomplishes in a surprising display in the final scene of the film.

The soul-searching jouissance depicted in the above-described scene restores the pre-lingual singularity in Elizabeth's resolve, and its affect bleeds over into the sacrificial and the abject during the ultimate scene of the film. Elizabeth assumes the pedestal of worship figuratively and physically after taking a knife and sacrificing her hair, connoting the transformation from her earthly/carnal self to the god/dess anomaly that she becomes in mimetic display as the Virgin Queen. In this final scene, she crosses the great hall in stone-cold makeup as the members of her court follow her with their shocked and collusive eyes. She then mounts the raised platform to sit at her throne as resolute as the illicit, complicit statue of the Virgin in her private chapel. She has become alone amongst her sex: queen, mother, wife, and sibling, that is, in excess of a subject, a singularity in progress.

# Works Cited

Barthes, Roland. *Image, Music, Text*. New York: Hill and Wang, 1977.

Elliot, Anthony, ed. *Contemporary Social Theory.* Oxford: Blackwell Publishers, 1999.

Getty, Adele. *Goddess: Mother of Living Nature.* London: Thames and Hudson, 1990.

Ian, Marcia. *Remembering the Phallic Mother: Psychoanalysis, Modernism, and the Fetish.* Ithaca, NY: Cornell University Press, 1993.

Kristeva, Julia. *Powers of Horror.* New York: Columbia University Press, 1982.

—. *Revolution in Poetic Language.* New York: Columbia University Press, 1984.

—. *Tales of Love.* New York: Columbia University Press, 1987.

Levin, Carole. *The Heart and Stomach of a King: Elizabeth I and the Politics of Sex and Power.* Philadelphia: University of Pennsylvania Press, 1994.

Parker, Emma. "From House to Home: A Kristevan Reading of Michele Roberts's *Daughters of the House.*" *Critique* 41 (2000): 153.

Reineke, Martha. *Sacrificed Lives: Kristeva on Women and Violence.* Bloomington: Indiana University Press, 1997.

Shell, Mark. *Elizabeth's Glass.* Lincoln: University of Nebraska Press, 1993.

Shlain, Leonard. *The Alphabet Versus the Goddess: The Conflict Between Word and Image.* New York: Viking Penguin, 1998.

Silverman, Kaja. *The Acoustic Mirror: The Female Voice in Psychoanalysis and Cinema.* Bloomington: Indiana University Press, 1988.

Tyndale, William. *Tyndale's New Testament.* New Haven, CT: Yale University Press, 1989.

Warner, Marina. *Alone of All Her Sex: The Myth and the Cult of the Virgin Mary.* New York: Alfred A. Knopf, 1976.

# CHAPTER FOURTEEN

# PENETRATION, CONCEPTION, AND THE CREATION OF A SUBSERVIENT FEMALE: A MUSIC-IMAGE ANALYSIS OF *THE MATRIX*

# JACK M. BECKHAM II

David Luty, in his 1999 film review, dubbed Larry and Andy Wachowski's *The Matrix* (1999) "a contradiction in terms, a big-budget action/science-fiction epic that's also riveting, ambitious, and intelligent" (54). Judging from the quantity of scholarly material published about this film since its release, Luty's comment about the intelligence of the film has clearly been confirmed by academia. And one trope that has certainly been discussed in relation to the film is that of birth/reproduction. In this vein, I see Samuel Kimball's particularly keen article, "Conceptions and Contraceptions of the Future: *Terminator 2*, *The Matrix*, and *Alien Resurrection*," as an excellent springboard for a discussion of *The Matrix* in reproductive terms. However, whereas Kimball's analysis is grounded in image, I utilize an audio-visual framework to analyze the film and, while maintaining his conclusions, highlight important developments that are not addressed by focusing on image alone.

Although Kimball is analyzing three films, he establishes five critical points early in his article to create a unique theoretical framework with which to investigate notions of conception and contraception within them. First, Kimball discusses Louis Althusser's notion of interpellation, stating that subjects are hailed before they are born: our thinking of them—how they will bear their father's name, for example—creates their subjectivity. However, a couple's choice not to conceive also addresses the subject; thus, a subject can be hailed out of being before it is conceived. This example of "contraceptive interpellation" shows that subjection precedes birth (Kimball 72). Therefore, subjectivity should not be understood in terms of life and death.

Second, Kimball discusses Judith Butler in relation to Althusser and the possibility of both conceptive and contraceptive interpellations. Quoting from *Bodies that Matter*, Kimball states that human beings are interpellated into sexual difference. He goes on to discuss how this sexual difference is established through both identifications and disidentifications. In other words, in order to identify with something, it is necessary to identify against it: identification occurs in relation to what that identification would exclude or abject. The subject, then, is constituted through abjection which produces an outside to the subject that is also inside the subject.

Third, Kimball argues that the Western intellectual tradition has literalized the metaphor of thinking as conceiving. He asserts that this tradition has established thinking as heterosexual, specifically male, and thereby a force of life. Drawing upon Butler's argument about identification and disidentification, Kimball announces that this metaphor of thinking as conceiving forestalls another type of thought that, when expressed, will appear to be "contraceptive, abortive, infanticidal, alternatively as monstrous, deformed, and always apocalyptic" (73).

Fourth, he provides a brief history of Western philosophy and how the Western world has literalized the thought-as-conception metaphor. Thought as conception is traced back to Plato and Aristotle; whereas Plato uses conception as a figure of speech, Aristotle implies that thinking is literally a masculine conceptive activity. Further, Aristotle suggests that thinking, being generative, is "self-begetting," it is self-conceptive, which makes conceiving of the future difficult in any terms other than as a continuation of life (Kimball 76-77).

Kimball takes a fifth step via Darwin, stating that the inevitable role of any species, including humans, is extinction. If thinking is conceiving, then it is impossible to conceive of the future because it requires conceptualizing an existence without human subjectivities, which is not conceptive but, rather, a termination (Kimball 79). Therefore, to think of the future is to have a nonconceptive thought, which is marked by the combination of apocalypse and infanticide as it "bumps up against the conceptualizations that would block its articulation" (79).

Kimball's central argument, then, is that *Terminator 2* (1991), *Alien Resurrection* (1997), and *The Matrix* all try to conceive of the future but do so in contraconceptive terms: these movies incorporate infanticidal imagery into storylines that revolve around threats of apocalypse. Further, because human thought is conceptive, the antagonists in these films are viewed as necessarily evil, since their existence poses the threat of human extinction. He then proceeds to discuss each film in terms of conception and contraception.

In Kimball's analysis of *The Matrix*, he argues that the protagonists' impetus to rebel against the machines in the film is being motivated by a type of male hysteria, which is derived from Morpheus's (played by Laurence Fishburne) and Zion's inhabitants' inability to imagine a future without conception. The machines, then, pose a double threat. For the people inserted into the Matrix, thought as a masculine conceptive activity is subordinated to the thought-system supplied by the Matrix program; second, because humans are grown by the machines rather than born, humans are menaced by an extirpation of heterosexual conception. In order to make the future conceivable, the film "heterosexualizes its narrative climax" by focusing on Neo's (played by Keanu Reeves) and Trinity's (played by Carrie-Anne Moss) heterosexual love and her erotic hailing which leads to his rebirth; by professing her love and kissing Neo, Trinity awakens in him the "inseminating generativity of the Morpheus father figure" (Kimball 93). Kimball argues that this allows Neo to perform the heterosexual act of impregnating the Matrix by penetrating Agent Smith (played by Hugo Weaving), an extension of the maternal Matrix, at the end of the film, thereby forestalling the contraconceptive designs of the evil machines (92-93).

Yet there is something beyond (or underneath) the heteronormative narrative climax that must be teased out, something that cannot be clearly read by focusing on image alone. By utilizing an audio-visual framework to analyze the film, one will see that Trinity must do more than simply profess her love and kiss Neo to awaken what Kimball calls the inseminating generativity of the father. Trinity and Neo must switch gender positions, with Trinity ultimately assuming a subservient role, to establish the heteronormative conclusion that the film requires, and this transfer can be witnessed by investigating three acoustical elements of the film: (1) the musical theme associated with penetration; (2) the appropriation of Trinity's musical theme by Neo; and (3) Trinity's de-acousmatization.

## Penetration, Conception, and the Pious Choral Voice

Cynthia Freeland's article "Penetrating Keanu: New Holes, but the Same Old Shit" can shed some light on the significance of the musical theme associated with penetration. It probes the value of human flesh and bodies in *The Matrix* and *eXistenZ* (1999), with Freeland's central argument being that *eXistenZ* foregrounds "vulnerable and connected bodies" while *The Matrix* seeks to endorse a fantasy of overcoming human flesh. She states that, in *The Matrix*, "the hero moves from being 'penetrated' and connected to others, to being self-controlling and intact—even immune to bullets" (205). She then proceeds to bifurcate her discussion of the two films and focus on how each male protagonist is penetrated.

In a section titled "Penetrating Keanu in *The Matrix*," Freeland discriminates between "violent penetration" and "good penetration" (207-208). Agent Smith's impregnating Neo with the bug-like tracking device, Trinity's aborting the bug with a gun-like apparatus, and Neo's awakening to find his "real" body pierced by several black wires and tubes are all given as examples of violent penetration. The first time Neo is "plugged in" after taking the red pill is also a violent penetration: Neo gives a silent scream as the metal spike is inserted into the back of his skull and his consciousness is uploaded into what Morpheus calls "the construct."

In contrast to these penetrations, Freeland asserts that Neo's being perforated with the acupuncture-like needles used to regenerate his muscles in Scene 35 is an example of good penetration, which is "emphasized by the religious-sounding choral music on the soundtrack" (208). A more vivid description of this choral music comes from J. Bond, who describes it as "hypnotic soprano vocals against minimalistic, Phillip Glass-like ostinatos" (43). Clearly, the music associated with this penetration is starkly different from the choral music of "The Power Plant" in Scene 30. That scene, which Freeland describes as a example of violent penetration, seems (to me) to be scored with a combination of tenor and alto vocals that are sung fortissimo against accelerando and sforzando horns—what Jonathan Broxton calls "low blatting brasses" (33). The vocals cease abruptly as the horns begin fading into dissonance.

At the end of the film, after Neo is reborn, there is no longer any penetration; Freeland states that the new Neo is "perfect, exciting, ... intact, closed-up, with no openings or flaws, no vulnerability—in short, with no relationship to his actual physical flesh-and-blood body. He has superseded the physical reality of the flesh" (209). Interestingly, while she notes the choral music accompanying the good penetration of Neo by the acupuncture-like needles, she does not mention the similar choral music—what I would describe as pianissimo mezzo-soprano vocals against string ostinatos and horns—that is heard after Neo's resurrection and when he freezes the agent's bullets in midair in Scene 213. Freeland explains this phenomenon using images rather than music: Neo is "even immune to bullets" (205). More than being immune, Neo is no longer *able* to be penetrated. I disagree with Freeland's notion that Neo has lost the relationship with his real body; indeed, after Neo dispels Agent Smith, Trinity yells "Neo" to his corporeal body and he hears her call from within the Matrix. I suggest that his inability to be penetrated signifies his recent heterosexualization and masculinization, a necessary development if Neo is to (as Kimball suggests) impregnate the Matrix and thwart its contraceptive machinations. Therefore, the type of religious-sounding choral music Freeland associates with good penetration is employed precisely due to Neo's *inability* to be penetrated. Being masculinized by the heterosexual call of the now-subordinate Trinity allows him to become an agent of penetration, rather than an object of penetration. Accordingly, he penetrates Agent Smith and, by extension, the Matrix. Because this penetration will ultimately end the war between Zion and the machines—ensuring conception—it can be seen in terms of Neo's and Morpheus' male hysteria as a good penetration, which is precisely why it is associated with the similar sort of non-threatening, pious choral voices referenced earlier.

## Strings and Horns: Leitmotifs and Appropriation

But how does the female protagonist become the now-subordinate Trinity to which I am referring? Freeland discusses Trinity in terms of subservience. She observes that the film opens promisingly with Trinity being portrayed as a strong female character who, at times, takes the lead but ultimately is relegated to the status of the "babe" and "sidekick" (Freeland 209-210). Alternately, the Neo at the end of the film—as the agent of penetration and the heterosexual savior of conception—is certainly different from the film's earlier Neo, "with his delicate eyelids" looking "as 'pretty' as a girl when we first see him sleeping [with] very fair skin [and] no body hair," one who has been "raped and impregnated" by Agent Smith (Freeland 207; Kimball 90). Trinity's metamorphosis from an autonomous and powerful female to an ancillary subject, like Neo's transformation into the all-powerful hero, can best be witnessed in terms of sound: specifically, how Neo appropriates Trinity's musical theme.

In *Unheard Melodies*, Claudia Gorbman asserts that one can "see music as 'meaning,' or organizing discourse, on three different levels in any film" (12). First, "pure musical codes" refer to a composition's musical structure itself. Second, "cultural musical codes" evoke enculturated reactions from the audience. Finally, "cinematic musical codes" allude to the way "music in a film refers to the film—that is, [music] bears specific formal relationships to coexistent elements in the film" (13). And it is this final musical discourse that is key here: Gorbman defines a theme as "any music—melody, melody-fragment, or distinctive harmonic progression—heard more than once during the course of a film"; she states that themes include "'theme songs,' background instrumental motifs, tunes repeatedly performed by or associated with characters, and other recurring nondiegetic music" (26). In relation to *The Matrix*, these musical themes—also called leitmotifs—establish Trinity as a character more dominant than Neo at the beginning of the film. However, as the diegesis progresses, Neo slowly adopts a version of Trinity's theme until his and her leitmotifs are combined and jointly inscribed onto his body. This joint inscription allows for Neo to remain familiar by way of retaining his own original leitmotif but also signals that he has changed into the autonomous character necessary to inseminate the Matrix.

From the very beginning of the film, Trinity is portrayed, both visually and aurally, as a character associated with action. In fact, her phone call to Cypher (played by Joe Pantoliano) within the first ten seconds of Scene 1 initiates the sequence of events that unfolds to become the film itself; even her voice, then, is associated with action. This phone call is bracketed by brass instrumentation, as is Trinity's dodging gunfire and diving off a roof and into the closed window of an adjacent building moments later in Scene 10. J. Bond admits that the musical cut "Trinity Infinity" captured his attention immediately: Davis treats "a slow-mo shot of Moss's glistening black form sprinting toward the camera with an explosion of arrhythmic brass that made my hair stand on end" (43). And, for almost the entirety of the film, Trinity continues to be associated with brass instrumentation. Specifically, this leitmotif is heard four minutes and thirty-seven seconds into the film in Scene 10, and it lasts for about six seconds. The best way to describe this musical theme is as two horns moving in contrary motion.

Kathryn Kalinak suggests that horns are used in film as a musical convention to convey a particular mood or emotion. These conventions assist in forming what Gorbman refers to as cultural musical codes. Kalinak states that "horns, with their martial heritage, are [an] obvious example [of a musical convention]. Because of their link to pageantry, the military, and the hunt, horns are often used to suggest heroism" (13). Trinity, however, is not the only character to be linked to horns. When Morpheus's other rebels are engaged in action, such as fighting or fleeing from an agent, their movements are associated with brass instruments as well, which also helps to imbricate Trinity's leitmotif with action.

In contrast to the heroic brass sounds associated with Trinity, Neo's leitmotif is an ethereal-sounding combination of strings. The musical theme associated with him first occurs fifteen minutes and fifty-one seconds into the film in Scene 18, and it lasts for approximately twenty seconds. Neo's leitmotif can be described as mirroring strings playing an ostinato; by "mirroring," I mean that one set of orchestral strings (call them "string set A") begins playing a certain musical sequence which is picked up, in the same key and tempo, by another set of orchestral strings (call them "string set B") and repeated shortly thereafter. For example, if the musical figure being repeated is five seconds in length, when string set A is in the third second of the figure, string set B begins its first second of the same figure; this continues several times, creating the mirroring ostinato and causing the music to appear as a cyclical form trapped by its own self-referentiality.

Kalinak suggests that the string family, "because of its proximity in range and tone to the human voice, is thought to be the most expressive group of instruments in the orchestra. For this reason strings are often used to express emotion" (13). Therefore, the very nature of the instrumentation, based on cultural musical codes, assists in portraying Neo as a less dominant character than Trinity and seems to further validate Freeland's argument about Neo's gender identity being questionable.

Second, the orchestration—a cyclical figure trapped by its own self referentiality—suggests a sort of stasis and represents Neo's inability to act.

And, indeed, he *is* unable to act. The scene in which this music plays shows Neo pacing and frantic, noting the insanity of scaling the outside of a Chicago skyscraper and in a quandary about why authorities have arrived at his workplace to place an innocent nobody, such as himself, in custody. In other words, the music is mirroring his mind's reeling away from action: Morpheus explains that the window ledge is the only way to avoid leaving the building in the authorities' custody, but Neo does not want to perform this action. This musical theme is punctuated with a variation of Trinity's leitmotif, in a slightly lower key than before, when Neo decides to take action and step out onto the ledge, but the brass is quickly evacuated by the mirroring strings again when he is gripped with fear and becomes frozen into inaction upon the ledge.

Trinity's theme is revisited in the film when she takes the lead. For example, her heroic brass motif can be heard in Scene 115 when she takes action to save Neo. In this scene, Cypher, Morpheus, Neo, and Trinity have been ambushed and are attempting to escape by crawling down the main plumbing wall. Morpheus is captured by an agent and tells Trinity that she must ensure that Neo makes it out. Again, Neo is frozen into inaction. The shooting script states: "Neo suddenly glimpses what is happening but is powerless to stop it" (79). Trinity's theme is heard as she "grabs [Neo's] ankle and they begin almost falling using the lath as a brake, skidding down the inside of the wall" (80).

However, Neo eventually begins to act, breaking out of his static cycle and, when he does, he begins to appropriate Trinity's theme, similar to the way the brass briefly punctuates his leitmotif of inaction in Scene 18. In Scene B195, when Neo is fleeing from the agents towards the Heart O' the City Hotel, one can hear traces of the Trinity leitmotif layered into the orchestral score. By the end of the film, Trinity completely surrenders her agency to Neo. She faithfully sits by his corporeal body aboard the hovercraft, while Neo is now the one who is jumping off buildings and dodging bullets. Whereas Neo was originally associated with emotion via his leitmotif, Trinity becomes the character who is overwhelmed with emotions—professing her inner heart and love for Neo— when he is killed by Agent Smith.

This reversal is also witnessed musically in Scene 211, after Trinity has professed her love and Neo has been resurrected. The orchestration includes Neo's leitmotif of mirroring ostinatos, Trinity's leitmotif of heroic brass, and the choral sounds of good penetration discussed in Freeland's article. Thus, Neo is symbolized both aurally and visually as an autonomous individual (i.e., he can see through the Matrix rather than be governed by it) who possesses the agency necessary to penetrate the Matrix and maintain the conceptive thoughts and deeds of humankind.

## The Acousmêtre and De-acousmatization

The final aural element that illustrates how Trinity surrenders her authority to serve the symbolic order involves her "de-acousmatization," a term coined by Michel Chion. One of Chion's main arguments is how film theory lacks a unique language to describe the meanings created by the union of sound and image. Thus, a major endeavor of his work *Audio-Vision* is to provide a working vocabulary with which to "audio-visually" analyze film, television, video art, music videos, and other media forms in which sound and image are working interdependently.

Chion's term "acousmêtre" is useful in discussing Trinity's loss of power. Acousmêtre is defined as "a kind of voice-character specific to cinema that in most instances of cinematic narratives derives mysterious powers from being heard and not seen. See acousmêtres in *The Invisible Man, 1000 Eyes of Dr. Mabuse, The Wizard of Oz*" (Chion 221). As opposed to a voice-over, which is understood as operating outside the diegesis, an acousmêtre is usually heard as a voice-off. Kaja Silverman describes a voice-off as "exceed[ing] the limits of the frame, but not the limits of the diegesis; its 'owner' occupies a potentially recoverable space" (48). However, different than one who is simply absent from the frame, Chion suggests that one quality inherent in the acousmêtre is its ability to be "instantly dispossessed of its mysterious powers when it is *de-acousmatized*, when the film reveals the face that is the source of the voice" (130).

I argue that Trinity is a character initially infused with the power of the acousmêtre. And although she inevitably surrenders her agency to aid in Neo's masculinization, the film begins with Trinity being fused to the concept of action: as stated above, her phone call to Cypher in Scene 1 initiates the sequence of events that unfolds on the screen. Because the phone conversation from Scene 1 is a voice-off, Trinity is initially established with the mysterious powers of the acousmêtre. However, while she is acousmatized in the beginning of the movie, she is de-acousmatized in Scene 4 when she says "shit" (she was visible in Scene 2, but this is the first chance to connect her voice with the voice-off from Scene 1). In contrast, Morpheus remains acousmatized until Scene 28. With a boom of thunder that signifies an almost elemental power, Morpheus' exclamation of "at last!" permeates the mise-en-scene. While Trinity's de-acousmatization is uneventful, Morpheus' leads to a type of de-acousmatization of the entire world. Rather than being dispossessed of his mysterious powers, Morpheus continues to intrigue Neo and the audience with his cryptic and enigmatic speech. Reality—or at least Neo's and the audience's conception of reality—is what loses its mysterious powers, not Morpheus.

This difference in de-acousmatization also signals a shift of power away from Trinity. In contrast to Morpheus, she relinquishes her acousmatic powers in jejune fashion early in the film to serve his will. Therefore, Trinity's de-acousmatization can be seen in the following terms: Morpheus, a sort of father figure, instructs Trinity to surrender her power by entering the Matrix and contacting Neo, whom Morpheus wishes to "adopt." This, of course, will eventually require Trinity to relinquish the remainder of her power and serve the patriarchy as an ancillary female in order to resurrect Neo and facilitate a transfer of Morpheus's inseminating generativity into him.

## Conclusion

The acoustical elements discussed here by no means account for all of the intricacies that are operating at the level of sound-image. However, investigating these musical elements in relation to the arguments raised by Kimball and Freeland articulates not only how Hollywood conventions sublimate Trinity and gradually position her into the standard role of the subservient female when a male lead enters the mise-en-scene, but also how an audio-visual reading of film can provide a richer analysis than one that focuses on image alone. Precisely because *The Matrix* has garnered so much critical, popular, and technical praise, it is important to investigate its role as a cultural artifact that perpetuates patriarchy and delimits female subjectivity in popular culture's visual products. Of course, this would also partially account for the large body of scholarly texts devoted to examining the film. And as employing music-image theory allows for the investigation of a work from multiple and simultaneous entry points, this chapter has sought to flesh out existing criticism by utilizing such an approach.

## Works Cited

Bond, J. "The Matrix." *Film Score Monthly* 4.6 (1999): 43.

Broxton, Jonathan. "The Matrix." *Soundtrack!* 18 (1999): 33.

Butler, Judith. *Bodies That Matter: On the Discursive Limits of Sex*. London: Taylor and Francis, 1993.

Chion, Michel. *Audio-Vision*. Trans. Claudia Gorbman. New York: Columbia University Press, 1994.

Davis, Don. *The Matrix: Original Motion Picture Score*. Varése Sarabande, 1999.

Freeland, Cynthia. "Penetrating Keanu: New Holes, but the Same Old Shit." *The Matrix and Philosophy*. Ed. William Irwin. Chicago: Open Court, 2002. 205-215.

Gorbman, Claudia. *Unheard Melodies*. Indianapolis: Indiana University Press, 1987.

Kalinak, Kathryn. *Settling the Score: Music and the Classical Hollywood Film*. Madison: University of Wisconsin Press, 1992.

Kimball, Samuel. "Conceptions and Contraceptions of the Future: *Terminator 2*, *The Matrix*, and *Alien Resurrection*." *Camera Obscura* 17.2 (2002): 69-107.

Luty, David. "The Matrix." *Film Journal International* 102 (1999): 54-55.

*The Matrix: The Shooting Script*. New York: Newmarket Press, 2001.

Silverman, Kaja. *The Acoustic Mirror*. Indianapolis: Indiana University Press, 1988.

# CHAPTER FIFTEEN

## IS MALKOVICH MALKOVICH?
## SEXUAL IDENTITY ON A STRING

## SARAH E. S. SINWELL

Explicitly addressing ideas of identity and identification, subjectivity and stardom, sexuality and simulacra, Spike Jonze's 2000 film, *Being John Malkovich*, poses puppets as the means of finding out who we are, and a hole in John Malkovich's head as "an entry point into the eternal" (Chang 9). Like a number of U.S. independent films introduced around the same time period, such as Steven Soderbergh's *Schizopolis* (1997) and Christopher Nolan's *Memento* (2001), *Being John Malkovich* plays with the multiplicity of identification, constantly shifting sexualities, and complicated gender ambiguities. By breaking Classical Hollywood Cinema's narrative and stylistic codes, these films question the idea of the unified subject, sutured together by continuity editing, verisimilitude in the mise-en-scene, and unobtrusive cinematography and use of sound. However, what makes Jonze's film even more extraordinary is the ways in which it manipulates puppets as a means of exploring sexuality, stardom, and spectatorship.

Blurring the lines between the characters on screen and the spectators in the audience, the film continually asks, How can we know who to identify with? We are constantly asking ourselves, Who am I? Is this me? Is that Malkovich? Am I me? Is Malkovich Malkovich? At the same time, the film's representation of language, desire, and embodiment interpenetrates with ideas of fractured identity and subjectivity. Throughout this chapter, I explore the intersections of psychoanalysis and postmodernism as a means of approaching the relationship between simulacra and the soul.

As the curtains open and the orchestra tunes up, *Being John Malkovich* begins. A wooden marionette is revealed on stage. The marionette's strings and joints are not hidden as it dances. As viewers, we are conscious of the presence of the puppeteer although, as yet, we cannot see the man behind the strings. Upon seeing its own reflection in the mirror, however, the marionette (despite the fact that we might imagine its wooden face incapable of expressing such emotions) seems shocked, surprised, disturbed. The marionette breaks the mirror and various objects throughout the room/stage, looks at himself, at his hands, and realizes he is a puppet. He looks above and sees Craig Schwartz (played by John Cusack) controlling the strings. All of this is expressed not only through the movements and gestures of the puppet, but also through the movement of the camera and the editing. As the marionette dances/panics/rages, the film intercuts between shots of Craig and the marionette. The marionette's performance ends as we hear the audience's applause. The film calls attention to its own filmicness, its own status as representation, as Craig shuts off the tape recording that included both the music and the audience's applause, and we realize that this performance lacked a true audience. Slumped against the wall, the marionette is still performing, wallowing in its sadness. We are invited to identify with both the puppet and the puppeteer, subject and master, ideal and real.

From its opening sequence, *Being John Malkovich* invites us to analyze its references to identity and cinematic identification. This point in the film seems to explicitly allude to Jacques Lacan's idea of the mirror phase, not only because of the presence of the mirror on screen, but also because of the presence of the puppet itself. In "The Mirror Stage as Formative of the Function of the I as Revealed in Psychoanalytic Experience," Lacan reviews his analysis of the child's development from the age of six months, when the child begins to recognize his own image in the mirror. He notes that, through the mirror stage, the child is able to move from an understanding of his body as separate from the image to one in which he recognizes its unity and totality. In *Being John Malkovich*, the puppet expresses distress at the sight of his mirror image (and here, the mirror image is reflected both in the mirror itself, as well as in Craig Schwartz, since the puppet seems to physically resemble the puppeteer). Here, the puppet recognizes that it is, indeed, a puppet. Seeing its own mirror image forces it to recognize the real, for as Lacan writes, the function of the mirror stage is "to establish a relation between the organism and its reality" (4). Lacan also defines the mirror stage as an identification, an aspect that, in this film, implies not only the puppet's identification with Craig and Craig's identification with the puppet, but the audience's identification as well.

*Being John Malkovich* constantly plays with ideas of identification. As we watch the opening of the film, are we to identify with the puppet whose character seems most linked to the camera, with Craig who we know controls the strings, or with John Cusack as a star? One means of approaching these questions is through Christian Metz's proposition, from *The Imaginary Signifier*, that there are two types of cinematic identification. For Metz, primary identification entails identification with the look of the camera and projector, whereas secondary identification entails identification with the actor, character, or star. However, the film questions even our identification with the unseen (but heard) audience by revealing that the sound of the audience's clapping is not real, but rather a recording. Thus, who are we to identify with? This is a question with which we must continue to grapple throughout our viewing of the film, as we are asked to identify not only with a puppet, but rather with a multitude of puppets, a chimp, John Malkovich, and a number of people who enter John Malkovich's head.

Identification can also be described as the search for similarities, particularly between the characters on screen and oneself. In "A Denial of Difference: Theories of Cinematic Identification," Anne Friedberg points out that "the process of identification is one of denying the difference between self and other. It is a drive that engages the pleasure of sameness" (40). When Craig Schwartz creates a puppet in his own image, he is attempting to express through his puppet what he cannot express through his own body. He tells his pet chimpanzee, Elijah, "You don't know how lucky you are being a monkey. Because consciousness is a terrible curse. I think. I feel. I suffer." And, yet, he cannot express those thoughts, feelings, and sufferings in front of others, only in the confines of his own home, and only through the movements of a puppet. If Craig himself had performed a "Dance of Despair and Disillusionment," we would find it socially taboo; but, as we shall see later in the film, in the guise of a puppet's performance, especially one in which the strings are held by a star, it is considered not only acceptable, but also creative and fascinating.

The idea of identification as a means of erasing difference and enjoying sameness can be linked to Jean Baudrillard's idea of the simulacrum. For Baudrillard, one of the characteristics of the postmodern era is that the difference between one and the other is disappearing (521). This erasure of difference can be revealed not only in the lack of separation between self and Other, but also between having and not having, between the real and the imaginary, between active and passive, between truth and fiction. In *The Secret Life of Puppets*, Victoria Nelson not only explicitly links the simulacra to puppets, but also to Baudrillard's notion of difference. She writes, "The simulacra functions as our evil twin, our alter ego, repository of all we refuse to acknowledge in ourselves" (262). Thus, Craig's use of puppets functions as a replacement for his own repressed desires; through the simulacrum of the puppet, he shares those desires which he is afraid to reveal on his own. Throughout this work, as I continue to analyze *Being John Malkovich*, I will continue to forge connections between real and imaginary, psychoanalysis and postmodernism, identity and identification, subjectivity and simulacrum.

The 7-1/2 floor of the Mertin Flemmer Building and Craig's filing job at Lestercorp also indicate the incorporation of mise-en-scene and language into this simulacrum. Because there are no jobs for puppeteers advertised in the classified section of the newspaper, Craig responds to the ad that is "Looking for a Man with Fast Hands." On the 7-1/2 floor of the Mertin Flemmer Building, where the ceilings are low enough not to dwarf "an adult lady of miniature proportions," Craig first meets Dr. Lester's secretary, who cannot understand a word Craig says. Then, upon meeting Dr. Lester (played by Orson Bean), Craig is given a test of his filing skills in which he is told to say which letter comes first. When Craig passes the test by pointing out that one of the letters is not a letter at all, he is given the job. As a result, Craig is also invited into Dr. Lester's "tower of indecipherable speech," for the secretary also misunderstands Dr. Lester, who therefore assumes he has a speech impediment. In this world, letters are confused with non-letters, language with nonsense. Even elements of time and space converge, for the ceilings on the 7-1/2 floor are so low that all but the tiniest people have to crouch in order to walk around. Indeed, the mise-en-scene in the Mertin Flemmer Building adds to our confused state of identification. For how can we identify with not only a puppeteer looking for work, but one who works under such bizarre circumstances? Whereas for Lacan, the entrance into the realm of language is one in which one journeys into the symbolic order, Nelson links this confusion—"bodily deformation, the decomposition of human speech, and the collapse of time and space" (114)—to the journey into madness.

Even Craig's attempt to find out Maxine's (played by Catherine Keener) name evokes notions of the entrance into the symbolic order, language, and madness. Upon asking Maxine if she will go out with him if he can guess her name, he finds her name through a bizarre manipulation of every woman's name he can think of, from "Bar-Ro-Bam-Kar-Sher..." to "Maxine." Throughout this scene, we see extreme close-ups of Craig's lips as he continues to converse, using Maxine's name unnecessarily over and over again. Thus, the film breaks with the continuity-editing system that it has privileged throughout the film up to this point and, as in the opening sequence, reminds us of the existence of the cinematic apparatus itself. As a response, we, as spectators, are caught between two poles. On the one hand, we are drawn into this mad world because we want to identify with the characters. At the same time, however, the film distances us as spectators by breaking the narrative and cinematic codes that are typical of the classical Hollywood system.

After meeting Maxine for a drink, Craig returns home to his wife, Lotte (played by Cameron Diaz), and to his workshop, where he (re)enacts a conversation with Maxine using Puppet-Craig and Puppet-Maxine.

PUPPET-MAXINE: Tell me, Craig. Why do you love puppeteering?
PUPPET-CRAIG: Well, Maxine, I'm not sure exactly. Perhaps it's the idea of being someone else for a while. Being inside another skin. Thinking differently. Moving differently. Feeling differently.
PUPPET-MAXINE: Interesting, Craig. Would you like to be inside my skin? Think what I think? Feel what I feel?

PUPPET-CRAIG: More than anything, Maxine.

After this dialogue, the puppets kiss as the camera circles around them in a parody of a Hollywood kiss. The camera cuts to a shot of Craig controlling the strings (seemingly to assure us of his connection to this fantasy) and we hear the voice-off of the real Maxine saying, "You're not someone I could get interested in, Craig. You play with dolls." When Craig attempts to use the dialogue he'd already rehearsed in his workshop, referring again to "the idea of being in someone else's skin and seeing what they see and feeling what they feel," Maxine responds with "Yikes."

In this sequence, reenacting the puppetry play performed in his workshop does not work. Maxine is not the puppet ideal that can be so easily manipulated with just a pull of the string, but rather a real person with her own will and opinions. We are again brought back to Baudrillard's simulacrum; he writes that "to simulate is to feign to have what one doesn't have" (522). The Craig and Maxine puppets function here not as replacements for the real, but as forms of wish-fulfillment for Craig. Through the puppets, Craig not only pretends to have Maxine, but he also pretends that Maxine would want to have him. This scene can also be linked to Friedberg's idea of identification. She writes:

> The process of identification is designed to encourage a denial of one's identity, or to have one construct identity based on the model of the other, mimetically repeating, maintaining the illusion that one is actually inhabiting the body of the ego ideal. (44)

However, Craig's denial of his identity and construction of the ego ideal are not limited to his performances in the puppet workshop. In the body of John Malkovich, Craig finds the perfect puppet ideal.

In the "deep storage" room, behind a filing cabinet, lies a tiny door that "takes you inside John Malkovich." Craig is the first of many in the film to enter this portal. After we see him slide down into the tunnel, the film cuts to a masked shot of someone reading *The Wall Street Journal*, eating toast, drinking coffee. It is only when we see this person look at his own image in the mirror that we realize that we are *within* John Malkovich (who is playing himself). He is even performing in front of the mirror, fixing his tie, checking his smile. Yet, this experience is so banal that in the middle of this out-of-body/in-the-body experience, the film cuts to a shot of Maxine on the telephone, rather than allowing us to see every moment of the world through Malkovich's eyes. Eventually, we return to "being" John Malkovich as he gets into a taxi. Though he is recognized as a famous actor, he is misidentified as Mapplethorpe and then as a character from a jewel-thief movie Malkovich himself insists he was never in. Again, the banality of being John Malkovich is emphasized when Craig is spit out into a ditch on the side of the New Jersey Turnpike (can you imagine a more banal location?) after his fifteen-minute ride is over.

We are returned to the "real" as Craig barges into Maxine's office to share his experience. Maxine's first words are, "Sounds great. Who the fuck is John Malkovich?" Neither Maxine nor Craig can name any of the films John Malkovich has starred in. As spectators, we are enveloped into this other world. Our consciousness of Malkovich's own star persona reflects upon our interpretation of the film. Can we, as viewers, recall the title of the jewel-thief film? Does it exist at all? Here, we are immersed in a simulacrum of identification. Are we to identify with Craig, with Craig within Malkovich, with Malkovich himself?

While we are in the mind of Malkovich, we not only identify with Malkovich but we *become* him, as the title of the film implies. As Dana Dragunoiu writes:

> The camera's radically subjective point of view when representing Malkovich's perspective suggests that the spectator does not merely identify with the male hero on screen but becomes him, controlling his thoughts and actions. (9)

Yet, it is not only the camera that allows us to become Malkovich, it is also our association with his star persona, and our immersion within the text of the film itself. As Craig Schwartz proposes, his trip into the mind of John Malkovich "raises all sorts of philosophical-type questions, you know, about the nature of the self, about the existence of a soul, you know. Am I me? Is Malkovich Malkovich?"

Just as Craig enjoys being in Malkovich's body because it is not his own, we, too, as spectators, enjoy being in Craig/Malkovich's body because it is not our own. As Friedberg writes, the pleasure of spectatorship lies not in identifying with our own image on screen, but rather our pleasure stems from denial. "The star's body is not the subject's body" (42). Indeed, we are in a simulacrum of different bodies at the same time; we are not only within Craig and Malkovich's bodies as characters within the film, but we are within the body of a famous actor, we are *being* John Malkovich. And, yet, is Malkovich's body a grotesque body? In *The Secret Life of Puppets*, Victoria Nelson references Mikhail Bakhtin's formulation of the grotesque body, "a body in the act of becoming. It is never finished, never completed; it is continually built, created, and builds and creates another body" (114). For Malkovich's body is continually in the act of becoming another self, not just another body. When Craig's wife, Lotte, "does" Malkovich, we are again forced to address the notion of the body and its becoming (female).

When Lotte first enters Malkovich, she sees herself/himself in the shower. She finds it sexy to be him, to feel him, to see him. She tells Craig, "Being inside did something to me. I knew who I was," to which Craig replies, "You weren't you. You were John Malkovich." Again, we are reminded of Lacan's mirror stage. For as Peter Lehman writes, "A male's development through the mirror stage establishes a powerful mechanism for pleasure in looking at the male body" (21). The pleasure here is given to the female within the male body, for when Craig entered Malkovich, he did not seem to long to be within Malkovich's body as Lotte does.

Lotte says, "I think it's kind of sexy that John Malkovich has a portal.... It's like he has a penis *and* a vagina. It's sort of like Malkovich's feminine side. I like that." Lotte likes being within Malkovich not just because she can be a man, but because she can be a man and a woman at the same time. She is attracted to both the masculine and feminine sides of Malkovich. Yet, there are "Some Psychical Consequences of the Anatomical Distinction Between the Sexes."

The division between masculine and feminine, active and passive, voyeurism and exhibitionism, sadism and masochism, thinking and feeling, is not as clear-cut and certain as our culture seems to imply. Rather, all human individuals (not just John Malkovich and the characters within *Being John Malkovich*) have both masculine and feminine characteristics. As Rosalind Minsky notes in *Psychoanalysis and Culture: Contemporary States of Mind*:

> The pure, biologically determined binary identities of "masculinity" and "femininity," historically purveyed by culture, are largely non-existent because children of both sexes are bisexual.... What culture calls "masculinity" and "femininity" emerge as forms of identity which refuse to be confined inside the boundaries of male and female bodies, leaving men and women as inherently bisexual mixtures of gender. (80)

Indeed, "pure masculinity and femininity remain theoretical constructions of uncertain content" (Minsky 77). The pure categories of gender rarely exist, if at all. *Being John Malkovich* plays with ideas of gender construction, bisexuality, and subjectivity through the simulacrum. It isn't simply that there is no longer a separation between self and Other, between Craig and Malkovich, between Lotte and Malkovich, but that fusion is occurring across gender boundaries. In fact, the entry into Malkovich is often described using sexual language. Maxine calls Craig her "man on the inside"—inside John Malkovich and, later, inside her *as* John Malkovich. Lotte asks Maxine, "Have you done Malkovich yet?," implying the sexual nature of entering his portal, explicitly compared to a vagina earlier in the film.

After being John Malkovich, not only does Lotte decide that she is a transsexual and wants to be a man, but Maxine decides that she wants

Malkovich only when Lotte is in his body. She tells Lotte, "Behind the stubble and the too-prominent brow and the male-pattern baldness, I sensed your feminine longing." Maxine wants Lotte-in-Malkovich. She even calls Malkovich "Lotte" as they are making love. Malkovich says he doesn't really mind. All of the characters are playing with gender-shifting, demonstrating the bisexuality that stems from within all of us. Minsky brings up "the issue of the extent to which passion depends on the repression of aspects of our gender so that our passions are ignited only by finding what we have unconsciously repressed in oneself, in the other" (82). Through Malkovich, both Lotte and Maxine discover what they were truly craving, both masculinity and femininity.

At the same time, however, we cannot forget how Malkovich's star persona fits into this narrative of desire, bisexuality, and subjectivity. It could be argued that much of the popularity and criticism that *Being John Malkovich* has received stems from the star's inclusion within the title, as well as the inclusion of stars such as John Cusack and Cameron Diaz within the film itself. Indeed, Cynthia Baron proposes that John Malkovich's popularity can be explicitly linked to his ambiguous sexual star persona. In her 2002 article "Buying John Malkovich: Queering and Consuming Millennial Masculinity," she proposes that "John Malkovich is a bankable media commodity because his star image plays into contemporary interest in ambiguous sexualities and gender identities" (18). Defined by the way his filmic identity functions as a pastiche of masculine and feminine traits, in *Being John Malkovich*, Malkovich conflates real and imaginary, truth and fiction, subject and object, inside and outside, mind and body, textual and extra-textual.

The first time we see Malkovich in the film without the trope of the eye mask that indicates someone else is within him, he is reading his lines in an exaggerated and "theatrical" manner. The film calls attention to his status as not only a star, but one that is identified with the theater as well as Hollywood. This identification reveals that he is a "real actor" who performs live and on stage, not only on the screen. Additionally, earlier in the film, the cabdriver also puts Malkovich's queer public image on display for us as viewers when he mistakes him for Mapplethorpe. Throughout the film, Malkovich's bisexuality is exemplified not only in his willingness to be called Lotte within the narrative itself, but also through the ways in which his star persona crosses gender boundaries extra-textually.

In an interview following the film's release, screenwriter Charlie Kaufman explained that Malkovich "was the writer's first choice…partly because of how funny his name sounds in repetition" (31). I imagine Kaufman had the scene in which Malkovich enters his own portal in mind when Malkovich was being cast for the film. For once Craig discovers that he can control Malkovich—forcing him to touch Maxine's breast and even making him speak; noting that "It's just a matter of practice before Malkovich is nothing but another puppet hanging next to my worktable"—Malkovich himself realizes that someone is controlling him and finds his way to JM, Inc. by following Maxine. He then insists on entering his own portal. When this happens, we see Malkovich's world through Malkovich's own eyes; again, the trope of the mask is used to indicate his subjective point of view. The scene links language to his subjectivity, because the only word in this world is "Malkovich" ("Malkovich" is even the only thing on the menu). In this subjective world, not only is Malkovich the only word used, but the only self is Malkovich: as a woman in a red dress, as a waiter, as himself, as a lounge singer. After he falls into a ditch by the New Jersey Turnpike, he tells Craig, "That was no simulation. I have been to the dark side. I have seen a world that no man should see…. It's my head, Schwartz." He notes that the experience Schwartz is selling for two hundred dollars a pop is real, not simulated, though it is the simulacrum at work, blurring truth and fiction, self and other, real and imaginary.

Again, the film calls attention to Malkovich's star persona as a fan drives by in a car off the turnpike and hurls a can at his head, yelling "Hey, Malkovich, think fast." One cannot help but notice that Malkovich's own personality must also have had something to do with the fact that he was chosen; few actors in Hollywood would be so willing to place themselves in his position (picture, if you will, Tom Cruise singing, "Cruise, Cruise, Cruise…").

*Being John Malkovich* again seems to explicitly reference Lacan's mirror phase and psychoanalytic theory in light of Lotte's relationship with her chimp, Elijah. When Craig locks Lotte up with Elijah, so that he can meet surreptitiously with Maxine as Malkovich yet again, we discover that Elijah really does have "feelings of inadequacy as a chimp," that the source of his ulcer is repressed childhood trauma. As Elijah looks at Lotte struggling with her tied wrists, the film cuts to Elijah's unconscious, specifically to a scene in which his family is attempting to untie the ropes they are captured in before the hunters/poachers/scientists(?) return. The subtitles translating the chimpanzees' screeching even indicate that his real name is Elijah. He recognizes his own image in that of Lotte and frees her from her binds. Thus, not only does the film allow us to search deep within our own psyches, within the psyches of the characters of the film, and within the psyche of the star, but also within the psyche of a chimpanzee. Indeed, it seems that even chimps can discover their repressed memories and their own totality and real past through the mirror image—here, through the image of the one he loves in binds.

Once she is freed, Lotte searches for Dr. Lester and discovers the secret of his eternal youth. He can live forever by leaping from vessel to vessel; indeed, he will be leaping into the "Malkovich vessel" on his forty-fourth birthday. If he fails to enter the vessel by midnight, he will be diverted into the infant vessel, "absorbed," "trapped, held prisoner in the host's brain, unable to control anything, forever doomed to watch the world through someone else's eyes." Thus, Lotte, Dr. Lester, and his friends wait for the chance to enter Malkovich's portal.

By the end of the film, Craig has made friends with the Malkovich body and completely taken it over. The proof is performed when Maxine asks him to do a puppet show for her with Malkovich. He repeats "Craig's Dance of Despair and Disillusionment," replacing the actual puppet he had used in the film's first scene with Malkovich's own body. This is one of the most astounding scenes in the film. As spectators, we believe that Malkovich is performing as a puppet. As in the opening scene, there is no diegetic sound of yelling, glass breaking, objects falling to the ground, only the music on the recording. Malkovich is a puppet who cannot speak, except through Craig himself. And, Maxine concurs, it's not just playing with dolls, "It's playing with people." Following his performance, Craig-Malkovich announces that he will use Malkovich's existing notoriety to launch his own puppeteering career. "From now on, the name John Malkovich will be synonymous with puppets," he explains.

Eight months later, Maxine is pregnant and Craig/Malkovich is watching a documentary of himself on TV. The documentary traces the life of "the man who reinvented how we view puppeteering," "the man behind the strings and the woman behind the man." The documentary, like *Being John Malkovich* itself, intersperses fantasy with reality. It reminds us of actual elements of Malkovich's career, his involvement in the Steppenwolf Theatre, and his performances in *Death of a Salesman* and *Dangerous Liaisons*. But then, the film includes an interview with Sean Penn, who mourns that perhaps he will be perceived as an imitator if he moves into puppeteering too quickly. Finally, Malkovich is seen teaching a Puppetry Master Class at Juilliard, where he urges his students that "Until the puppet becomes an extension of you, it's a novelty act." The film notes that "Malkovich shows us a reflection of ourselves, our frailties, and our desperate humanity." As Nelson writes, "Manipulation of the puppet would require total identification of operator and puppet: the operator himself would have to dance" (62). Indeed, Malkovich dances when Craig dances; Malkovich is not only an extension of Craig, he *is* Craig. Yet, if Malkovich is a reflection of ourselves, who are we? Would we have made the same choices that Craig made? Would we, too, have the world on a string?

In an attempt to force Craig to leave Malkovich's body so they can enter it, Dr. Lester kidnaps Maxine. When Lotte confronts Maxine, both Maxine and Lotte enter Malkovich's portal, his subconscious. Malkovich's subconscious includes all of the stereotypical Freudian moments from the childhood past. He witnesses the primal scene; he rocks in his basement, repeating "I am bad, I am bad" over and over again to himself; he sniff's women's underwear; he is teased. Then, both Lotte and Maxine end up on the side of the New Jersey Turnpike just before Craig himself leaves Malkovich's body, finally deciding that he will save Maxine's life though it never needed to be saved. Just in time, Dr. Lester and his friends enter Malkovich.

Seven years later: Lotte and Maxine play with their daughter, Emily, on the beach (Lotte-as-Malkovich is the father). Craig looks at Maxine through Emily's eyes and tells her to look away. But, she doesn't. He can't control her. He entered the Malkovich portal too late and is now doomed to spend eternity looking at Maxine, and the world, through Emily's eyes. As the closing credits roll on screen, we are invited to swim through all eternity within the body of Emily, imagining ourselves in Craig's position, as a prisoner trapped in her subconscious. Thus, jumping from body to body, from subjectivity to subjectivity, becomes not only an emancipatory opportunity but also a risk: that in replacing someone else's subjectivity, one might lose one's own.

Indeed, one of the aspects of the film that Nelson brings to mind in *The Secret Life of Puppets* is the relationship between simulacra and the soul. For Nelson, "In the history of puppets...we can read—in a backward image, like a reflection in a mirror—the underground history of the soul" (31). As we watch *Being John Malkovich*, we tend to get caught up in the self-reflexivity of the narrative and forget the metaphysical can of worms it has opened. For in being John Malkovich—by exploring identity, identification, stars, psychoanalysis, and postmodernism—we have discovered the secret to eternal life.

## Works Cited

Baron, Cynthia. "Buying John Malkovich: Queering and Consuming Millenial Masculinity." *Velvet Light Trap* 49 (2002): 18-38.
Baudrillard, Jean. "The Precession of Simulacra." *Media and Cultural Studies.* Ed. Meenakshi Gigi Durham and Douglas M. Kellner. Malden, MA: Blackwell Publishers, 2001. 521-549.
Chang, Chris. "Head Wide Open." *Film Comment* 35 (1999): 6-9.
Dragunoiu, Dana. "Psychoanalysis, Film Theory, and the Case of *Being John Malkovich.*" *Film Criticism* 26 (Winter 2001-2002): 1-18.
Friedberg, Anne. "A Denial of Difference: Theories of Cinematic Identification." *Psychoanalysis and Cinema.* Ed. E. Ann Kaplan. New York: Routledge, 1990. 36-45.
Lacan, Jacques. "The Mirror Stage as Formative of the Function of the I as Revealed in Psychoanalytic Experience." *Ecrits: A Selection.* Trans. Alan Sheridan. London: Tavistock Publishers Ltd., 1977. 1-7.
Lehman, Peter. *Running Scared: Masculinity and the Representation of the Male Body.* Philadelphia: Temple University Press, 1993.

Metz, Christian. *The Imaginary Signifier: Psychoanalysis and the Cinema.* Trans. Celia Britton, Annwyl Williams, Ben Brewster, and Alfred Guzzetti. Bloomington: Indiana University Press, 1977.

Minsky, Rosalind. *Psychoanalysis and Culture: Contemporary States of Mind.* New Brunswick, NJ: Rutgers University Press, 1998.

Nelson, Victoria. *The Secret Life of Puppets.* Cambridge, MA: Harvard University Press, 2002.

# Part V
## Gay Men on Film and Video

CHAPTER SIXTEEN

BLURRING THE LINES OF SEXUALITY AND
PATRIARCHAL POWER: ALTERNATIVE POWER
STRUCTURES IN *MY OWN PRIVATE IDAHO*

CHRISTINE E. PACE

Gus Van Sant's film *My Own Private Idaho* (1991) raises many questions about gay men and the male-dominated society of the patriarchy. It blurs the lines of masculinity and sexuality by featuring a group of male hustlers who do not easily fall into a definition of gay or straight. In order to decode this symbolic masterpiece, the usual categories used to evaluate cultural notions—such as race, class, gender, and sexual orientation—hold little relevance to deciphering the underlying implications of its cultural dynamics. However, the theories of Fredric Jameson and Roland Barthes allow an interpretation of this film to emerge without a need for objectivity or authorial intent. The subject's uncovering of the characters' and the film's political unconscious contribute to discovering this work's cultural significance. With these interpretative tools, a dialogue centered on the binary opposition of patriarchy/anti-patriarchy surfaces which not only questions the male-dominated society, but also the problematic role of gay men in U.S. society's cultural politics.

In summary, this road movie, based loosely on William Shakespeare's *Henry V*, tracks two hustlers, Mike Waters (played by River Phoenix) and Scott Favor (played by Keanu Reeves), on a quest to discover their identities amongst their divergently dysfunctional families. It opens with a definition of the word "narcolepsy": "a condition characterized by brief attacks of deep sleep." We soon discover that Mike suffers from this disorder and falls asleep during various stressful situations. We also learn that Scott comes from a powerful family, one that values wealth and status above all else. Scott's father is the mayor of Portland, and he is completely opposed to his son's hustler lifestyle. Following the themes of *Henry IV*, Scott plans to renounce his devious life as a hustler once he reaches his twenty-first birthday and inherits his father's fortune. With his birthday just a week away, the leader of the street boys, Bob Pigeon (played by William Richert), hopes to benefit from Scott's newfound wealth and prosperity.

Amid the hustlers' dates (with both men and women), robberies, and excursions, Mike discovers a need to reconnect with his family and find his long-lost mother. Thus begins Mike and Scott's road trip to Idaho in order to find Mike's brother, who turns out to be not only his brother, but his father as well. Mike and Scott continue their search on the road and travel eventually to Rome, where the trail to Mike's mom is lost and Scott meets the woman of his dreams, abandoning Mike. We soon discover that Scott's father has died and Scott is ready to abandon his excessive lifestyle in order to assume his proper role in the patriarchy.

In interpreting this film, the theories of Fredric Jameson and Roland Barthes serve well to help decode the unconscious underpinnings of the film's cultural politics with a study of the subject and not the object. Jameson's shift in emphasis differs from that of other academic disciplines which encourage objectivity. In his work *The Political Unconscious: Narrative as Symbolic Act*, he contends that exposing the paths of interpretive categories leads to the revealing of the political unconscious of a work, which is more beneficial to scholarship than a study of the forms or content of a text (Jameson 9).

Jameson's conception of the political unconscious has empowered scholarship with a mode of interpretation that is meant to be self-reflective. Interpretation of any piece will inject into the discourse at hand the presuppositions of the individual involved in the act of deduction. Jameson argues:

> The political unconscious accordingly turns on the dynamics of the act of interpretations, and presupposes, as its organizational fiction, that we never really confront a text immediately, in all its freshness as a thing-in-itself. Rather, texts come before us as the always-already-read; we apprehend them through sedimented layers of previous interpretations, or—if the text is brand-new— through the sedimented reading habits and categories developed by those inherited interpretive traditions. (9-10)

Therefore, the act of interpretation does not lead us to a creation of something new and original, but rather recreates something that has already been read with the use of the tools or codes that we choose.

In a similar vein as Jameson, Barthes, in *Image, Music, Text*, endorses the importance of the reader (or, in this case, the viewer) of the artifact more than the relevance of the author. The author creates a foreclosure on the subject of the text and the fortified language becomes cemented within itself, protected from interpretations. Barthes explains:

> Once the Author is removed, the claim to decipher a text becomes quite futile. To give a text an Author is to impose a limit on that text, to furnish it with a final signified, to close the writing. Such a conception suits criticism very well, the latter then allotting itself the important task of discovering the Author (or its hypostases: society, history, psyche, liberty) beneath the work: when the Author has been found, the text is "explained"—victory to the critic. (147)

According to Barthes, in order to open the text to the status of signifier rather than signified, the author must be removed from the variable of study. To transplant the author out of the equation allows the reader a space for interpretation and allegorical analysis. Barthes concludes, "The birth of the reader must be at the cost of the death of the Author" (148). In other words, Barthes gives the reader authority to enter the dialogue of the established writing and render interpretations without limit.

With Barthes' criteria for interpretation and the framework of Jameson, *My Own Private Idaho* can effectively be analyzed. One of the important dialogues in this film involves the role of the patriarchy for men who are not members of its traditional power structure. The movie questions this masculine order of society under the leadership of the almighty father. According to theorist Kaizaad Kotwal, the binary opposition of patriarchy/anti-patriarchy comes to light with the character of Scott Favor (5). He argues, "Scott's refusal of his father's power symbolizes his rejection of the larger social patriarchy at hand" (2). In essence, the patriarchy and the anti-patriarchy differ in the ways the dominant males in a society utilize their power. In the patriarchy, power resides in an unemotional control of money and political sway, while the anti-patriarchal structure uses love and pleasure as a means of control. This noteworthy dimension represents a political unconscious of the film.

When the film first introduces Scott, he appears well dressed and well mannered, but when Scott succumbs to his father's summoning, he appears disheveled and delinquent. His father wonders what he has done to deserve such a son, and he wishes for him to accept his role in the capitalistic order. Scott asserts that once he is needed to fulfill his role in the patriarchy, he will rise to the occasion. Scott then reaches toward his father for an embrace, which causes a flutter in the man's failing heart, illustrating the lack of caring in this strong, male figure. Therefore, Scott's power to love has overtaken the love of power, which his father represents.

The leader of the hustlers, Bob, represents the political unconscious of the anti-patriarchy. While Mayor Favor emanates respect and power, the followers of Bob perceive their leader to be a lovable joke, one who exerts his power through love. Bob leads his flock of social and sexual "deviants" as their "psychedelic papa" and acknowledged king of the streets. Scott, as the favored "son" of Bob, assumes the position of prince to the group of deviants. Although the kingdom of Bob represents an anti-patriarchic system, it still contains a social order, with Scott as Bob's second. There seems to be a genuine bond of love between Bob and Scott that is not seen between Mayor Favor and his son.

The emotion that Scott expresses to his psychedelic papa does not fit neatly into the patriarchic system. This expression generates another binary opposition of emotion/money. Here, the power of love is juxtaposed with the power of wealth. For example, when the police and a member of Mayor Favor's group discover Scott at Bob's headquarters, he jumps into bed and simulates a sexual act with Mike. Scott consciously plays on the fears of his father, which transforms Scott into the manifestation of the fear hidden in his father's political unconscious. Not only is his father represented as unemotional, but he also appears physically impotent in his wheelchair, which reveals that Mayor Favor's ability to love has been foreclosed. The political unconscious of Scott and his father involves a contest for superiority; the chest pains of Mayor Favor demonstrate that he has been overpowered by his son.

Outside of this situation, Scott represents a paradox to the emotion/money binary. Although Scott states to both of his fathers that he will return to his expected birth role when the time has come, his siding with wealth over love calls into question the degree to which Scott is truly separated from the patriarchy's ideology. While he verbally expresses his feelings of love to Bob, he also denies the act of homosexual sex when money is not involved. In the magazine scene featuring a number of the boys posing as cover models for pornographic publications, Scott talks about the advantages of doing such photos. He then goes on to express fear that the photographer might want more than just pictures. He declares that he would not want to take part in a sexual exchange with the photographer unless it involved money. This statement makes trouble for the idea of Scott being part of the anti-patriarchy. While he refuses the lifestyle of the patriarchy, he still unconsciously holds on to its ideals by not separating the act of love from the act of making money.

Mike, on the other hand, comes from a much different background than Scott. The film introduces the audience to Mike on the road, recognizable to him by its "fucked-up face." Here, Mike shares his view with the audience by making a telescope with his hand, joining the audience's viewpoint with his gaze of the road, its distant hills and shrubbery resembling a deformed face. Kotwal uses Freud's work *The Interpretation of Dreams* to argue that this recognition generates from the déjà vu emanating from Mike's memory of his mother (2). After this recognition of familiarity, Mike falls into the first of many narcoleptic sleeps. His narcolepsy restricts his functioning in the patriarchic world and brings him into his subconscious search for his mother. As we literally enter Mike's unconscious, many loaded symbols appear. We see Mike's mother happily dancing with him as an infant, and then another scene with Mike resting his head on her lap. Kotwal states that this latter image of his mother refers to the roads "untraveled, back to the mother's genitals" (3). This initial scene foreshadows his mission throughout the film to find his mother.

Kotwal utilizes a Freudian framework to examine Mike's search for his mother, home, and family. He regards the images of Mike's mother and the farmhouse as symbolizing "the fossilized remnants of Mike's development into the pre-Oedipal" (3). This repressed desire to be joined with his mother leads Mike on a journey to fulfill the missing link to his psychological development. The repressed thought symbolically enters his consciousness when the orgasm from a john manifests into a farmhouse crashing on the road. After this, Mike encounters a woman on the street who looks like his mother, and his growing obsession eventually leads him to his brother. This troubling encounter with his brother reveals that Mike is a product of incest. When his brother/father embraces him, Mike leaves, rejecting the abnormal patriarchy in favor of the continued search for his mother.

Before Mike and Scott meet with Mike's brother/father, a campfire scene occurs within which Mike questions Scott about what it would be like to have a "normal" family.

SCOTT: When I left home, the maid asked me where I was going off to. I said, wherever, whatever. Have a nice day.
MIKE: You had a maid?
SCOTT: Yeah.
MIKE: If I had had a normal family, a good upbringing, then I would have been a well-adjusted person.
SCOTT: Getting away from everything feels good.... Depends on what you call normal.
MIKE: Yeah, it does. You know, like a mother and a father and a dog and shit like that. Normal. Normal.
SCOTT: So you didn't have a normal dog?
MIKE: No, I didn't have a dog.
SCOTT: You didn't have a normal dad?
MIKE: No. No normal dog, and no normal dad. Anyway, what's a normal dad?

Kotwal reveals that this moment in the film represents the point at which the goals of Mike and Scott come closest to converging (5). While the two discuss the ideals of family and fathers, they are unable to identify what "normal" signifies. Mike makes the claim that if he had had a normal family, then he would be "well-adjusted." Yet Scott, who benefits from at least having a complete family, does not comment in response. From this conversation, the maid seems to fit the ideal of a caring family member better than any other representation Scott has portrayed.

While their trajectories do converge for a moment, the moment passes before the scene concludes. Mike confesses his love to Scott, yet Scott rejects Mike's affections. Scott has acted as a mother-figure, sheltering Mike from harm throughout the film, not as a father-figure, as Kotwal argues. For example, after Mike suffers a narcoleptic attack as a result of the stress caused by Hans' (played by Udo Kier) advances in their first meeting, the scene turns to Scott holding Mike's sleeping body in a pieta-like manner representative of Mary holding her fallen son, Jesus. Therefore, the logical result of Mike's feelings for Scott would be a mother-son relation, not a father-son relation.

Ironically, it is at this point in the film that Scott re-exposes his political unconscious and the lasting patriarchic difference between love and money. When he rejects Mike on the notion that he "only has sex with men for money," he claims that Mike is his best friend and that it is impossible for two guys to love one another. Because he is unable to believe that two men can truly love each other, Scott, like his father, chooses the value of money over love itself. In contrast, the love that Mike projects onto Scott culminates from his unconscious desire to have sex with his mother and fulfill his Oedipal fantasy so that, in this case, the child would not be defeated by the father. However, Mike does not get to live out his fantasy, and the search for his mother resumes.

The next scene of foreclosure takes place for both Mike and Scott in the Italian countryside, where Mike believes his mother is now residing. Once Mike arrives, he ignores Carmella (played by Chiara Caselli), the woman taking care of the house, and starts calling for his mother, whom he presumes is there. He searches the house to find his mother absent; meanwhile, Scott gets to know the Italian girl who puts an end to his hustler life. When Mike learns that his mother is gone and his quest has ended, he turns to his mother-substitute, Scott, who turns away from him to pursue the love of Carmella. When looking back at the discussion of family in the campfire scene, Carmella-the-Italian-maid fits the mold of the caring mother-figure that Scott fondly recalls as having questioned him about his whereabouts. So, instead of Mike finding his mother, Scott finds his ideal female figure and instantly falls in love with her. Shortly thereafter, Scott leaves with Carmella, telling Mike that he wants to "take some time off." Scott soon learns that his father has died, hence making him the head of the family.

Without the nurturing of Scott, Mike readily returns to a lifestyle of hustling and falls into more narcoleptic states, now without a protector. Once he returns to America, Scott drives by Mike sleeping on the street without even blinking an eye. Then, Bob sees that his prince has returned with his new wealth. In the hopes of being saved from his poverty, he approaches Scott. Inside a crowded restaurant filled with members of the upper crust, Bob positions himself on one knee and asks for recognition from his son. Scott replies:

I don't know you, old man. Please leave me alone. When I was young and you were my street tutor, I was planning a change. There was a time when I had the need to learn from you, my former and psychedelic teacher. And although I love you more dearly than my dead father, I have to turn away. Now that I have, and until I change back, don't come near me.

Scott does not even grace Bob with his gaze until he issues his final warning. Bob, paralyzed by the words of his prince, cannot even walk out of the restaurant on his own. His heart has literally been attacked by Scott; he is visibly weakened by the betrayal of his prince. By denying Bob, Scott not only rejects his old ways, but he also assumes the political unconscious of his father and therefore rejects Bob with it. In accepting his role, Scott fully takes on the yoke of the patriarchy, along with the money and responsibility that go along with it. However, unlike his father, Scott's powerful lack of love is not impotent, because in his rejection of Bob he actually facilitates Bob's death that evening of a broken heart.

The dual funeral scene that results crystallizes the values of both the patriarchy and the anti-patriarchy. The scene opens with the funeral of Mayor Favor. As the priest reads from a Bible, the unemotional crowd, clothed in black, listens passively. Then, music comes from the other side of the cemetery, where Bob's funeral is taking place. There, his faithful followers sing, yell, and joyously lament their fallen leader with shouts of "BOB!" The noise reaches Scott, who stares intently, showing no emotion. The parishioners of Bob take part in an orgiastic ritual that gives off a sense of hope, rather than despair. While the conservative priest continues stoically, Scott and Mike lock eyes. As they gaze at each other, Mike continues to scream Bob's name, while Scott looks on without reaction, each reaffirming their now-permanent place in their chosen social order.

The film then ends with Mike once again stranded on the unknown road. Unlike the road with the "fucked-up face," this road has pronounced green grass on one side, and brown grass on the other. Mike's concluding words reiterate his position, reminiscent of the film's beginning: "I am a connoisseur of roads. I've been tasting roads my whole life. This road will never end. It probably goes around the world." Mike soon falls asleep, after which a car drives up and two men emerge to steal Mike's bag and shoes. Minutes later, a second car approaches. Its driver removes Mike from the road and drives away with him. The theft of his bag and shoes symbolizes the end of Mike's journey; however, the actions of the man in the second car, who drives away with Mike, can only be decoded ambiguously. He could be out to help or to hurt Mike; there is no way to be certain. However, the colors of the grass on either side of the road appear to symbolize a shift in Mike's life, from the hardship and turmoil he has endured to the greener pastures of an unknown future.

The film as a whole projects a political unconscious for the paradoxical view of queers in American society. On the one hand, Mike is represented as a gay character through his love for Scott; on the other, Scott never identifies himself as being gay. Scott accepts the patriarchal family order, while Mike has no way to join it. Film scholar Matt Bergbusch argues that this movie reminds viewers, through Mike's search for his mother, that the woman's inability to be reached symbolizes "the exclusion of gays by conventional definitions of family" (214). The dreams of the film, Bergbusch believes, function as "an alternative solution to psychosocial disorientation (metaphorized by Mike's narcolepsy) initially produced by many gay people by their exclusion from such biologistic reifications as 'Family' and 'Home'" (214). Because gay men cannot have the nuclear family in the same sense as heterosexual couples, Mike is lost in his own idealized state of "Idaho" where he can repeat the family fantasy forever.

Bergbusch also exposes a gay and lesbian response to the film as being "pessimistic and depressing" (215). In most respects, the tale of Mike is a tragedy. He never achieves independence and, ironically, despite the love that he carries, he lacks a person to share it with. However, the ambiguous ending could lead to a home or it could just be another stopover for Mike until he reaches another road. After the concluding shot of the car driving off with the still-sleeping Mike, the vehicle fades into the distance. Then, there is the image of the now-familiar farmhouse, followed by an intertitle that reads "Have a Nice Day." This series of images can either be taken as a procession of the directions that Mike's life may lead, or a sarcastic snide that the fate of Mike will continue in a never-ending circle. Here, the viewer is left to decide whether to have a nice day or not.

In conclusion, this film's rich interweaving of narcoleptic dreams and harsh realities not only leads to questions about the meaning of homosexuality, but also of how to qualify the power structures used in describing U.S. culture. When all is said and done, *My Own Private Idaho* leaves its audience members open to evaluate their own notions of love and wealth and which will fare better in the American landscape.

## Works Cited

Barthes, Roland. *Image, Music, Text*. Trans. Stephen Heath. New York: Hill and Wang, 1977.

Bergbusch, Matt. "Additional Dialogue: William Shakespeare, Queer Allegory, and *My Own Private Idaho*." *Shakespeare Without Class*. Eds. Donald Hedrick and Bryan Reynolds. New York: Palgrave, 2000. 209-227.

Jameson, Fredric. *The Political Unconscious: Narrative as Symbolic Act.* Ithaca,
   NY: Cornell University Press, 1981.
Kotwal, Kaizaad. "Psychedelic Papas and the Oedipal Mama: Lonesome
   Trajectories within the Flesh and Psyche in Gus Van Sant's *My Own Private
   Idaho.*" *The Film Journal* 8 August 2003. <http://www.thefilmjournal.
   com/issue3/myownprivateidaho.html>.

# CHAPTER SEVENTEEN

# ROOMS WITH DIFFERENT VIEWS: RESTORING GAY IMAGES TO THE PAST IN CONTEMPORARY COSTUME FILM

# ALINA PATRICHE

Western culture has inherited a literary and visual past purged of images of "deviant" sexuality. Although representations of homosexuality had enjoyed an underground circulation in the nineteenth century and the first seven decades of the twentieth century, sexual otherness was generally edited out of the mainstream culture of that period. The homosexual author E. M. Forster wrote only one novel dealing openly with gay relations, *Maurice* (1914), and he never tried to publish it during his lifetime. In the late nineteenth century, the British poet and essayist John Addington Symonds wrote his autobiography, revealing his "abnormal" relations with other men, but the manuscript was kept from publication until 1984 by a strict embargo meant to protect the writer's descendants from embarrassing connections. In early silent films, male actors were kissing one another on the mouth to express such feelings as friendship or family bond, but homosexual associations were kept as far as possible from the moviegoers' minds by the media's silence on the topic, or by their presenting it as an unfortunate disease or a criminal transgression.

Set in 1985, in the midst of the "Reagan era," Tony Kushner's Broadway hit *Angels in America* (adapted for television in 2003 by HBO) pointed at the tragic consequences that this conspiracy of silence pertaining to homosexual issues had on the gay community in the United States. Kushner's magic-realist play was part of the media's efforts to raise awareness, at the beginning of the 1990s, about the toll that the generally ignored AIDS pandemic was taking on gay males. While theatrical or film productions such as *Angels in America* are crucial in promoting the current homosexual "cause" in today's society, a group of recent period movies, based primarily on literary fiction (e.g., *A Room with a View, Maurice*) or biographies (e.g., *Carrington, Wilde*) and labeled "heritage" by British critics, played a vital role in restoring images of homosexuality to history. By integrating homosexual characters among the "regular" people populating the streets and drawing rooms of the nineteenth and early twentieth centuries, these period films add a crucial piece to the historic puzzle of sexual manifestations in the Western world.

Gay individuals are not only today's tragic victims of AIDS or the young men who perform handy makeovers on fashion-challenged people; they may also have been our ancestors. As gay media scholar Richard Dyer points out in his 2000 essay "Nice Young Men Who Sell Antiques: Gay Men in Heritage Cinema," "Heritage cinema did address issues of gay history. In part, they did what so much early gay history did: they showed that we were there" (44). Furthermore, due to their aesthetic and intellectual significance in the contemporary cultural landscape, heritage films that equated homosexuality with normality (e.g., *Another Country*, *Gosford Park*, *Maurice*) played an important role in the integration of queer representation into the mainstream culture, contributing to the increasing acceptance of gay sexuality in today's society.

Regarded as a threat to the patriarchal laws dominating human societies for centuries—with religion commonly used as vital support for these laws—homosexuality has been constructed as a perversity not worth talking about socially and virtually ignored in terms of artistic or cultural representation. Primarily due to religious edicts against sodomy, homosexuality has been legally considered a crime in many cultures, despite its status as a consensual act. In England, Henry VIII introduced the first legislation against homosexuals with the Buggery Act of 1533, making "buggery" punishable by hanging, a penalty not finally lifted until 1861 (Bailey 145). In 1885, the British Parliament enacted the so-called Labouchere Amendment, which prohibited "gross indecency" between males, a broad term that encompassed most or all male homosexual acts (Lancaster 29). It was the law under which Oscar Wilde suffered his well-known conviction and imprisonment in 1895. The Wolfenden Report in the United Kingdom was a turning point in the legalization of homosexuality in Western countries. In 1957, a departmental committee chaired by John Wolfenden published a favorable report on "homosexual offenses," stating that "homosexuality cannot legitimately be regarded as a disease, because in many cases it is the only symptom and is compatible with full mental health in other respects" (*Wolfenden* 11). Sexual acts between two adult males were made legal in England in 1967 and, in the United States, sodomy laws were declared unconstitutional in 2003 by the Supreme Court's decision in the case of Lawrence vs. Texas (Lawrence n. pag.).

While the courts were busy convicting those guilty of the "abominable and detestable crime against nature," as Sir William Blackstone referred to homosexuality in the 1760s, mass media were busy keeping the topic far from the general public's perception. Recognizing the increasing capacity of motion pictures to influence the film audiences' opinions and behaviors, Hollywood producers adopted, in 1930, a self-imposed censorship formula, known as The Production Code of the Motion Picture Producers and Directors of America (which remained in effect until 1968, when it was replaced by the rating system). The second chapter of the Code regulates the representation of sex in movies:

> The sanctity of the institution of marriage and the home shall be upheld. Pictures shall not infer that low forms of sex relationship are the accepted or common thing.... Sex perversion or any inference to it is forbidden. (Phillips 386)

The production details of a well-received 1936 movie, *These Three*, stand as a significant example of film censorship intended to maintain the silence surrounding the gay issue. In 1934, Lillian Hellman's play *The Children's Hour* became a Broadway hit. It was a tale of gay awakening, in which a schoolmistress becomes aware of her lesbianism when one of her pupils makes up a story about a love affair going on between the heroine and her best friend, another school teacher who is engaged to be married. Samuel Goldwyn bought the rights to Hellman's work, but he was obliged to remove all references to lesbianism when he turned it into a movie script. (In 1934, no lesbian manifestations were permitted on screen, although Hollywood itself was no stranger to gay characters. Ramon Navarro, still popular at that time, was gay, and two of the biggest stars of the day, Marlene Dietrich and Greta Garbo, were enjoying lesbian affairs.) The film, rewritten by Hellman herself, kept the same plot line—three people are ostracized when a schoolgirl says one of them is secretly in love with the other—but instead of harboring a secret love for her friend, the spinster teacher now pines for her friend's fiancé, Joe. The director of *These Three*, William Wyler, later went back to Hellman's original story and, in 1961, he remade *The Children's Hour*, with Shirley MacLaine as the closeted lesbian and Audrey Hepburn as the object of her affection.

Thus, beginning in the 1960s, when the sodomy laws began to change and the Production Code was replaced with the rating system, images of homosexuality began to penetrate the wall of silence that had isolated them from the mainstream culture. However, although present-day homosexuality is represented in reality shows, commercials, and popular television series such as *Queer as Folk*, we seem to lack those images in the past. The heritage film genre, developed over the last three decades, has proven crucial in restoring images of homosexuality to the past. In their much-noted efforts for authenticity in recreating the past, heritage movies pay particular attention to non-dominant sexual identities. Accurate period costumes and settings often form the backdrop for authentic sexual diversity rarely shown in previous representations of history.

In their manifest efforts for authenticity, brought about by the media's prolonged denial of sexual difference, most heritage films that bring up the topic of gay sexuality base their portrayals of homosexual characters on real-life figures. For example, released in 1984 and directed by Marek Kanievska, *Another Country* tells the story of Guy Bennett, a gay politician who fled Britain and became a spy for the Soviet Union. The character of Bennett, played by the now-openly gay actor Rupert Everett, is quite obviously based on a real-life character, Guy Burgess, a flamboyantly gay diplomat in the 1930s and 1940s who spied for the Soviet Union and finally fled to Moscow in 1951. According to the film's official website, two other British historic figures, John Cornford and Esmond Romilly, served as sources of inspiration for the upper-class leftist character Tommy Judd (played by Colin Firth), Bennett's heterosexual best friend and schoolfellow at Cambridge. In 1995, Christopher Hampton wrote and directed *Carrington*, a biopic based on Michael Holroyd's biography of the homosexual essayist and historian Lytton Strachey. The film focuses on the lifelong relationship between Strachey (played by Jonathan Pryce) and another Bloomsbury personality, the bisexual painter Dora Carrington (played by Emma Thompson).

Although it does not explicitly deal with gay relations, Sally Potter's 1992 version of Virginia Woolf's mock biography *Orlando* (1928) contains a theoretical exploration of gender identity: Orlando is a man born around 1500, who turns into a woman in the late seventeenth century, at the age of thirty, and gives birth to a child in the mid-nineteenth century. Generated by Woolf's own shifting sexuality, this book was inspired by, and is dedicated to, the writer's once lesbian lover Vita Sackville-West, a British socialite and novelist who could trace her aristocratic roots to the Elizabethan time. In the film version of *Orlando*, the director actually illustrates the idea of gender performativity by using just one performer, actress Tilda Swinton, to play Orlando as both man and woman, and by casting the famous cross-dresser and gay icon Quentin Crisp in the role of Queen Elizabeth I.

Along the same "biographic" lines, Julian Mitchell wrote and Brian Gilbert directed the 1997 film *Wilde*, a sexually explicit though highly reverential biopic of Oscar Wilde, based on Richard Ellman's "near-definitive biography" of the writer (Porton 8). In a 1998 interview for *Cineaste*, Stephen Fry, the gay actor who plays Wilde in Gilbert's film, points out the absurdity of avoiding clear references to the writer's homosexuality in older cinematic approaches to Wilde's eventful life. Talking about 1960's *The Trials of Oscar Wilde* (which starred Peter Finch in the title role), Fry remembers "being baffled by this man being sent to prison for patting people on the head. That's not the fault of the film, of course, that's the fault of the age" (Porton 9). In the same interview, Fry discusses the general silence in the Victorian drawing rooms and mass media on the subject of "sexual inversion" as one possible reason why Wilde carried out the apparently masochistic venture of suing the Marquess of Queensberry for calling him a "sodomite" (or, more accurately, a "somdomite"). Because no one talked about sexual perversion in society, or even about sex in general, it was difficult for Wilde to imagine that the legal representatives, during the public trial, would inquire about such graphic details as the state of the sheets. As Fry hypothesizes, the Victorian writer did not understand "that the legal process was quite as frank as it was, because it wasn't reported in the papers.... I don't think he knew that courtrooms were places where erections and semen were talked about. These things were never talked about in polite society" (Porton 10-11).

Set in 1932 at a British country estate, Robert Altman's *Gosford Park* (2001) not only sets the spotlight on a real-life gay artist, Ivor Novello, but also puts homosexuality back into the entertainment business of the 1930s. Three of Sir William's guests for a shooting weekend at Gosford Park are connected with the movie industry: the fictional character Morris Weissman (played by Bob Balaban) is a Hollywood producer doing research for his studio's next Charlie Chan mystery, which would be set at a country estate in England; Henry Denton (played by Ryan Philippe), also a fictional figure, is an aspiring actor who puts his talent to the test by faking a Scottish accent and pretending to be Weissman's British servant; and Ivor Novello (played by Jeremy Northam) was a real-life British actor, writer, and composer, a matinee idol regarded as the Rudolf Valentino of England. All of these characters who represent the entertainment industry are gay. Weissman is the older homosexual man who brought with him his protégé and love interest, Denton. In his turn, Denton audaciously offers sexual favors both to Lady Sylvia, his glamorous hostess (played by Kristin Scott Thomas), and to the dashing Ivor Novello.

Although Novello chooses to reject Denton's advances, he is craftily characterized as gay. Not only is his character uninterested in any of the available ladies at the party, but the screenplay also has him singing and playing a song written by Novello himself, the lyrics of which encode subtle references to the "love that dare not speak its name." Asked by his blasé hosts to perform some of his popular musical bits while they are driving away their boredom by flirting and playing cards, Novello opens his recital with a song describing an escapist heaven: "another land" where unconventional love is not hindered by common rules. Although playful, the tone of the lyrics remains sad, reflecting the artist's awareness of the insurmountable barriers separating gay sexuality from social acceptability: "We shall never find that lovely land of Might-Have-Been/I shall never be your king nor you shall be my queen." Altman further employs this song as the musical background for the end credits of *Gosford*

*Park* and, in his commentary on the alternative DVD soundtrack, refers to Novello's lyrics as "the lament of the gay existence" in an intolerant, heterosexist society.

Despite their openness to the incorporation of non-dominant sexuality in their recreation of the past, heritage films have formed the object of severe disapproval, especially from British film scholars, for their almost exclusive focus on the English upper classes. The term "heritage" itself was initially used by leftist British critics such as Andrew Higson and Tana Wollen to connect these movies' infatuation with history with the Thatcherite/New Right program regarding the preservation of national identity through re-enacting the British past. In her article "Nostalgic Screen Fictions," Wollen posits that "Britain seemed to have been squashed into the south-east corner of England and the hearth gods were the breezy middle classes who languished in sumptuous *ennui*" (182). Indeed, most of the characters in these films belong or are otherwise connected to the upper classes, apparently justifying such labels for the heritage genre as "white flannel films" or "white linen suit movies" (Monk 116).

Nevertheless, most heritage narratives foreground the figure of an artist or intellectual with distinctly liberal views. Their progressive attitude places these figures in the position of outsiders in their own conservative world (e.g., Maurice and Clive Durham in *Maurice*, Guy Bennett and Tommy Judd in *Another Country*, and Ralph Touchett in *The Portrait of a Lady*). These characters usually function as thoughtful observers of nuances, which escape more obtuse witnesses and very often invite audience identification. The casting of gay characters in the role of the outsider/observer, who usually serves as a point of identification for the film spectator, shatters the perception of the British upper crust as the homogenously heterosexual social group to which audiences are supposed to relate. The homosexual identity of these liberal observers consistently challenges the classist and patriarchal values typically associated with political conservatism by shifting the focus toward creativity and analytical power, and away from the social, economic, or patriarchal authority of the empire rulers. The gay characters are consistently conceived as "others" in relation to the conservative values of the dominating social structures, and they are often rejected by the representatives and promoters of those values.

The construction of the gay characters in Altman's *Gosford Park* casts a revealing light on the way this film genre positions itself in relation to class and nationality. Morris Weissman, Henry Denton, and Ivor Novello are outsiders in more than one way in the class-driven, patriarchally structured English aristocracy: the Hollywood producer invited to an English shooting party is not only American, but also Jewish and vegetarian; his "boy-toy," Denton, also

American, fakes a Scottish accent for most of the film and is sexually ambiguous; and the movie star, Novello, is of lower-class, Welsh extraction (he was born David Ivor Davies in Cardiff, Wales). They represent the world of popular entertainment, which seems inherently at odds with the upper classes; in a memorable scene, the Countess of Trentham (played by Maggie Smith) does not understand Weissman's reservations in giving away the ending of his upcoming film, as none of the aristocratic guests would dream of going to the movies anyway.

Weissman is the outsider who carefully observes the British aristocracy and its rules, and the results of his "research" are almost instantly transmitted to Hollywood over the telephone. The American producer thus becomes a guide for the film spectators who can identify with him as he discovers the rules of the aristocratic game. In his audio commentary on the alternative DVD soundtrack, scriptwriter Julian Fellowes asserts that he conceived of Weissman as the representative of the audience in that "trip on the moon," the character who would make them feel they "have a friendly alien on screen."

Based on Julian Mitchell's eponymous play (first staged in 1982), *Another Country* provides dramatic examples of the ways by which the British colonial system rejects intellectual figures who question the powerful elite's patriarchal rules rather than conforming to them. Set at Cambridge in the early 1930s, the story explores the effects of the university education on a few students involved in the struggle for power within colleges, a circumstance that anticipates and mirrors the struggle for political and financial power in which they will later be involved as representatives of the ruling class. The film centers on two figures at odds with the rules of the establishment: Guy Bennett, who dreams of a career within the system while coming to terms with his homosexuality, and Tommy Judd, a committed Marxist who wants to abolish the entire colonial government.

Bennett and Judd become the ultimate outsiders in an educational system that denies individuality, favoring blind subjection to social and sexual rules. They are characterized in clear contrast to the other students who, despite their sharing Judd's democratic convictions or Guy's sexual preferences, are ready to deny them in order to fit the mold of "empire ruler." The character that best embodies the picture-perfect empire ruler is the stupid, aggressive, and militaristically inclined Fowler (played by Tristan Oliver), the leader of the Gascoigne house. Judd sums up the colonial system's reliance on "Fowlers" for its survival:

> He's precisely what this school was designed to produce. Not empire builders—dear me, no. Building empires needs imagination. Empire rulers.... Licensed bullies. Fowler will go from the King's African Rifles straight into the Colonial Service—you wait and see. (Mitchell 20)

In this film, only Bennett and Judd continue to resist assimilation. Despite his political ambitions, which require him to adhere to the heterosexual norm, Bennett refuses to give up his gay relationship with the young and handsome James Harcourt (played by Cary Elwes). Likewise, Judd denies the moral legitimacy of the colonial system by refusing to accept any function in his house's hierarchy. In the end, both Bennett and Judd are rejected by their fellow students, with Bennett having to give up his dream to join the leaders of the house after a humiliating corporal punishment and public exposure of his homosexuality. In the film version, their opposition to the system takes active forms, as Judd joins the Republican forces against Franco in the Spanish Civil War (and dies there), while Bennett becomes a Russian spy and defects to the Soviet Union. The entire movie is constructed as a flashback: it opens in the present with the old and crippled Guy Bennett telling his story to a British journalist who visits him in Russia. This way, the colonial system's inflexible rejection of any kind of "deviancy" from its patriarchal, conservative norms becomes the explanation for Bennett's betrayal of his country.

Another film that draws on the notion of intellectual and sexual awakening of upper-class youth during their years at Cambridge is Merchant Ivory's *Maurice* (1987), based on E. M. Forster's partially autobiographical novel by the same title. Here, the title character (played by James Wilby), representing the writer's alter ego and inviting audience identification, is depicted in contrast to his friend and love interest, Clive Durham (played by Hugh Grant), with regard to their willingness and ability to conform to the patriarchal rules. It is "clever" Clive, with his "tranquil and orderly brain" (Forster 37), who first understands his own homosexuality and opens Maurice's eyes about his. However, despite Maurice's passionate response to his advances, Clive ultimately chooses to deny his true nature in order to pursue his political ambitions. Like Guy Bennett in *Another Country*, Clive faces social rejection if his "deviance" from the heterosexual norm becomes public. The movie further dramatizes Clive's need to make a choice by introducing an episode in which the character has the traumatic experience of witnessing his friend Risley's trial and conviction for homosexuality.

As in *Another Country*, at the end of *Maurice* we see both Clive and Maurice as outsiders. Clive, who has taken his place in the upper-class, patriarchal order by getting married and becoming a politician, is bound to loneliness and isolation from his inner self. Maurice, who has found love not only outside of the heterosexual norm but also outside of his class through his fulfilling relationship with gamekeeper Alec Scudder, will forever be an outsider in the upper-class world for which he was raised.

In fact, the plot of *Maurice* mirrors the choices that real-life intellectuals had to make in the nineteenth century and the first half of the twentieth century if their sexual orientation did not conform readily to the establishment's heteronormativity. One notorious example is that of Oscar Wilde, whose trial for homosexuality and conviction to years of hard labor likely inspired the Risley episode in the film version of *Maurice*.

Other homosexual artists, such as E. M. Forster himself, kept silent during their lifetimes about their "deviance," both socially and professionally. For instance, although written between 1913 and 1914, *Maurice* was not published until 1971, a year after Forster's death. Despite awareness of his own homosexuality from an early age, Victorian poet and essayist John Addington Symonds (1840-1893) chose Clive Durham's path: he got married, fathered four daughters, and apparently lived the straight life expected of a Victorian gentleman. However, he secretly wrote an autobiography documenting both his struggle with his sexual "inversion" (under pressure from the heterosexual upper class into which he was trying to fit) and his liberating homosexual experiences consummated abroad, in Italy and Switzerland. Aware of the negative social impact the publication of his memoirs might have on his family, especially his children, Symonds left instructions that his confessions should not be published for years after his death. The manuscript was left in the custody of the London Library in 1925 by Symonds's executor, with a fifty-year ban against reading it. A subcommittee of the London Library examined it in 1954 and advised against its publication (Symonds 9-11). Not until 1984 could Canadian scholar Phyllis Grosskurth finally edit and publish the autobiographical work under the title *The Memoirs of John Addington Symonds: The Secret Homosexual Life of a Leading Nineteenth-Century Man of Letters*.

A more subtle treatment of the thinker who observes the world apparently from the outside is given to the character of Ralph Touchett (played by Martin Donovan), Isabel Archer's cousin in Henry James' *The Portrait of a Lady*. Probably a stand-in for the writer himself, Ralph carefully scrutinizes his American cousin and seems to be the only one able to understand her free spirit. Therefore, he renounces part of his inheritance in her favor, hoping she will make the best use of her financial freedom. The most obvious way by which Ralph is constructed as an outsider is his fatal illness: slowly dying of tuberculosis, he knows it will be pointless for him to get seriously involved with Isabel (played by Nicole Kidman), despite his unmistakable admiration for her. However, as many critics have noted, Ralph is also encoded as sexually different: what seems to be conspicuously lacking in his close relation with Isabel is his sexual desire for her. Moreover, both film versions of James' novel, the 1967 BBC series and Jane Campion's 1996 movie, hint subtly at Ralph's homosexuality. The authors of the BBC adaptation cast Richard Chamberlain, a gay actor, in the role of Ralph. In Campion's film, Ralph's death seems to be connected with a mysterious illness, rather than with the recognizable signs of consumption. As John Carlos Rowe observes in his recent essay on Campion's adaptation, images of Ralph on his deathbed are meant to evoke the image of AIDS patients in the modern spectator. Rowe further argues that the construction of Ralph as a gay character is one of the ways by which the director challenges phallocentrism. According to Rowe:

> Campion plays with the historical context of the novel to suggest that Ralph embodies the late-nineteenth-century decadent or aesthete, bringing to mind such figures of the aesthetic and sexual avant-garde as Lytton Strachey, Oscar Wilde, and John Addington Symonds. (201)

In addition to deconstructing the clichés of the British patriarchal upper and middle classes, the promotion of an intellectual/artistic figure at the center of the highly literate heritage narratives contributed to the increasing recognition of homosexuality as part of the mainstream culture. The gay characters were offered as objects of identification for increasingly diverse categories of viewers, in aesthetically influential art-house films that reached mass audiences due to the development of video and DVD technology. Backed up by the prestigious literary authorship of E. M. Forster and by the well-respected Merchant Ivory production label, *Maurice* was the first gay movie to cross over and become a mainstream success. As such, it likely contributed to the gradual acceptance of homosexuality in the late 1980s. In his online review of *Maurice*, posted on <amazon.com>, a gay American viewer thus greeted the release of this film on DVD at the beginning of 2004: "This was a very important film to me as it was instrumental in my own coming out process. I have waited a long time for the DVD version to appear" (7 Mar. 2004). Another member of the audience, characterizing himself as "a senior gay person," declared Merchant Ivory's *Maurice* to be his "favorite movie." This spectator's testimony of his complete identification with the characters and situations in Forster's gay coming-of-age story appears to confirm Richard Dyer's assertion that heritage films have put gay men back into history:

> This film speaks directly to me; it reflects wonderfully the frustrations that I felt growing up in the '50s.... It is a movie that reaffirms, over and over again, my very existence. (<amazon.com> 24 Sept. 2002)

Finally, even when the narrative is not centered on a homosexual story or character, the visual style of heritage cinema often proves particularly "friendly" to gay male (or women) spectators. While heritage texts provide a dwelling for historically marginalized social groups, the mise-en-scene in heritage films also places women and gay men in a privileged spectator's seat as main target audiences. As Claire Monk points out in "The British 'Heritage Film' and its

Critics," in offering the male body instead of the female body as the object of spectators' gaze, heritage films tend to favor the female and the gay-male gaze, as opposed to the heterosexual-male gaze addressed by classical narrative cinema (120). For example, Merchant Ivory's first commercial success, the 1986 adaptation of E. M. Forster's *A Room with a View*, focuses on the heterosexual love story between the upper-class English rose Lucy Honeychurch (played by Helena Bonham-Carter) and the penniless but appealing representative of the working class, George Emerson (played by Julian Sands). However, one show-stopping moment in this adaptation portrays a bathing scene in which three naked men playfully take a dip in the "secret lake" near the Honeychurch country estate. Although conceived in the homosocial rather than the homoerotic or homosexual sphere (e.g., none of the characters is gay, and there is no hint of sexual attraction among them), this scene sprang from the pen of the homosexual writer E. M. Forster, and its occurrence in the movie appeals primarily to gay-male spectators. In his online review of the movie, a lover of period romances, apparently heterosexual and most probably male, seemingly fails to pick up on the homosexual undertones in this Forster adaptation and finds the male nudity in the bathing scene offensive enough to spoil his visual and narrative pleasure:

> Being a romantic and loving old-fashioned movies, I rented *A Room with a View* after reading comments by other viewers. I watched the movie and it was a promising film. That was until I saw the bathing scene. I'm not one to enjoy watching frontal nudity, especially male frontal, and I couldn't understand why it was added to the movie to begin with. That scene destroyed the movie for me. (<amazon.com> 6 July 2002)

Although not considered part of the heritage canon, Luchino Visconti's *Death in Venice* (1971) is one of the first literary adaptations to display the heritage themes and visual style, which include homoeroticism. Based on Thomas Mann's eponymous novella (first published in 1912), *Death in Venice* more explicitly focuses on the male body as the object of the gaze. The story revolves around German composer Gustav von Aschenbach (played by Dirk Bogarde), who travels to Venice to recuperate after the death of his daughter and the fiasco of his last musical composition. In Venice, the artist has an epiphany as he encounters the epitome of his ideal beauty in the person of Tadzio, a Polish teenage boy vacationing there with his mother and sisters. As Aschenbach follows Tadzio on the beach and around the city, the camera identifies with his gaze and idealizes the boy's beauty. The movie reaches its climax when the middle-aged composer dies on the beach, watching his idol walking into the sea. In the film's memorable finale, Tadzio resembles a

Michelangelo sculpture as he stands in the water, bathed in the soft sunlight under the dying artist's gaze.

 Gay motifs have come to be considered a main characteristic of heritage filmmaking and often form the target of genre parodies. The 1997 *Stiff Upper Lips* (directed by Gary Sinyor) is a declared spoof of the Merchant Ivory adaptations, although the parody expands to include other heritage movies marked by homosexual undertones. One theme amply parodied in *Stiff Upper Lips* is the homosexual awakening, which forms the subject matter of *Maurice*. Like Clive Durham and Maurice Hall in the original, best friends Cedric and Edward go through their own sexual initiation in *Stiff Upper Lips* and become a gay couple. During Cedric's visit with Edward at Ivory Hall, the two young men bathe in a pond, Cedric fully dressed and speaking in Latin; later in the same scene, the handsome peasant George actually gets naked and plunges into the pond, in an incident reminiscent of the naked bathing moment in *A Room with a View*. Another moment between the latent homosexuals Cedric and Edward clearly references similar sequences in Visconti's *Death in Venice*. During their trip to Italy, Cedric is shown sitting in a chaise longue on the beach; close-ups of his desiring eyes are intercut with shots of Edward playing in the water under (but unaware of) his friend's gaze. The scene clearly alludes to Visconti's montage sequence between Aschenbach, the voyeur, and Tadzio, the object of his gaze. Also, the musical piece used as acoustic background for this sequence in *Stiff Upper Lips*, the Adagietto from Gustav Mahler's Fifth Symphony, comprises the musical theme of Visconti's movie.

 Thus, despite some critics' accusations that these movies attempt to promote a false, idyllic image of the past as historical reality, heritage films reveal a deep awareness of the social problems faced by those who failed to conform to the sexual norms of the patriarchal upper-class system. Acclaimed heritage productions such as *Another Country, Carrington, Gosford Park, Maurice,* and *Wilde* restore images of homosexuality to a past world that persistently attempted to erase them. While offering positive points of identification for various types of audience members and subtly gratifying the gay (as opposed to the heterosexual) male gaze, these intellectually and aesthetically influential films have substantially contributed to the acceptance of homosexuality in the mainstream culture.

## Works Cited

Bailey, Derrick Sherwin. *Homosexuality and the Western Christian Tradition.* London: Longmans/Green, 1955.
Blackstone William. *Commentaries on the Laws of England.* Chicago: University of Chicago Press, 1979.

Dyer, Richard. "Nice Young Men Who Sell Antiques: Gay Men in Heritage Cinema." *Film/Literature/Heritage: A* Sight and Sound *Reader*. Ed. Ginette Vincendeau. London: BFI, 2001. 43-48.

Forster. E. M. *Maurice*. New York: Signet Classic, 1973.

Lancaster, Roger, and Micaela Di Leonardo. *The Gender/Sexuality Reader: Culture, History and Political Economy*. New York: Routledge, 1997.

*Lawrence vs. Texas*. <http://en.wikipedia.org/wiki/Lawrence_v._Texas>.

Mitchell, Julian. *Another Country*. London: Amber Line Press, 1982.

Monk, Claire. "The British 'Heritage Film' and its Critics." *Critical Survey* 7.2 (1995): 116-24.

Phillips, William. *Film: An Introduction*. New York: Bedford/St. Martin's, 1999.

Porton, Richard. "The Actor as Critic: An Interview with Stephen Fry," *Cineaste* 23.4 (1998): 8-12.

Rowe, John Carlos. "For Mature Audiences: Sex, Gender and Recent Film Adaptations of Henry James's Fiction." *Henry James on Stage and Screen*. Ed. John Bradley. New York: Palgrave, 2000. 190-211.

Symonds, John Addington. *The Memoirs of John Addington Symonds: The Secret Homosexual Life of a Leading Nineteenth-Century Man of Letters*. Ed. Phyllis Grosskurth. Chicago: University of Chicago Press, 1984.

*The Wolfenden Report: Report of the Committee on Homosexual Offenses and Prostitution*. New York: Stein and Day, 1963.

Wollen, Tana. "Over Our Shoulders: Nostalgic Screen Fictions for the 1980s." *Enterprise and Heritage: Crosscurrents of National Culture*. Ed. John Corner and Sylvia Harvey. New York: Routledge, 1991. 178-193.

# CHAPTER EIGHTEEN

# SKIN-TO-SKIN: BAREBACK COMMUNITY, PORNOGRAPHY, SUBJECTIVITY

# HOLLIS GRIFFIN

Bareback pornography, the depiction of anal sex without condoms, has become an increasingly popular subgenre in gay adult video since the late 1990s. In the face of massive casualties in the gay community at the hands of AIDS during the 1980s and 1990s, some gay film scholars advocated the use of pornography for "the re-education of desire" (Dyer, "Coming," 27), which, in effect, has meant the depiction of condom use during anal sex. During that period, HIV/AIDS educators regarded condoms as the best way to stem the tide of gay-male deaths as a result of AIDS-related illnesses and, as such, the pro-condom preventative discourse surrounding the AIDS pandemic made filmic portrayals of safe anal sex *de rigeur* during that time. But the recent surge in popularity of bareback pornography is part of a larger movement within the gay community that is related to bareback sex. In active resistance to the endless warnings from the HIV/AIDS-education establishment and the seemingly never-ending link of gay male sexuality with death, some gay men have formed bareback communities wherein they pursue condomless sexual trysts and the perceived homophobic connotations that attend them.

The temptation to create a causal link between the consumption of bareback pornography and "real world" participation in the bareback community flies in the face of decades of well-established communication theories, and I have no intention of trying to make such a connection here. I do, however, intend to show how bareback pornography has emerged as an increasingly popular category in gay adult video for some of the same reasons that contributed to the rise of the barebacking community and, in fact, may even be considered a visual articulation of the goals of that project. As a result, an examination of the portrayal of condomless anal sex on video necessitates an examination of the practice of condomless anal sex in real life. From there, I will discuss the discourse surrounding the notion of "pornography as fantasy" and how the bareback videos' popularity can also be seen as a result of less explicitly political readings by viewers.

I want to highlight that this analysis willfully leaves aside notions of repetition-compulsion and the death drive. The application of psychoanalysis has for too long been the means by which gay men and homosexual acts are uniformly pathologized. At face value, the rise of the bareback movement—both on video and in real life—fits well with such an application. But my aim here is to offer an alternative narrative in a particular instance when psychoanalysis leaves room for little more than a sweeping dismissal and assignation of blame, discursive elements that have overwhelmingly and problematically shaped societal understandings of gay-male sex acts in the wake of AIDS. I wish to identify possible community-building impulses that prompt gay men to engage in condomless anal sex, and I intend to carve out a more positivist stance on gay men's spectatorial involvement with bareback pornography. Formal analyses of bareback videos illustrate how they differ from their pre-AIDS predecessors; as such, I also intend to demonstrate how they make trouble for much of the scholarship that is used to study pornography and understand sexuality in the academy today.

## The Condom Code and the Rise of Bareback Culture

After the AIDS pandemic decimated certain segments of the gay community during the mid-1980s, many community leaders and AIDS activists recognized an urgent need for safer-sex education programs. Gabriel Rotello refers to these strenuous efforts as "the condom code," whereby "once it became widely accepted that HIV was the viral cause of the new syndrome, and once it was demonstrated that HIV could indeed be blocked with latex condoms,…the advice to use condoms became the central tenet of the new gay sexual ecology" (100).

It is important to note the condom code's centrality in safer-sex education programs because it places anal sex at the center of the gay-male sexual experience, much as gay scholars and community leaders had been doing since the birth of the gay rights movement. Of course, this link between sexuality and anality is a reason why, historically, people have viewed homosexuality as being dirty and obscene. As a result, many gay activists and scholars often reclaim this link. With the outbreak of AIDS in the 1980s, many men in the gay community believed that the condom code initiated by AIDS activists "was too judgmental and implicitly devalued a central aspect of gay sex—namely, unprotected anal sex" (Rotello 101). This foreshadowed the barebacking movement that would develop more than a decade later.

While scientists and AIDS activists hailed the dramatic decrease in HIV-infection rates among gay men during the late 1980s and early 1990s as the obvious sign of the condom code's victory over the pandemic, a sharp increase in infection rates among gay men during the mid-1990s mitigated their celebrations. A cover story in *The New York Times* from December 11, 1993 brought mainstream attention to a "second wave" of HIV infections. Reporter Jane Gross highlighted that many of the men newly infected with HIV were reporting that they had been practicing unsafe anal sex all along. Furthermore, the highest levels of new infections were among the youngest groups of gay men, those who had less experience with death and grief in the wake of AIDS (Rotello 118). Yet, in fact, the dip in new infections in the gay community during the late 1980s and early 1990s could be attributed, mathematically, to the high rates of AIDS-related deaths in the community during that period. In short, the condom code wasn't working and may never have worked at all. Rather, the condom code helped to create a backlash that, in turn, has given rise to a new barebacking movement among gay men.

The term "barebacking" was coined as a way to refer to the deliberate practice of anal sex without condoms. Its connection to the unbridled virility of riding a horse without a saddle is obvious and intentional, connoting a choice fraught with risk and establishment scorn.

> Barebacking may be viewed as reinforcement of sexual identity, resistance to imposed behavioral norms, creation of a new sexual and political identity, or a continuation of practices unaffected by organized messages aimed at stopping such practices. (Yep, Lovaas, and Pagonis 4)

While conscious, deliberate unprotected anal sex has been a reality for many gay men all through the AIDS pandemic, scholars point to 1996-1997 as the period of the development of a barebacking consciousness, "the point at which there emerged a heightened eroticization, premeditation, and form of structured organizing devoted to the practice of unsafe sex" (Scarce n. pag.). This occurred via the utilization of websites, listservs, and chatrooms; the rental and purchase of amateur and professional videos; and attendance at sex clubs and private parties. Here, the jargon and slang terminology developed and traveled, and the barebacking movement was born.

The question of interest here is, if all scientific literature concludes that unprotected anal sex is a "good" way to transmit HIV, why are so many gay men knowingly engaging in it, even celebrating it? Rotello states that drug use, cruising for sex in public areas, promiscuity, and unprotected sex are often key features of the gay experience for young men living in urban centers (138). Michael Scarce stresses the multitude of reasons that gay men engage in bareback sex, including increased physical sensation, the exhilaration of defying prevention campaigns, and the symbolic act of bonding that many barebackers attach to the practice of sharing semen.

Michelangelo Signorile attributes another factor to the rise of the barebacking community: the success of protease inhibitors in managing the illnesses and extending the lives of people with AIDS and the attendant media coverage that focused on the manageability of the disease as opposed to its horrors. He states:

> Many of us believed the hype about drug cocktails consisting of protease inhibitors being some sort of "cure." We reveled in the idea that…the epidemic was over. (n. pag.)

The truth is, of course, that no cure exists for the virus. Rotello also calls attention to this false sense of faith in emerging AIDS treatments as one of the key myths informing what he identifies as a trend wherein many gay men feel invincible in the face of AIDS (10).

Gust Yep, Karen Lovaas, and Alex Pagonis examine research about the emotional element of unprotected anal sex, concluding that some gay men regard unprotected sex as inherently more intimate and feel that protected sex is overly detached, even impersonal (6). The practice of barebacking, therefore, often serves as a way to intentionally strip the practice of unprotected anal sex of its negative connotations and reframe it as a way to convey positive feelings and emotions for a sexual partner or partners. These researchers point to several studies in which emotional involvement with a partner was the key factor that determined sexual behavior (as opposed to any kind of HIV-risk assessment), particularly with regard to young gay men. Many of these young men expressed, in surveys and interviews, that being in love with someone meant having unprotected anal sex with him (6).

Of course, HIV-positive gay men have faced unique issues regarding their practice of unprotected anal sex. Research suggests that some view the practice positively as a result of a desire to escape the pressures of life with the disease and that many HIV-positive gay men have engaged in unprotected anal sex because they feel they have nothing left to lose (Yep, Lovass, and Pagonis 7). While the AIDS panic of the 1980s cast HIV-positive gay men in the role of the undesirable Other in their own community, the barebacking movement has created a wholly different political overtone regarding an individual's decision to forgo the use of condoms. I contend that it is forging a new kind of alliance between HIV-negative and HIV-positive gay men who participate in barebacking communities, whereas the condom code had previously caused a large rift that frequently seemed insurmountable.

The risk of using a phrase such as "many gay men" in the context of this argument is that it will be generalized across the entire population, or at least a larger percentage than is appropriate. Nevertheless, while the barebacking movement is but one element of the larger gay community, I would argue that it is an increasingly popular one.

## Representing Condomless Anal Sex on Video

While some attention has been paid to gay bareback sex in academic, mainstream, and gay publications, scholars and journalists have paid less attention to its representation on video. The information that has been published deals primarily with the issue of representational accuracy. Deeply ingrained in this literature is the deliberate blind eye that these videos turn toward the safer-sex warnings and practices that HIV/AIDS educators have so strenuously tried, and continue to try, to ingrain in the gay consciousness.

Bareback video producer Paul Morris argues that, over the last decade or so, gay pornography has become overly sanitized and normalized, drastically reducing the types of acts and kinds of bodies that appear in the genre. He points to condoms in gay pornographic offerings as symbols of forced stylization, political correctness, and the absolute unavailability to the viewer of the physical communion that the video promised to portray, which is why he believes condom use during anal sex is more a filmic convention than a real-life fact. John Burger concurs, stating that one of the biggest problems with mainstream gay video pornography in the age of AIDS is its failure to integrate the application and use of condoms into depicted sex acts (28). He notes:

> Footage involving the application of the rubbers is usually edited. Also edited are initial scenes of anal penetration.... What the viewer sees are two men in the midst of anal intercourse. Subsequent close-up shots of penetration usually reveal that the fucker is wearing a rubber.... For the climax shot, the magic of editing makes the condom disappear. (28)

The end result is a video clip with little or no continuity, as the viewer watches condoms appear and disappear within depictions of anal sex, and the scene has little (or none) of the erotic charge of the real-life act.

As a result, Morris argues that all pornography should move toward a more documentary format whereby, rather than declaring acts as being safe or unsafe, filmmakers can capture their subjects' sexual and erotic individuality non-categorically. Morris charges that the use of condoms in mainstream gay pornography portrays not the reality of gay life and gay sex, but rather what gay men *think* that should look like, based on the strictures of the safer-sex establishment. He also argues that bareback sex is a more widespread practice in the gay community than most people realize and/or are willing to admit, and he dismisses mainstream pornography as little more than a sanitized performance for the sake of commerce and political correctness.

My own research involving bareback videos confirms the notion that they tend to have a documentary feel. The use of amateur actors is common in bareback videos; one reason for this, I believe, is that producers want to eroticize the fact that "real men" are partaking in this act. Another reason is companies that produce and distribute bareback pornography do so outside the framework of the mainstream pornography industry. Because bareback sex repudiates the safer-sex guidelines of the AIDS-prevention establishment, industry insiders fear that the commingling of actors in bareback pornographic works with actors in mainstream pornographic offerings (i.e., with condoms) will result in a wave of new HIV infections (Morris n. pag.).

*Smooth, Cute, and Young Bareback* (2000) is an all-amateur offering, produced and distributed by Gaslamp Videos, that involves little in the way of characterization and narrative and is shot with a hand-held camera, giving the production the "shaky" quality of a documentary. The video begins— without opening credits—with a shower scene in which two young, white, athletic actors engage in various acts of oral and anal sex. There is then a cut to a scene in a hotel room, where the actors engage in anal intercourse and the camera focuses on the point of insertion, drawing viewer attention to the fact that no condom is being used. An important point to note is that the actors attempt three different positions before a successful insertion is achieved, something that would likely have been eliminated readily with editing in mainstream pornography. Furthermore, the actors engage in dialogue with the cameraman and, at one point, the bottom even says, "This isn't working." At that point, the top ceases to attempt insertion and moves to the side, in order to ejaculate via masturbation. All through this sequence, edits and cuts are minimal, the end result of which, I maintain, is a stressing of the fact that the viewer is witnessing an unstaged act.

*Bareback Orgy #11* (2000) is another all-amateur offering produced and distributed by Gaslamp Videos. This video features as many as eleven actors at a time engaged in a variety of sexual configurations. Again, edits and cuts are minimal, and a strong emphasis is placed on the point of insertion during scenes that depict anal intercourse. Additionally, anal sex is shown from a variety of different angles—from below, the side, and on top—in order to better illustrate the fact that the insertive partner is not wearing a condom. As with *Smooth, Cute, and Young Bareback*, this video features no characterization or narrative, and its production qualities are very poor. An important difference lies in the variety offered in *Bareback Orgy #11*: the video includes actors from a wide range of ages, races, and body types. It serves as an example of Morris' contention that the documentary-style bareback pornography format tries to do a better job of representing the range of people who actually consume videos than does the mainstream industry.

*Seattle Bareback Boyz, Vol. 1* (2003) calls more attention to the fact that it is an all-amateur production. It is marketed with the following copy by GAE Boy Video:

> Many of the guys in our videos have never performed sexually in front of a camera before and have chosen to have consensual adult sex for fun in an effort to perform for an audience. If you are used to viewing professionally produced adult films, you will find ours very different yet uniquely erotic. There is no cheesy music, no studios, no script, no unnecessary dialog[ue], no major editing, no fancy effects, fades or graphics, just attractive guys having sex. All the sound is live, so there are no audio insertions of guys moaning and groaning and all the scenes are real. There are no fake sexual encounters and no forced dialogue.... Sometimes the guys cum, sometimes they don't.... With films of this nature anything goes, that's what makes them fun, unique and erotic.

Thus, it can safely be concluded that the producer/distributor presents the bareback video as an articulation of actual gay men, not actors, engaging in what is considered to be an illicit but erotic sexual practice.

Casey McKittrick points to the proliferation of studios devoted exclusively to the production and distribution of bareback videos as a sign of bareback pornography's increasing popularity (5). While I agree with this claim, I also think that it raises important issues about spectatorial involvement. Are the multitudes of gay men who are embracing bareback pornography *all* embracing it as an overtly political act? And how has this popularity transformed it?

## Depoliticized Fantasy and the Transgression of Genre Boundaries

I believe that the subgenre's increasing popularity may be resulting in a move away from documentary style. *Hardcore Habits* (2003), a video produced and distributed by Hot Desert Knights Productions, exhibits a dramatic improvement in production values over the amateur productions discussed previously. This video features settings in and around posh homes in Palm Springs, California, as well as intricate camerawork and editing. Furthermore, I would argue that, in recent years, a star system has developed in the bareback video industry. Because of the controversy surrounding bareback videos and the increased potential for health risks among actors who appear in them, a strict dividing line has developed between actors who work in the mainstream gay adult video industry and those who work in the bareback industry (Slezak n. pag.). This may have been a factor that contributed to the use of all-amateur casts in the bareback pornography's infancy; however, mainstream pornography stars such as Jeff Palmer and Jackson Price have moved from the mainstream industry in recent years in order to work exclusively with bareback studios. With the genesis of this star system, videos produced by the bareback industry can be seen as the creation of a filmic fantasy and not just a politicized articulation of an illicit sexual practice. Price's star billing in *Hardcore Habits* underscores this fact.

An important point to note is that both Palmer and Price are openly HIV-positive, a reality that calls attention to the industry debate about the representation of bareback sex. In the wake of AIDS, the perceived industry recognition and status of bareback videos and the studios that produce them have generated strong opposition from the porn actors who participate in HIV/AIDS education and fundraising efforts. For example, actor and activist Will Clark charges:

> It's socially irresponsible for us to produce these videos as an industry. And it's poor business practice to provide entertainment that endangers behavior that could increase infection for a virus that has no cure. (qtd. in Slezak n. pag.)

One sign that the production of bareback videos is not necessarily always a political statement is the fact that videos produced and distributed by Hot Desert Knights feature intertitles about safe sex before any action takes place. These intertitles state:

> This video is designed as a fantasy. The men in this production have made an
> informed consensual choice not to use condoms during the making of this
> product. Whether or not you choose to use condoms and/or practice safe sex is
> a decision that only you can make after knowing all the facts.

Of course, this could be perceived as being a concession due to the
tremendous amount of controversy that has surrounded the depiction of
condomless anal sex. Nevertheless, my contention is that this can also be
seen as a deliberate attempt at distanciation, particularly because this intertitle
is followed by a series of others that relate the various ways by which HIV
can be transmitted sexually.

Pornography as fantasy material is, of course, a longstanding debate in
gay discourse, and its utility for these purposes is perhaps most powerful in
the post-AIDS era. Dennis Altman states that pornography "provides a safe
outlet for fantasies that most people recognize cannot easily be acted out in
real life" (qtd. in McNair 78). Yet Burger advocates an even more radical
reading of bareback videos as fantasy:

> I opt to recast the role of the porn star involved from that of unsafe
> practitioner to that of martyred saint—one who practices what I can no longer
> enjoy. (79)

But if bareback videos function as fantasy material for some gay men, do
they recall the gay pornography from the halcyon days of the pre-AIDS era?
By comparing videos depicting condomless anal sex from before the
mainstream industry-wide gentlemen's agreement to use condoms in the late
1980s to those depicting bareback sex today, it can be seen that the current
videos cause trouble for many of the assumptions that currently ground the
study of pornography in the academy. Bareback videos' relative lack of
narrative, as well as their portrayal and foregrounding of anal versatility—
men who act as either the "insertive" or "receptive" partner during anal
intercourse—between and among sexual partners are marked departures from
their pre-condom ancestors. Additionally, the bareback videos have adopted
new formal conventions in their depictions of "the money shot," a shot
widely considered to be a hallmark of all pornography. They move away
from external, visible depictions of ejaculation, a marked departure from pre-
AIDS condomless gay (and most other) pornography.

For my purposes here, I am defining narrative in Richard Dyer's terms.
He argues that narrative is "the very basis" of gay-male pornography,
charging that even in scenes that do little more than depict two men engaging
in sexual activity "there are the following narrative elements: the arrival on

the scene of the fuck, establishing contact,...undressing, exploring various parts of the body, coming, parting" ("Coming" 28). These narrative details may be as small as the inclusion of a leather jacket in a character's wardrobe to invoke a kind of "renegade" persona, or a character shown driving a truck to connote his working-class status. My contention is that, comparatively speaking, current bareback videos do not as frequently foreground minimal character elements and iconography. In most cases, they do not include them at all—scenes often open with actors already engaged in sexual relations.

One of the hallmarks of pre-condom gay pornography was its relatively comic use of setting and characterization to create a narrative and contextualize the depiction of sex, however thinly. In *These Bases are Loaded* (1982), for example, a baseball team engages in group masturbation and sex in the locker room after a game, and in *Frat House Memories* (1984), one of the fraternity brothers joins his roommate in seducing a handyman who is completing electrical work at their house. In *Pacific Coast Highway* (1981), Troy Richards and Steven Richards are shown engaging in oral and anal sex while camping in a tent on the side of the road, and in *Brother Load* (1983), actors Bobby Madison and Paul Madison are cast as brothers who engage in aggressive anal sex in their parents' home. Conversely, as discussed previously, many of the current bareback videos include little or no narrative build-up or characterization along such lines, nor do they include any real mise-en-scene.

The portrayal of versatility among partners during anal sex is not a convention for much of gay pornography for several reasons. Burger states that the number of straight-identifying actors appearing in gay adult videos increased considerably during the early and mid-1980s (27). My contention is that, among the gay-for-pay actors, societal prejudices about the allegedly inherent femininity in being the receptive partner during anal intercourse likely resulted in their insisting on portraying the "top" role. It is one thing to appear in gay pornography for money; it is a different story entirely to get anally penetrated for anyone to see. If a heterosexual male presence in the industry was as commonplace as Burger alleges, I contend that this would vastly curtail the filmic depictions of anal versatility.

Dyer discusses how an exclusivity of sexual positions on screen lends an actor an aura of unavailability that can be very valuable in marketing videos: viewers know what to expect of an actor, and he can help to build a following by playing on that star image (*Culture* 195). Furthermore, gay adult film star Scott O'Hara has stated that he was always cast as the insertive partner during anal-sex scenes while he worked in the industry during the early

1980s because he fit the traditional image of masculinity that directors and producers linked to the insertive role in anal sex (86).

Yet, anal versatility is foregrounded in bareback videos. In *Bareback Orgy #11*, nearly every actor plays both top and bottom roles in anal-sex scenes. In *Bareback Lovers*, a scene featuring actors Scott Thornton and Matt Douglas, as well as a scene with Thomas Bjorn and Keb Sanders, involves the tops and bottoms switching positions. The opening scene of *Seattle Bareback Boyz, Vol. 1* runs nearly an hour long and features both actors ejaculating as a result of being the insertive partner. A striking example is a scene in *Hardcore Habits*, in which actors Guy Franck and Dillian McFate switch positions, insertive to receptive, several times while engaging in anal sex.

Linda Williams states that, by the late 1970s, hardcore pornographic movies had adopted the formal convention of "showing external ejaculation of the penis as the ultimate climax—the sense of an ending—for…the money shot assumed the narrative function of signaling the climax of a genital event" (93). True to form, in each of the pre-condom movies I viewed, every sex act culminated in the visible external ejaculation of all of the actors involved in the scene. But Casey McKittrick contends that the post-AIDS bareback video has ushered in a new formal convention—the "depiction of a money shot followed by a reinsertion of a still-ejaculating penis into the submissive sex partner"—which draws attention to the fact that the actors are having unsafe sex (2). In a scene depicting actors Ben Archer and Jackson Price engaging in anal sex in *Hardcore Habits*, the image fades to a second scene in which Archer is standing behind Price and masturbating. When Archer begins to ejaculate, he reinserts his penis into Price's anus and continues to ejaculate there. In *Bareback Orgy #11*, several of the anal-sex scenes that are depicted end with internal ejaculation. Additionally, GAE Boy Video's marketing materials for *Seattle Bareback Boyz, Vol. 1* warn that some of the actors "may have accidentally cum away from the camera or while he was still 'inside' (heck, that's the way we all like it, right?)." While not a universal convention in the bareback videos I viewed, I would definitely consider this to be a recurring pattern.

Naturally, these generic developments beg an obvious question: Why do these differences exist? Regarding the bareback videos' lack of narrative details, it is important to note their historical context. Bareback videos have emerged during a cultural moment when gay-male representation in the mainstream media seems to be ever-increasing. Current filmic portrayals of gay-male life illustrate romance, family, work, and friends, yet these portrayals rarely, if ever, include actual gay sex. I contend that the widespread desexualized depictions of gay men in mainstream media have, at least in part, resulted in a deliberate elimination of narrative details in some pornographic videos as a political statement similar to the intentional exclusion of condoms. In the face of mainstream representations that deliberately hide gay sexuality, bareback pornography can be interpreted as purposefully reducing portrayals of gay sex to their basic, genital events. Furthermore, I believe that the foregrounding of anal versatility in bareback videos is the direct result of a move toward representational accuracy. Rotello and many other gay scholars underscore the fact that, while not universal, insertive/receptive versatility is extremely common among gay men (76). As such, filmic representations of men who "refuse to flip" seem firmly outside the goals of cultural products created in order to more truthfully represent desire.

Dyer argues that the goal of every filmic male sexual encounter is visible ejaculation ("Coming" 28). Yet with a video such as *Seattle Bareback Boyz, Vol. 1*, in which intertitles state that some of actors may not ejaculate, or *Bareback Orgy #11*, in which some of the anally insertive partners ejaculate internally, this is clearly not the case. In the instance of the amateur videos, non-professional actors have not necessarily perfected the art of control over their ejaculatory impulses in the same way that most porn stars have. Furthermore, limited access to editing and camera equipment may make it extremely difficult, or even impossible, for amateur pornographers to close every scene with a visible ejaculation. Still, Archer and Price's aforementioned anal-intercourse scene in the professionally produced *Hardcore Habits* points to a deliberate adoption of the new formal convention. I think that by depicting the ejaculation of an insertive partner inside the anus of the receptive partner, without a condom—or outside followed by re-insertion—bareback pornographers are re-eroticizing this event. In the case of *Hardcore Habits*, it is clearly the intentional reclamation of an act made taboo by the condom code.

Others have argued that the internal-ejaculation shot used in bareback pornography might be used to signify the deliberate transmission of HIV (McKittrick 7). A controversial article in *Rolling Stone* magazine written by Gregory Freeman, as well as the 2003 documentary film *The Gift*, drew mainstream attention to this practice—called "bug chasing" or "gift giving"—in which some HIV-negative gay men eroticize, and seek out, viral infection. The popularity of this practice is unknown and debated, and there is an inherent difficulty in representing this on film given that viral transmission cannot be confirmed until months after the incidence of condomless anal intercourse, and only then by blood test. Furthermore, I have attempted in this chapter to illustrate that participating in bareback sex and consuming bareback pornography can be something radically different than willfully seeking out HIV transmission. Nevertheless, this is an issue that needs to be examined more closely, perhaps even specifically, with greater attention than I can give it here.

## Conclusion

In phallocratic society, gay-male sexuality is illicit sexuality and, in the age of AIDS, this illicitness is only augmented by the fact that some gay men are ignoring years of vociferous warnings from the establishment and are purposely, defiantly engaging in anal intercourse without using condoms. Gay men engage in bareback sex for a variety of reasons, including wishes to forge more intimate connections with partners and find like-minded individuals in order to build a sense of community for themselves. Relatedly, amateur bareback videos foreground the notion that bareback sex is a conscious choice via their employment of extreme close-ups on the point of insertion during anal intercourse. The documentary style of many bareback videos might be interpreted as an attempt at representational accuracy, something that many members of the bareback community believe the mainstream pornography industry has forsaken in the interests of profit and political expediency.

I do not wish to suggest a linear relationship between the more documentary-style bareback videos and the more streamlined productions that have appeared in the marketplace more recently, but the recent proliferation of bareback pornography in the gay adult video industry makes trouble for the notion that those who produce and distribute such offerings will always do so with an explicitly political agenda. Bareback pornography's increasing popularity lends itself to interpretations that account for a wider scope of intentionality among those who produce it, as well as more varied readings among those who consume it. I want to reiterate here that no straight line can be drawn between the activities depicted in the videos and the viewers who consume them. As such, bareback pornography's potential statuses as a business and a generator of fantasy, as well as a document and a representation of something lived, are very much a reality. In addition, bareback videos differ from their pre-AIDS condomless predecessors on several fundamental levels, namely their relative backgrounding of narrative, their emphasis on anal versatility, and their reframing of the money shot. This research is offered as a starting point for a larger discussion of the ideological conflicts underpinning bareback pornography, the environments in which the bareback videos are produced, and the contexts in which such offerings are consumed.

## Works Cited

Burger, John R. *One-Handed Histories: The Eroto-Politics of Gay Male Video Pornography.* Binghamton, NY: The Haworth Press, 1995.

Davis, Murray S. *Smut: Erotic Reality/Obscene Ideology.* Chicago: University of Chicago Press, 1983.

Dyer, Richard. "Coming to Terms: Male Gay Porn," *Jump Cut* 30 (1985): 27-29.

—. *The Culture of Queers.* New York: Routledge, 2002.

Freeman, Gregory A. "Bug Chasers." *Rolling Stone* 6 Feb. 2003. 20 Nov. 2003.<http://www.rollingstone.com/news/story/_/id/5933610?rnd=11339 58691223&hasplayer=true&version=6.0.12.1212>.

GAE Boy Video. Company website. 20 Nov. 2003. <http://www.gaeboy video.com/>.

Morris, Paul. "No Limits: Necessary Danger in Male Porn." *Visual AIDS: Gay Male Porn and Safer Sex Pedagogy.* 28 May 1999. 10 Nov. 2003. <http://hivinsite.ucsf.edu/InSite?page=pa-2098-4218>.

McKittrick, Casey. "Structures of Plenitude and the Death Drive in Contemporary Gay Bareback Video." Society for Cinema and Media Studies Conference. Minneapolis. 3 Mar. 2003.

McNair, Brian. *Mediated Sex: Pornography and Postmodern Culture.* New York: Arnold, 1996.

O'Hara, Scott. *Autopornography: A Memoir of Life in the Lust Lane.* Binghamton, NY: Harrington Park Press, 1997.

Rotello, Gabriel. *Sexual Ecology: AIDS and the Destiny of Gay Men.* New York: Dutton, 1997.

Scarce, Michael. "Back to Barebacking." *NY Blade* 21 Aug. 1998. 10 Nov. 2003. <http://www.managingdesire.org/scarcebtb.html>.

Signorile, Michelangelo. "AIDS at 20: Complacency Returns." *Gay.com.* 6 June 2001. 15 Oct. 2003. <http://www.signorile.com/articles/ gca20.html>.

Slezak, Michael. "Raw Footage." GayHealth.com. 26 Jan. 2001. 10 Oct. 2003. <http://www.gayhealth.com/templates/1065654964579377590678 00001/sex?record=392>.

Williams, Linda. *Hard Core: Power, Pleasure, and the "Frenzy of the Visible."* Berkeley: University of California Press, 1989.

Yep, Gust A., Karen E. Lovaas, and Alex V. Pagonis. "The Case of 'Riding Bareback': Sexual Practices and the Paradoxes of Identity in the Era of AIDS." *Journal of Homosexuality* 42 (2002): 1-14.

# CONTRIBUTORS

**Jack M. Beckham II** is a Ph.D. student in English at the University of California, Riverside. His research interests include film and visual culture, cultural studies, and American literature with a specific focus on the U.S.-Mexico border. His recently published articles on film and visual culture include "Border Policy/Border Cinema: Placing *Traffic*, *The Border*, and *Touch of Evil* in the American Imagination" and "From Seedy ROMs to DVDs: Virtual Sex and the Search for Control."

**Jaime Bihlmeyer**'s research focuses on the imaging of cultural groups and women in mainstream movies. He has published in *Cinema Journal, Essays in Philosophy,* and *The Journal for the Speech and Theatre Association of Missouri*. His most recent publication is a chapter in the book *Images and Imagery—Frames, Borders, Limits—Interdisciplinary Perspectives.*

**Nate Brennan** is a graduate student in the Department of Cinema Studies at New York University. He received his bachelor's degree in English and theatre production from the University of Delaware in 2005. His essay in this collection was part of his senior thesis project on the science fiction films of Jack Arnold.

**Catherine R. Burke** is a freelance library researcher living in New York City. In addition to advanced degrees in library science from Columbia University and the University of Pittsburgh, she has earned a master's degree in cinema studies from the College of Staten Island.

**Mattias Frey** is a Ph.D. candidate at Harvard University, where he is affiliated with the Department of Germanic Languages and Literatures and the Department of Visual and Environmental Studies. His writings have appeared or are forthcoming in *Literature/Film Quarterly, Quarterly Review of Film and Video,* and *Senses of Cinema*. He also writes film reviews for the *Boston Phoenix.*

**Jane M. Greene** is an assistant professor in the Department of Cinema at Denison University. She received her Ph.D. in film studies from the University of Wisconsin-Madison. Her current projects include a book on industry censorship and romantic comedy in the 1930s and research on trends in contemporary horror films.

**Hollis Griffin** is a doctoral student at Northwestern University. He has published articles and book reviews in *Spectator* and *The Velvet Light Trap*, respectively, and has served as the senior features editor of *FLOW*. Prior to beginning his graduate work, Griffin worked as a publicist in the publishing industry.

**Kylo-Patrick R. Hart** is chair of the Department of Communication and Media Studies at Plymouth State University, where he teaches courses in film studies, television studies, and popular culture. He is author of the book *The AIDS Movie: Representing a Pandemic in Film and Television*, as well as numerous research essays that have appeared in academic journals (including *Journal of Film and Video* and *The Journal of Men's Studies*) and media anthologies (including *Television: Critical Concepts in Media and Cultural Studies* and *Gender, Race, and Class in Media: A Text-Reader*).

**Cynthia Lucia** is an assistant professor of English and cinema studies at Rider University. She is the author of *Framing Female Lawyers: Women on Trial in Film* and has written extensively for *Cineaste,* for which she has served on the editorial board for more than a decade. Her essays appear in *Feminism, Media and the Law*, and *The Process of Adaptation*.

**David M. Lugowski** received his Ph.D. in cinema studies from New York University. He is currently an associate professor of English and director of the Communication Studies Program at Manhattanville College. He has published in *Cineaste, Cinema Journal, The Encyclopedia of Documentary Film, The International Encyclopedia of Queer Culture, Senses of Cinema*, and elsewhere, including several scholarly anthologies.

**Heather MacGibbon** is completing her dissertation on abortion in U.S. cinema at New York University. Her research areas include gender and sexuality, documentary history and theory, and theories of race and nationalism.

**Tamar Jeffers McDonald** is Senior Lecturer in Film at Buckinghamshire Chilterns University College. Her current research interests include different filmic strategies for the representation of virginity, film costuming, Doris Day, and romantic comedy. She is the author of *Romantic Comedy: Boy Meets Girl Meets Genre*, which explores the confluence of several of these themes.

**Melissa Ooten** received her Ph.D. in history from the College of William and Mary in 2005. She is currently the assistant director of the Women Involved in Living and Learning (WILL) Program at the University of Richmond, where she teaches in the Women, Gender, and Sexuality Studies Department.

**Christine E. Pace** recently received her master's degree in liberal studies from Dartmouth College. While her undergraduate studies focused on history and classics, her graduate studies concentrated on contemporary U.S. culture with particular emphasis on theories of popular culture, anthropological theories of violence, and American religious culture.

**Mary E. Pagano** is a doctoral candidate in the Radio/Television/Film Program at Northwestern University, where she is also earning a graduate certificate in gender studies. Her dissertation explores the intersections and dialogue between representations of women in U.S. television sitcoms and the development of second-wave feminism during the 1960s and 1970s.

**Alina Patriche** earned her M.A. in British literature from the University of Illinois at Urbana-Champaign in 1998 and her Ph.D. in film studies from that same university in 2003. Since 1997, she has taught composition, literature, and film in the English Department of the University of Illinois and media literacy in the Communication Department at Carthage College. Her research interests include identity construction in genre films, contemporary British cinema, and visual literacy.

**Sarah E. S. Sinwell** is currently a doctoral candidate in the Department of Communication and Culture at Indiana University, Bloomington. Her dissertation focuses on contemporary American independent cinema and the ways in which fluid subjectivities, embodied sexualities, and multiple identifications are constructed through feminist, queer, and postmodern frameworks.

**Whitney Strub** is completing his dissertation, *Perversion for Profit: The Politics of Obscenity and Pornography in the Postwar United States*, in the history department at UCLA. He is fascinated by cultural battles at the local level and the rise of the New Right social agenda. He intends to explore the politicization of "family values" in his future work.

# INDEX